Canada's Resource Industries

This is Volume 14 in the series of studies commissioned as part of the research program of the Royal Commission on the Economic Union and Development Prospects for Canada.

The studies contained in this volume reflect the views of their authors and do not imply endorsement by the Chairman or Commissioners.

Canada's Resource Industries

JOHN WHALLEY
Research Coordinator

*Published by the University of Toronto Press in cooperation
with the Royal Commission on the Economic Union and
Development Prospects for Canada and the Canadian
Government Publishing Centre, Supply and Services Canada*

University of Toronto Press
Toronto   Buffalo   London

Grateful acknowledgment is made to the following for permission to reprint previously published and unpublished material: The American Assembly; *Canadian Water Resources Journal*; Council on Foreign Relations; International Institute of Applied Systems Analysis; Miller Freeman Publications Incorporated (*Pulp and Paper International*); Resources for the Future; University of California Press; World Bank.

Printed in Canada
ISBN 0-8020-7256-9
ISSN 0829-2396
Cat. No. Z1-1983/1-41-14E

CANADIAN CATALOGUING IN PUBLICATION DATA

Main entry under title:
Canada's resource industries

(*The Collected research studies / Royal Commission on the Economic Union and Development Prospects for Canada,*
ISSN 0829-2396 ; 14)
Includes bibliographical references.
ISBN 0-8020-7256-9

1. Natural resources — Economic aspects — Canada — Addresses, essays, lectures.
2. Canada — Industries — Addresses, essays, lectures. I. Whalley, John. II. Royal Commission on the Economic Union and Development Prospects for Canada.
III. Series: The Collected research studies (Royal Commission on the Economic Union and Development Prospects for Canada) ; 14.

HC113.5.C35 1985   338'.0971   C85-099608-2

PUBLISHING COORDINATION: Ampersand Communications Services Inc.
COVER DESIGN: Will Rueter
INTERIOR DESIGN: Brant Cowie/Artplus Limited

CONTENTS

FOREWORD

When the members of the Rowell-Sirois Commission began their collective task in 1937, very little was known about the evolution of the Canadian economy. What was known, moreover, had not been extensively analyzed by the slender cadre of social scientists of the day.

When we set out upon our task nearly 50 years later, we enjoyed a substantial advantage over our predecessors; we had a wealth of information. We inherited the work of scholars at universities across Canada and we had the benefit of the work of experts from private research institutes and publicly sponsored organizations such as the Ontario Economic Council and the Economic Council of Canada. Although there were still important gaps, our problem was not a shortage of information; it was to interrelate and integrate — to synthesize — the results of much of the information we already had.

The mandate of this Commission is unusually broad. It encompasses many of the fundamental policy issues expected to confront the people of Canada and their governments for the next several decades. The nature of the mandate also identified, in advance, the subject matter for much of the research and suggested the scope of enquiry and the need for vigorous efforts to interrelate and integrate the research disciplines. The resulting research program, therefore, is particularly noteworthy in three respects: along with original research studies, it includes survey papers which synthesize work already done in specialized fields; it avoids duplication of work which, in the judgment of the Canadian research community, has already been well done; and, considered as a whole, it is the most thorough examination of the Canadian economic, political and legal systems ever undertaken by an independent agency.

The Commission's research program was carried out under the joint direction of three prominent and highly respected Canadian scholars: Dr. Ivan Bernier (*Law and Constitutional Issues*), Dr. Alan Cairns (*Politics and Institutions of Government*) and Dr. David C. Smith (*Economics*).

Dr. Ivan Bernier is Dean of the Faculty of Law at Laval University. Dr. Alan Cairns is former Head of the Department of Political Science at the University of British Columbia and, prior to joining the Commission, was William Lyon Mackenzie King Visiting Professor of Canadian Studies at Harvard University. Dr. David C. Smith, former Head of the Department of Economics at Queen's University in Kingston, is now Principal of that University. When Dr. Smith assumed his new responsibilities at Queen's in September 1984, he was succeeded by Dr. Kenneth Norrie of the University of Alberta and John Sargent of the federal Department of Finance, who together acted as Co-directors of Research for the concluding phase of the Economics research program.

I am confident that the efforts of the Research Directors, research coordinators and authors whose work appears in this and other volumes, have provided the community of Canadian scholars and policy makers with a series of publications that will continue to be of value for many years to come. And I hope that the value of the research program to Canadian scholarship will be enhanced by the fact that Commission research is being made available to interested readers in both English and French.

I extend my personal thanks, and that of my fellow Commissioners, to the Research Directors and those immediately associated with them in the Commission's research program. I also want to thank the members of the many research advisory groups whose counsel contributed so substantially to this undertaking.

DONALD S. MACDONALD

At its most general level, the Royal Commission's research program has examined how the Canadian political economy can better adapt to change. As a basis of enquiry, this question reflects our belief that the future will always take us partly by surprise. Our political, legal and economic institutions should therefore be flexible enough to accommodate surprises and yet solid enough to ensure that they help us meet our future goals. This theme of an adaptive political economy led us to explore the interdependencies between political, legal and economic systems and drew our research efforts in an interdisciplinary direction.

The sheer magnitude of the research output (more than 280 separate studies in 70+ volumes) as well as its disciplinary and ideological diversity have, however, made complete integration impossible and, we have concluded, undesirable. The research output as a whole brings varying perspectives and methodologies to the study of common problems and we therefore urge readers to look beyond their particular field of interest and to explore topics across disciplines.

The three research areas, — *Law and Constitutional Issues*, under Ivan Bernier; *Politics and Institutions of Government*, under Alan Cairns; and *Economics*, under David C. Smith (co-directed with Kenneth Norrie and John Sargent for the concluding phase of the research program) — were further divided into 19 sections headed by research coordinators.

The area *Law and Constitutional Issues* has been organized into five major sections headed by the research coordinators identified below.

- Law, Society and the Economy — *Ivan Bernier and Andrée Lajoie*
- The International Legal Environment — *John J. Quinn*
- The Canadian Economic Union — *Mark Krasnick*

- Harmonization of Laws in Canada — *Ronald C.C. Cuming*
- Institutional and Constitutional Arrangements — *Clare F. Beckton and A. Wayne MacKay*

Since law in its numerous manifestations is the most fundamental means of implementing state policy, it was necessary to investigate how and when law could be mobilized most effectively to address the problems raised by the Commission's mandate. Adopting a broad perspective, researchers examined Canada's legal system from the standpoint of how law evolves as a result of social, economic and political changes and how, in turn, law brings about changes in our social, economic and political conduct.

Within *Politics and Institutions of Government*, research has been organized into seven major sections.

- Canada and the International Political Economy — *Denis Stairs and Gilbert Winham*
- State and Society in the Modern Era — *Keith Banting*
- Constitutionalism, Citizenship and Society — *Alan Cairns and Cynthia Williams*
- The Politics of Canadian Federalism — *Richard Simeon*
- Representative Institutions — *Peter Aucoin*
- The Politics of Economic Policy — *G. Bruce Doern*
- Industrial Policy — *André Blais*

This area examines a number of developments which have led Canadians to question their ability to govern themselves wisely and effectively. Many of these developments are not unique to Canada and a number of comparative studies canvass and assess how others have coped with similar problems. Within the context of the Canadian heritage of parliamentary government, federalism, a mixed economy, and a bilingual and multicultural society, the research also explores ways of rearranging the relationships of power and influence among institutions to restore and enhance the fundamental democratic principles of representativeness, responsiveness and accountability.

Economics research was organized into seven major sections.

- Macroeconomics — *John Sargent*
- Federalism and the Economic Union — *Kenneth Norrie*
- Industrial Structure — *Donald G. McFetridge*
- International Trade — *John Whalley*
- Income Distribution and Economic Security — *François Vaillancourt*
- Labour Markets and Labour Relations — *Craig Riddell*
- Economic Ideas and Social Issues — *David Laidler*

Economics research examines the allocation of Canada's human and other resources, the ways in which institutions and policies affect this allocation, and the distribution of the gains from their use. It also considers the nature of economic development, the forces that shape our regional and industrial structure, and our economic interdependence with other countries. The thrust of the research in economics is to increase our comprehension of what determines our economic potential and how instruments of economic policy may move us closer to our future goals.

One section from each of the three research areas — The Canadian Economic Union, The Politics of Canadian Federalism, and Federalism and the Economic Union — have been blended into one unified research effort. Consequently, the volumes on Federalism and the Economic Union as well as the volume on The North are the results of an inter-disciplinary research effort.

We owe a special debt to the research coordinators. Not only did they organize, assemble and analyze the many research studies and combine their major findings in overviews, but they also made substantial contri-butions to the Final Report. We wish to thank them for their perfor-mance, often under heavy pressure.

Unfortunately, space does not permit us to thank all members of the Commission staff individually. However, we are particularly grateful to the Chairman, The Hon. Donald S. Macdonald; the Commission's Exec-utive Director, J. Gerald Godsoe; and the Director of Policy, Alan Nymark, all of whom were closely involved with the Research Program and played key roles in the contribution of Research to the Final Report. We wish to express our appreciation to the Commission's Administrative Advisor, Harry Stewart, for his guidance and advice, and to the Director of Publishing, Ed Matheson, who managed the research publication process. A special thanks to Jamie Benidickson, Policy Coordinator and Special Assistant to the Chairman, who played a valuable liaison role between Research and the Chairman and Commissioners. We are also grateful to our office administrator, Donna Stebbing, and to our sec-retarial staff, Monique Carpentier, Barbara Cowtan, Tina DeLuca, Françoise Guilbault and Marilyn Sheldon.

Finally, a well deserved thank you to our closest assistants: Jacques J.M. Shore, *Law and Constitutional Issues*; Cynthia Williams and her successor Karen Jackson, *Politics and Institutions of Government*; and I. Lilla Connidis, *Economics*. We appreciate not only their individual contribution to each research area, but also their cooperative contribu-tion to the research program and the Commission.

IVAN BERNIER
ALAN CAIRNS
DAVID C. SMITH

PREFACE

This volume on Canada's resource industries and water export policies is one of six dealing with various aspects of Canada's international trade policies and Canada's interaction with the global economy. These volumes collectively represent the research output of the group of scholars who worked on international trade issues for the Economics branch of the research effort of the Royal Commission. The other volumes deal with such issues as Canada-U.S. free trade, Canada and the multilateral trading system, industrial policies and trade, and influences from abroad on Canada's domestic policies.

In the present volume two issues of major importance are discussed in separate commissioned papers. In the first, Bruce Wilkinson of the University of Alberta assesses export prospects for Canada's resource industries. He provides an item-by-item evaluation of the potential of our various resource-producing industries, concluding that the demise of Canadian resource industries, which some have predicted for the years ahead, is unlikely to occur. While the rapid expansion of the 1950s and 1960s in these industries is unlikely to be repeated, prospects for their continued vitality, in terms both of output and of exports, seem to be good. He also cautions that the choice between resource and "high-tech" industries, which is sometimes presented, is also spurious, since many resource industries now involve high-technology extraction and processing methods.

In the second paper, Anthony Scott, John Olynyk and Steven Renzetti of the University of British Columbia discuss the design of water-export policy in Canada. Their main conclusion is that each water-export project should be assessed separately, using benefit-cost analysis on a project-by-project basis. They propose that this be achieved through a government review process involving both federal and provincial governments, using economic criteria to determine the desirability of exports.

The topics covered in these papers are clearly central to current trade-policy debates. Resources are a traditional export area for Canada, and water-export policy has long been a contentious issue. The papers are therefore a welcome addition to the research output of the Commission, and will, I am sure, contribute both to current and to future policy debate for many years to come.

JOHN WHALLEY

ACKNOWLEDGMENTS

Many people were involved in the trade policy research effort in the economics branch of the Commission's research program and we would like to acknowledge their help. The Commission's Research Advisory Group on Trade Policy (Economics) provided valuable assistance in selecting the topics to be covered and in commenting on papers and on the issues before the Commission. They also participated extensively in the research symposia held by the Commission on trade policy topics.

The following were the members of the group: Peter Cornell (Economic Council of Canada), John Curtis (Institute for Research on Public Policy), Richard G. Harris (Queen's University), Gerald K. Helleiner (University of Toronto), James Markusen (University of Western Ontario), Ronald McKinnon (Stanford University), A. Edward Safarian (University of Toronto), Ronald Shearer (University of British Columbia), Rodrigue Tremblay (University of Montreal), Bruce W. Wilkinson (University of Alberta) and Ronald Wonnacott (University of Western Ontario).

We are grateful for the assistance of the Commission's economic research staff, particularly Dr. I. Lilla Connidis, Barbara Cowtan, Tina DeLuca, Donna Stebbing and Marilyn Sheldon, and Donald Wilson of the Institute for Research on Public Policy. We also acknowledge the support and guidance of David Smith, John Sargent and Kenneth Norrie, co-directors of research in economics for the Commission. We are particularly grateful to Ruth Crow, the editor of the economics volumes on trade policy.

J.W.

Canada's Resource Industries:
A Survey

BRUCE W. WILKINSON

Introduction

> . . . some countries have progressed much faster than others, while some
> have not progressed at all. The explanation for these differences does not
> seem to lie mainly in the realm of factor endowments. . . . My hypothesis is
> that the single most important explanatory variable is political organization
> and the administrative competence of government.
>
> Lloyd Reynolds (1983)

Long before Canada became a nation, its abundant endowments of fish,
trees and fur-bearing animals made it a magnet for seafarers from
Europe, who filled their ships with products to sell in their native
countries. As settlement commenced, the prime concern of the early
residents was to have access to European markets for their raw materials. From the time these lands we now call "Canada" became a British
colony, they enjoyed privileged access to British markets until the
withdrawal of the Corn Laws in 1846 took away this privilege. The
colonial province of Canada responded in 1847 with its own general tariff
on imports from all countries. The early special tie with Britain was
broken, never to be the same again, in spite of attempts to restore it
through the British Preferential Tariff around the turn of the century.
Eyes were cast to the United States for new markets and new trading
relationships. The chief concern was still access to markets for Canadian
resource products. Accordingly, the Reciprocity Treaty with the United
States, which lasted from 1854 to 1866, related to natural products
involving limited amounts of processing. In addition to the traditional
fish, furs and lumber, new commodities were involved: grain and flour,
meat and dairy products, and coal.

Since those early years, Canada has become an industrialized nation producing a wide range of manufactured products and supplying a host of different services. During the same period, the resource-producing sector has expanded dramatically, too. The traditional exports are still strong: Canada is today the world's largest exporter of fish products, and supplies over one-quarter of the world's imports of softwood lumber. But many other natural commodities or products of natural commodities have been added to the list of exports; these include grain, particularly wheat and barley, which meet about one-fifth of the world's import needs, a range of metals and non-metallic minerals from nickel to asbestos, and woodpulp and newsprint. All these became important exports in the last century and the early part of this one. In the last four decades, still other raw material exports have augmented the list: petroleum and natural gas, uranium, iron ore, sulphur, potash, electricity, and canola (formerly called "rapeseed"). Expansion of traditional products to new markets has also occurred; coal and copper, for instance, have been sold to Japan, and zinc has been sold to both Japan and the European Community (EC).

Simultaneously, however, Canada's pre-eminence in some products has diminished dramatically. Canadian nickel accounted for 80 percent of the world's supply in 1950, but comprises less than 25 percent today. Over the same period, the share of Canadian asbestos has decreased from 65 percent to less than 40 percent.

Yet, in spite of setbacks in some sectors, resource-based products in crude, semi-processed or final form still provide Canada with sizeable surpluses in its total commodity trade, outweighing the nation's consistently huge deficits in many highly manufactured goods. This fact is evident from Table 1-1. Particularly noteworthy is the large surplus in forest products, although the contributions to the trade surplus of energy, agricultural, and mineral products are also significant.

The actual resource-producing industries themselves are quite small relative to the total economy, whether measured by shares of employment or shares of gross domestic product (GDP). As Table 1-2 indicates, agriculture, forestry, fishing, trapping and the working of mines, quarries and oil wells together account for only 7 percent of total employment in Canada and 6 percent of GDP.

Although rather small in themselves, these industries provide the inputs for processing industries as well, thereby making these secondary industries possible in Canada. The best example of this spin-off effect is forestry, which yields the basic resource for the powerful lumber, woodpulp and newsprint industries. These secondary industries together account for over 85 percent of forest-product sales abroad. The employment and GDP they involve are, of course, counted in manufacturing and comprise 13 and 14 percent respectively of the entire manufacturing sector.

TABLE 1-1 Canadian Trade Balances,
by Major Commodity Group, 1983

	1983
	($ billions)
Agricultural products	4.60
Forest products	11.91
Crude minerals (except energy products)	2.06
Energy products	7.68
Semi-processed minerals	2.92
Automobiles and parts	1.92
Other highly manufactured goods	−18.70
Special transactions (trade)	−0.77
Fishing and marine	1.13
Total	12.75

Source: Statistics Canada, Summary of External Trade: December 1983 (Ottawa: Statistics Canada, 1984).

TABLE 1-2 Employment and Gross Domestic Product at Factor Cost
by Major Sector, 1982–83

Sector	Employment, 1983 Numbers in Thousands (1)	Percent (2)	Gross Domestic Product, 1982 Constant 1971 Prices (3)
Goods Producing			
Agriculture	485	4.5	2.8
Fishing, trapping and forestry	110	1.0	0.7
Mines, quarries and oil wells	162	1.5	2.5
Subtotal: primary industries	757	7.0	6.0
Manufacturing	1,884	17.7	20.0
Construction	562	5.3	5.8
Subtotal: goods producing	3,203	30.0	31.8
Services Producing			
Transportation, storage, communication and other utilities	862	8.2	14.2
Trade	1,840	17.3	12.2
Finance, insurance and real estate	601	5.6	13.9
Community, business and personal services	3,377	31.7	20.7
Public administration	774	7.3	7.3
Subtotal: services producing	10,657	100.0	100.0

Sources: Column (1) and (2): Statistics Canada, The Labour Force: December 1983 (Ottawa: Statistics Canada, 1984). Column (3): Statistics Canada, System of National Accounts, National Income and Expenditure Accounts (Ottawa: Statistics Canada, 1983).

Although, relative to the total economy, the primary industries may not seem impressive in size, for some provinces their significance is greater than that of manufacturing. This is particularly so for Saskatchewan and Prince Edward Island, where the agricultural sector involves 20 percent and nearly 14 percent respectively of the labour force. It is also true for Alberta, where agriculture and the oil industry, as Table 1-3 shows, are important commodity-producing sectors.

While it may be tempting to leap on the high-technology bandwagon with the belief that focussing on it is the secret to Canada's maintaining a healthy international trading position, to do so to the exclusion of detailed attention to the resource sectors would be a mistake. Similarly, if we devote all our time and talents just to ensuring that Canada achieve, by one method or another, the economies of scale in manufacturing that are possible in today's world, we shall again be shortchanging ourselves. Either of these reactions or both of them together, while extremely important, entail too narrow a focus to promote Canadian success in the world trading environment. The world is rapidly changing. New sources of minerals and forestry products are being developed around the globe. Some developing countries are subsidizing the export of their resources, as well as of processed forms of these resources. New technologies create substitutes for Canadian natural products. Protectionism in the world is expanding and hindering trade, particularly of processed resources.

We need, therefore, to ask questions about the future of primary product exports, as well as that of processed exports based on our resource endowments. What will the world supplies and demands for these resources be in the future? What changes are taking place in world markets, and what additional changes can be foreseen? Are new, cheaper sources of supply coming onto the markets? Are new technologies making our resources less important? Are tastes changing? What do these and other changes imply for Canada's trade in primary and resource-based commodities? What shall we be able to sell and at what prices? What policies and adjustments are necessary within Canadian industries to make them competitive internationally? These are the types of questions that immediately come to mind when one thinks of the changing world economy in which Canada has to function.

We cannot hope in this study to answer all of these questions thoroughly, given the time and resources available. But we can highlight some of the major trends and issues that must be considered in any continuing developmental plans that Canada may have. We shall approach this task by bringing together, from as wide a range of sources as possible, the information available about world and domestic resource developments. We shall weigh and assess this information and the implications for Canada derived from it. We shall devote a section to each of the major resource-producing sectors and give attention, also,

TABLE 1-3 Employment by Province, December 1983

	Nfld.	P.E.I.	N.S.	N.B.	Que.	Ont.	Man.	Sask.	Alta.	B.C.
					(percent)					
Agriculture	0	11.3	1.8	2.5	2.7	3.0	8.4	19.9	7.9	2.5
Other primary industries	7.3	6.3	5.2	3.7	1.5	1.0	1.4	2.8	6.0	4.3
Total	7.3	17.6	7.0	6.2	4.2	4.0	9.8	22.7	13.9	6.8
Manufacturing	9.7	7.5	12.2	13.2	20.7	23.1	12.3	5.1	8.3	12.9
Construction	5.5	7.0	6.1	5.3	4.3	4.4	4.5	5.6	6.5	5.7
Transportation	11.5	7.5	7.9	11.1	7.7	7.2	9.5	6.7	8.9	9.5
Trade	18.2	17.0	19.2	20.2	17.9	17.0	18.4	18.1	17.5	19.3
Finance, insurance, and real estate	4.2	2.1	4.6	3.7	5.6	6.4	5.0	4.9	5.2	6.2
Service	31.5	30.0	34.1	32.9	32.4	31.6	32.1	28.8	32.6	33.4
Public administration	12.1	11.3	9.1	7.4	7.2	6.3	8.4	8.1	7.1	6.2
	100.0	100.0	100.0	100.0	100.0	100.0	100.0	100.0	100.0	100.0

Source: Statistics Canada, The Labour Force, December 1983 (Ottawa: Statistics Canada, 1984).
Note: Numbers may not add up to 100 because of rounding.

where appropriate, to the industries based on these resource sectors. The following section will focus on agriculture. Sections on energy products, fisheries, forest products, and minerals (excluding energy products) will follow in that order. We shall also devote a short section to the possibility of water-resource exports. The final section will summarize our findings and present some general observations and conclusions.

Agriculture

> Just as it is in the self-interest of a producer to seek market power, it is in the short-term self-interest of a nation to protect domestic industry from world competition. . . . But in both cases, consumers pay the price and total income flow and wealth are diminished.
>
> William Vogley (1984)

This section will focus primarily on agricultural products trade, its potential, and the constraints that may influence it. The proportion of the Canadian labour force engaged in agriculture per se is only about 5 percent. Yet the total agri-food sector comprises a sizeable segment of the economy and accounts for over 15 percent of the total labour force. Hence the international competitiveness of agriculture and the trade flows it generates are of great importance in the total economy. We shall commence with a brief review of production and trade for this sector. Next we shall outline the global outlook for agriculture and Canada's prospects in the world economy. We shall then examine possible constraints on Canadian competitiveness and draw a few conclusions.

Canadian Output and Trade: The Record

The relative importance of production from the various segments of agriculture is summarized in Table 1-4. Grains and oilseeds form the largest portion, accounting for over one-third of farm-cash receipts. Cattle and dairy receipts make up another third. All other products comprise the balance. Surprisingly, perhaps, the total of vegetables, fruits and tobacco make up only 11 percent of farm receipts.

When we turn to net trade balances, the significance of grains of oilseeds becomes much more pronounced, for Canada's consistent surplus in agricultural products trade is almost entirely attributable to the competitiveness of these products in world markets (Table 1-5). Noteworthy, too, is the growing trade deficit in fruits, vegetables, nuts and other products. Some of these products are, however, complementary: that is, they are products not normally grown in Canada, such as citrus and tropical fruits, nuts, tea, coffee and cocoa. Imports of these products have grown at an annual rate of 11 percent over the past 10 years, compared to a 7.9 percent growth rate for products competitive with domestic sources of supply.

TABLE 1-4 Canada's Farm Cash Receipts by Major Category, 1982

	$ Million	% of Total
Cereals	5,671	30.6
Oilseeds	840	4.5
Cattles and calves	3,478	18.8
Dairy	2,903	15.7
Hogs	1,943	10.5
Poultry and eggs	1,198	6.5
Potatoes, fruits, vegetables, tobacco	1,974	10.6
Other	514	2.8
	18,521	100.0

Source: Statistics Canada, *Farm Cash Receipts, 1982* (Ottawa: Statistics Canada, 1983).

TABLE 1-5 Canada's Net Trade Balance for Agricultural Commodity Groups

	millions of current dollars			
	1971–75 average	1976–80 average	1981	1982
Grain and grain products	1,846	2,848	4,827	5,400
(wheat and wheat flour)	(1,411)	(2,326)	(3,723)	(4,360)
Oilseed and oilseed products	121	266	498	342
Animal feeds	46	98	135	181
Animals, meat, and other animal products	6	205	400	663
Dairy products	12	32	115	192
Poultry and eggs	−5	−33	−17	−30
Fruits and vegetables	−504	−1,030	−1,427	−1,474
Other	−551	−1,110	−1,362	−984
Total net trade in agricultural commodities	852	1,276	3,169	4,209
Net trade in all commodities	382	2,050	1,855	13,903

Source: Adapted from T. Veeman and M. Veeman, *The Future of Grain* (Ottawa, Canadian Institute for Economic Policy, 1984).

Because grains (especially wheat) form the bulk of Canadian exports, they deserve special attention. The major grain-export markets for the past three crop years are shown in Figure 1-1. The Soviet Union dominates as a destination for Canadian grains (mostly wheat and barley), although Japan and increasingly China are also large buyers.

Wheat

Canada's wheat production, standing at about 27 million tonnes in 1982, amounts to 5.5 percent of world output. Canada's output is exceeded by only four other nations: the U.S.S.R., the United States, China and India (which has recently become self-sufficient in food production).

FIGURE 1-1 Major Importers of Canadian Grain, 1980–81, 1981–82, 1982–83

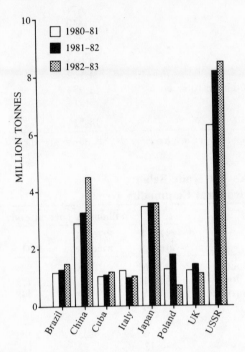

Source: T. Veeman and M. Veeman, *The Future of Grain: Canada's Prospects for Growing Oilseeds, and Related Industries* (Ottawa: Canadian Institute for Economic Policy, 1984).

World wheat exports and changing market shares of the main exporting nations are shown in Table 1-6. Trade in wheat has about doubled over the last 20 years, representing an annual growth rate of 3.5 percent. Canada's share of world exports has hovered at around 20 percent, declining in the late 1970s and early 1980s and rising again in 1983–84. The decline was a function of lower-than-usual production, bottlenecks in the grain transportation and handling system, and concentration of exports on traditional but rather slow-growing markets at the expense of faster-growing markets for a different quality of wheat varieties from the usual Canadian hard red spring wheat with its high protein content (Veeman and Veeman, 1984a; Konandreas and Hurtado, 1978). Export subsidies and aggressive marketing techniques by competitor countries have also been important in challenging Canada's position. The EC, for example, increased its export-market share from 8 percent in the early 1970s to nearly 16 percent in recent years, by means of a complicated system of subsidies and export credits. The maximum subsidy was $83 per metric tonne in 1979–80. Grain disposal alone cost the EC $1.4 billion

TABLE 1-6 World Wheat Exports[a] and Market Shares

Exporters	Average				1980–81	1981–82	1982–83[b]	1983–84[c]
	1960–64	1965–69	1970–74	1975–79				
	(million tonnes)							
United States	19.5	19.0	25.6	31.8	41.9	49.1	41.5	38.0
Canada	11.0	11.3	12.7	13.9	17.0	17.8	21.0	21.5
Australia	6.1	6.5	7.5	9.8	10.6	11.0	7.5	11.0
EC	3.3	4.2	4.9	7.6	14.7	15.5	15.5	15.5
Argentina	2.6	3.4	1.9	3.9	3.9	4.3	8.5	6.5
Other	5.7	8.2	7.5	5.2	6.2	4.5	6.2	4.9
Total[d]	48.2	52.6	60.2	72.2	94.2	102.2	100.2	97.4
	(percent share of exports)							
United States	40.5	36.1	42.5	44.0	44.5	48.0	41.4	39.0
Canada	22.8	21.5	21.1	19.3	18.0	17.4	20.9	22.1
Australia	12.7	12.3	12.5	13.6	11.2	10.8	7.5	11.3
EC	6.8	8.0	8.1	10.5	15.6	15.2	15.5	15.9
Argentina	5.4	6.5	3.2	5.4	4.1	4.2	8.5	6.7
Other	11.8	15.6	12.5	7.2	6.6	4.4	6.2	5.0
Total	100.0	100.0	100.0	100.0	100.0	100.0	100.0	100.0

Source: T. Veeman and M. Veeman, *The Future of Grain* (Ottawa: Canada Institute for Economic Policy, 1984).
a. July/June, excluding intra-EC.
b. Preliminary.
c. Forecast.
d. Numbers may not add up to 100 because of rounding.

in 1980 (Cole and Horton 1983). If the EC were to eliminate its protective policies, its grain production could diminish by about 40 percent (Koester, 1982).

Canada's recent improvement in export performance has been attributed to higher production levels, few if any rail and handling bottlenecks (partly a result of the reduction in other rail traffic caused by the recession and partly because of enhancement of the grain-transportation and -handling system), lack of rainfall in Australia, and poor U.S. relations with the U.S.S.R. (Veeman and Veeman, 1984a).

Barley

Although Canada is still the world's largest producer of barley (14 million tonnes in 1981–82), its share of world exports has declined over the last decade from about 27 to 23 percent. At the same time, the European share of exports has risen from 45 to 52 percent, again because of EC export subsidies. Increasingly, corn (or maize) is taking a larger share of the world coarse grain market (68 percent of such trade in 1981, compared with 17 percent for barley).

Oilseeds

These crops, particularly rapeseed/canola, have become an important Canadian export (2 million tonnes in 1981–82). World rapeseed output accounts for around 7 percent of total world oilseed output. (Soy beans comprise over half of world oilseed output.) Canadian exports of canola have expanded greatly since the early 1970s, when plant researchers developed varieties no longer detrimental to health. In 1979, Canada was the world's largest producer of rapeseed, accounting for about one-third of total world production. More recently, China has taken over the leading position as Canada's share diminished to about 15 percent in 1982–83. Simultaneously, Canada's export share dropped from 83 to 55 percent.

Live Animals, Beef and Pork

These have been significant Canadian exports. The United States is still Canada's major market (taking 70 percent of pork and 90 percent of beef exports), but since 1970, Japan has become increasingly important especially for pork. Exports to Japan fluctuate considerably, however, and various provincial hog-marketing boards and private processors have been attempting to develop exports to Japan through long-term contracts.

The Global Outlook for Agriculture

Global projections vary depending on the assumptions made about population growth, output and income expansion, and income and price elasticities of demand, as well as the agricultural and commercial policies of both importing and exporting nations. Consequently, one has to be careful not to put too much stock in any one set of estimates. For developing countries, the U.S. Council on Environmental Quality and Department of State, *Global 2000 Report to the President* and Food and Agriculture Organization (FAO), *Agriculture: Toward 2000*, among other reports, conclude that even given optimistic assumptions about the performance of agriculture in these countries, they will require huge increases in imports in future years. Under the FAO's most favourable assumptions about the performance of less-developed countries, it is anticipated that by the year 2000, their cereal imports will have to amount to 149 million tonnes annually, or about triple their 1975 level, if the number of undernourished people in their populations is to be reduced even marginally. Generally, though, agricultural imports by developing nations will grow at a slower pace than the 5.7 percent a year of the period 1961–80, possibly at about 3.8 percent annually to the year 2000. Centrally planned economies are generally expected to continue their dependence on grain imports, although at a lower pace in the 1990s than in the past (Farrell et al., 1984; Cole and Horton, 1983).

Recent overall world growth rates of consumption and production to the years 2000 and 2020 for major agricultural commodity groups are summarized in Table 1-7. For cereals, the 1.8 percent expansion rate to 2000 is down considerably from the 2.6 percent annual growth rate of the 1970s. Yet it is higher than the projection of the International Wheat Council for 1980 to 2000 of 1.2 percent (Veeman and Veeman, 1984a, p. 40). The 2.1 percent expected growth rate for oilseeds is about one-half that of the 1970s. For the years 2000 to 2020, the expected rates of growth are lower again, although the same pattern prevails, with the anticipated expansion of the consumption of meat and oilseeds being more rapid than that for milk products and cereals. Most of the 21st-century increases are expected to have to come from improved yields.

The world trade flows for the year 2000 as compared with 1978–80 are summarized in Table 1-8. They show that North America will be by far the largest source of supply for cereals and oilseeds. For milk and meat products, however, North American net exports will be negligible, although significant trade between the United States and Canada is likely to continue. Also noteworthy are the expected large EC surpluses of cereals and milk products, resulting from the continuation of the highly protectionist and export-subsidizing Common Agricultural Policy. The U.S.S.R.'s grain imports are expected to level out, while Sub-

TABLE 1-7 Projections of World Production and Consumption

	1980–2000	2000–2020
	(annual compound percentage growth rates)	
Cereals	1.8	1.4
Oilseeds	2.1	1.9
Meats	2.4	2.0
Milk products	1.5	1.1

Source: Kenneth R. Farrell, Fred Sanderson, Trang T. Vo, and Michael F. Brewer, "Meeting Future Needs for United States: Food, Fiber and Forest Products" (Washington, D.C.: Resources for the Future, 1984).

Saharan Africa, South and East Asia, as well as the centrally planned economies of Asia, are expected to expand their imports of cereals.

As for prices of agricultural products, the evidence is mixed and opinions vary. Recent projections tend to be more conservative than those of a few years ago. On the one side are those who foresee growing scarcities of food and an increase in real food prices that reflects this situation. The report *Global 2000: Implications for Canada* (Barney, Freeman, and Ulinski, 1981) and the later work *Challenge for Growth: An Agri-Food Strategy for Canada* (Canada, Department of Agriculture, 1981), based upon this report, project that real food prices will rise by about 1 to 2 percent a year from the mid-1970s to the year 2000. Veeman and Veeman (1984a), in contrast, suggest that real prices of grain could continue to fall at a modest rate as they did for about 60 years up to 1972. Agriculture Canada envisages real prices remaining much as at present, with a strong possibility of a decline of about 1 percent per year from 1984 to 2000. The only certainty is that instability will be common, as it has been in the past.

Projections for Canada

The 1980 *Global 2000* report for Canada (Barney, Freeman, and Ulinski, 1981) projected that Canada's wheat exports, although they rose by nearly one-third from 1970 to 1985, would be cut in half over the following 15 years. This pessimistic perspective has, however, been dismissed as overstating both supply constraints and domestic demand for grains for livestock feed (Veeman and Veeman, 1984a).

For the period to 1990, other estimates by both the Canadian Wheat Board and the Canada Grains Council forecast that grain and oilseed exports will continue to expand to 36 million tonnes annually. Table 1-9 provides some detail and comparisons with earlier years. The 1990 figures do not appear to be beyond reason. Wheat exports in 1982–83 already stood at 21 million tonnes, only 1 million tonnes short of the 1990 target, even though much of the world was in recession and markets were rather depressed. The projected exports would require domestic produc-

TABLE 1-8 Projected World Trade

Regular	Meats		Milk Products		Cereals		Oilseed	
	1978–80	2000	1978–80	2000	1978–80	2000	1978–80	2000
North Africa/Middle East	−0.7	−3.9	−6.3	−12.9	−24.1	−46.5	−1.4	−5.4
Sub-Saharan Africa	0	−0.1	−0.7	−1.3	−4.4	−29.3	−1.4	−5.4
European Community	−0.4	1.0	8.0	14.8	−1.2	20.0	−30.4	−39.3
Other Western Europe	−0.2	−0.2	1.0	1.0	−9.7	−8.3	−5.1	−7.4
U.S.S.R.	−0.5	−0.5	−3.0	−2.0	−24.6	−29.8	0	1.1
Eastern Europe	0.6	1.0	−0.1	−0.1	−14.2	−19.7	−6.9	−8.2
South Asia	0	0	−0.5	−0.5	−2.1	−13.8	2.7	2.1
East Asia	−0.8	−1.2	−1.7	−2.6	−29.8	−53.1	−5.9	−16.6
Centrally planned economies of Asia	0.2	0.4	−0.2	−0.6	−15.0	−31.6	−1.1	1.8
Oceania	1.6	5.0	5.9	9.3	14.0	25.3	0.1	−1.2
Latin America	0.5	−1.6	−2.1	−3.9	−5.8	−9.8	15.2	19.7
North America	0	0.1	−1.1	−1.1	122.9	196.6	34.2	54.4

Source: Kenneth R. Farrell, Fred Sanderson, Trang T. Vo, and Michael F. Brewer, "Meeting Future Needs for United States: Food, Fiber and Forest Products" (Washington, D.C.: Resources for the Future, 1984).

(−) = imports

TABLE 1-9 Canadian Grain and Oilseeds Exports, Actual and Projected

	Actual		Target	Projected
	1978–79[a]	**1982–83**[b]	**1990**	**2000**
	(millions of tonnes)			
Wheat	13.0	21.4	22.0	44
Coarse grains	4.1	5.7	8.5	12
Oilseeds	2.8		6.5	NA

Sources: Historical numbers: Statistics Canada, *Cereals and Oilseeds Review, 1983* (Ottawa: Statistics Canada, 1984).
1990: Canadian Wheat Board.
2000: S. Borland and G. Robertson, "A Sectoral View of the Longer-Term: Agriculture," in *Long-Term Economic Prospects for Canada: A Symposium*, volume 23 of the research studies prepared for the Royal Commission on the Economic Union and Development Prospects for Canada (Toronto: University of Toronto Press, 1985).
a. Exports at the time the 1990 target was initially set.
b. Most recent year available.
NA = not available

tion of some 52 million tonnes; the expansion in output would come from bringing new acreage into cultivation (21.3 percent), reducing acreage presently put into summerfallow (48.5 percent) and improving yield (30.2 percent) (Veeman and Veeman, 1984a).

Grain and oilseeds projections to the year 2000 are naturally more tenuous. The expansion in wheat exports to 44 million tonnes, as projected by Borland and Robertson (1985), implies an annual growth rate from 1990 to 2000 of 7.5 percent. To achieve the estimate for barley, a much more modest though still challenging growth rate of 3.5 percent would be necessary. These exports, even at current nominal prices, would imply an increase over 1983 levels of 70 percent in the value of agricultural exports. They would also require an expansion of acreage in crops of 1.2 percent annually in Western Canada (to 65 million acres), along with an annual decline of 3.5 percent in summerfallow acreage and yield increases of 1.0 percent per year.

One contemporary development not reflected in these figures is the potential for increased corn or maize production. Only 2 million acres are now in corn, whereas at least 4.2 million acres are quite suitable for this purpose, and another 16.5 million acres are marginally suitable (Nowland et al., 1982).

Forecasts to the year 2000 of growth in production and domestic disappearance of red meats, poultry and eggs, and dairy products are summarized in Table 1-10. The numbers given imply that little net change in trade balances for these products is anticipated in the years ahead. It is well known that red meats will likely continue to be exported to the United States and, to a lesser extent, to Japan, particularly if the Canadian dollar remains at about U.S. $0.73 and Canadian costs do not

TABLE 1-10 Projected Growth Rates in Canada's Livestock Needs, 1984–2000

	Beef	Hog	Poultry	Dairy
	(average annual percent change)			
Production	1.2 – 2.1	0.6 – 3.0	1.0	0.9
Disappearance	1.6	1.4	1.0	1.0

Source: S. Borland and G. Robertson, "A Sectoral View of the Longer-Term: Agriculture," in *Long-Term Economic Prospects for Canada: A Symposium*, volume 23 of the research studies prepared for the Royal Commission on the Economic Union and Development Prospects for Canada (Toronto: University of Toronto Press, 1985).

rise much faster than those in the United States; under current policies, on the other hand, restrictions on imports will continue to be necessary to preserve the poultry and dairy industries as they exist today. Price projections are for increases that roughly approximate inflation (5.8 percent) for beef and fall somewhat short of inflation increases for poultry, pork and, especially, for eggs. But for dairy products, Target Return and Support Prices are projected to rise more rapidly than inflation, that is, by about 7 percent (Borland and Robertson, 1985).

In general, then, future growth in trade surpluses in agricultural products will occur (unless unforeseen changes take place in either the domestic or world economy) in the traditional wheat and course grain sector, as well as in canola and red meats.

Actual and Potential Constraints on Canadian Performance

A variety of concerns has been raised relating to the ability of the agricultural sector to meet future export objectives and to compete with imports. These can most easily be discussed with reference to the major product groups.

Grains and Oilseeds

The issues surrounding these products can be categorized into two sets of topics: those involving the maintenance of the extent and quality of the land base and those relating to international marketing. Although we shall consider them in turn, the two are closely related. Because there is much confusion and apprehension about these topics, particularly with respect to land quality and productivity, we shall consider them at some length.

Many concerns are voiced about constraints on increasing production: the possible limits on the availability of additional suitable land; the loss of land to urbanization, coal mining and like processes; the deterioration of soil quality because of increasing salinity, reduced organic matter, wind and water erosion, and soil acidity; and the presence of large quantities of compacted solonetzic soils (Whelan, 1983). The short answer to these concerns is that they are manageable if Canada is prepared to take two types of action: first, commit far more resources to intensive research on the wide range of problems that exist; and second, show greater flexibility in farming practices and in methods of grain licensing, grading, handling and transportation.

Consider the land base. Whelan (1984) states that between 1961 and 1981, losses from urbanization in Canada amounted to 9.6 million acres. Yet between 1971 and 1981, the improved agricultural land base in the prairies actually expanded by 2.2 million acres (Statistics Canada, 1972, 1982). More important, in Alberta, which has had one of the highest rates of loss of farm land to urbanization, estimates to the year 2000 suggest that in terms of the acreage equivalent of existing average dryland-farming productivity, there could well be an increase of over 4.6 million acres. The significant aspect of this estimate is that while it allows for continued losses to urbanization (amounting to over 1 million acres), various types of new energy-production locations (nearly 0.5 million acres) and salinity (0.5 million acres), it excludes any allowance for increases in acreage equivalents from reduction to summerfallowing (a topic to be treated more fully below). The gains come, instead, from improving unimproved land, from northern development, and from expanding irrigation. It is estimated that there are about 18 million acres in Alberta alone that could be improved (Macdonald, 1984). As there is increasing awareness of the problem of prime farmland losses to urbanization, we can expect to see new policies developed to minimize this loss; some policies have already been instituted, especially in British Columbia, Quebec and Prince Edward Island (Manning, 1983).

The problems of the decline in quality of soil are real, but not unmanageable. About one-third of the organic matter in prairie land has been lost since cultivation began, and this loss, in turn, makes that land more susceptible to erosion. Salinity results from excessive unutilized water absorbing salts as it moves down through the soil and then seeping to the surface in other, lower areas. It is estimated to affect somewhere between 2.7 and 4.0 percent of all dryland in Western Canada (or between 3.7 and 5.5 million acres) and over 20 percent of irrigated acreage, which lies mostly in southern Alberta. It is increasing at a rate of about 10 percent annually (Vander Pluym, Paterson, and Holm, 1981; Vander Pluym, 1983). Precise estimates of losses from wind and water erosion are not available, although it is known that in the southern prairies, wind losses are substantial in dry years, and that in some parts of northern Alberta, eastern Saskatchewan, and southern Manitoba, water losses have been large on occasion (Coote 1984). Significant topsoil losses have also been recorded in other places, such as Prince Edward Island (20 tonnes per hectare on potato land), and Ontario (as much as 50 tonnes per hectare on corn land). Acid soils now comprise about 6.5 million acres on the prairies, 70 percent of which are in Alberta (Hoyt, Nyborg and Ukrainetz, 1981). In addition to being the natural result of carbon dioxide in the soil, acid soil is caused by the use of fertilizers (especially nitrogen) and emissions from natural gas-processing plants, thermal power plants, and smelters. Solonetzic soils (comprising nearly 20 million acres on the prairies) involves highly compacted, impervious subsoils that limit root and water penetration (Racz, 1984, p. 365).

Initial research has suggested that the first two of these land-quality problems can be handled in a relatively straightforward manner, although more work needs to be done on them. The addition of lime to acid soils and the deep-plowing of solonetzic land are profitable investments to make under a range of assumptions about prices and costs (Alberta, Alberta Agriculture 1984a, 1984b). Remedies for salinity, for the declining organic matter in soils, and for erosion are more complex.

Consider salinity. Its control in dryland farming requires one or more of the following techniques: surface water drainage of the recharge areas causing the saline seeps; subsurface drainage (although this approach is often too expensive); the growing of alfalfa or other deep-rooted crops in and around the main recharge areas, to soak up soil moisture to a considerable depth (salt-tolerant cereal crops with shallower root structures will not prevent the increase of salinity); the cessation of summerfallowing in the remainder of the recharge area; and switching to rotating annual crops. The saline-seep areas may be reclaimed (providing the recharge area is simultaneously being controlled) by the growing of salt-tolerant, high-moisture-use crops. How long this process may take is not always clear. In Montana, some experiments with high-moisture-use crops not only lowered the water table in the recharge area, but also reclaimed the downslope saline seep within three years (Vander Pluym, Paterson, and Holm, 1981; Govindasamy, 1984).[1] A key problem in all of this is that the recharge area that causes the problem may be on one farmer's land whereas the seepage or discharge area where the salinity occurs may be on another farmer's acreage. For the first farmer, there may be little incentive to change what he is doing, and yet, unless he does, the neighbouring farmer's attempts to cope with the salinity will be unsuccessful. Once recharge areas are identified through research, legislation may be the only way to ensure that salinity is countered.

A key factor in coping with salinity, and indeed with the reduction of organic matter in the soil, as well as with erosion, is the cutting out of the summerfallow practice. Summerfallowing began primarily as a means of storing moisture for a year so that a better crop could be produced the following year. Weed control became a second major motive for the practice. The share of cultivated prairie acreage under summerfallow grew from 30 percent in 1931 to 40 percent in 1961 and still stood at 36 percent in 1976. But summerfallowing retains only a relatively small percentage (7 to 14 percent) of the year's precipitation for the following year's crop (Hedlin, 1980, p. 5). The remainder passes down through the soil, even in the dry "brown" soil area of the Palliser Triangle, often to form a salt seep elsewhere. Continuous cropping helps greatly to absorb the excess moisture, and when an annual legume crop is included in the rotation, restores organic matter and nitrogen to the soil while also reducing the possibility of erosion.

Initial economic analysis (Zentner, 1984; Wolashyn, 1984; and Alberta, Alberta Agriculture 1984a, 1984b) has suggested that continuous cropping is profitable on "black" and "grey" soils, which comprised over 50 percent of the prairie soils in crop or fallow in the late 1970s. It is also profitable, or at least equivalent to summerfallowing every second or third year, on "dark brown" soils, which comprise about 28 percent of cropped and fallowed land, assuming that crop prices are average or better. If they (or stubble yields) fall significantly below average (say, by 20 percent), summerfallowing may continue to provide better returns. On "brown" soils, comprising the remaining 20 percent of cultivated acreage, continuous cropping does not appear to be profitable to farmers, particularly given present and projected world prices, unless spring moisture in the land is well above average, or rains in the growing season are adequate and fall at the right time.

In general then, even using today's usual farming technology, summerfallowing could be substantially reduced on at least 50 percent of the total cultivated acreage on the prairies and possibly much more than this. Some scepticism has been expressed about the willingness of farmers to take this step even where it seems profitable to do so (McGill, 1982, pp. 97–98). Yet in Alberta, between 1976 and 1981, summerfallowed acreage actually diminished from 30.2 to 23.7 percent (Kelly and Moreau, 1982, p. 145) and in North Dakota, reductions are occurring even more rapidly (Anderson and Associates, 1981, p. 109). Thus it is not unreasonable to expect that as farmers become better educated about the long-run adverse effects of summerfallowing, they will move more and more away from it wherever possible.

Other changes in farming methods will have to occur, however, particularly in the "dark brown" and "brown" soil areas, if summerfallowing is to be reduced as much as is desirable. One of these changes will be in snow- and other moisture-management practices. Planting grass barriers across fields at intervals of about 15 metres, cutting swaths in varying heights (Nicholaichuk, 1983; Nicholaichuk and Read, 1980), and leaving the stubble on the fields over the winter all trap much more snow (as much as double). Stubble will also retain 80 percent of the melted snow water, and it reduces evaporation by 40 percent as compared with fallowed fields. Zero-tillage methods mean more spring water, too, with accompanying increases in crop yields (Lindwall and Dubetz, 1984). The testing of soil for moisture content in the spring will help to identify where seeding of stubble is appropriate. Regular testing for soil nutrients will enable the appropriate amount of fertilizers to be employed, which in turn will increase the efficiency with which crops use moisture by at least 25 to 50 percent and will enable crops to handle greater salinity and to resist weeds and fungal infections (Rennie, 1980, p. 5). More fertilizers will, in general, have to be used: phosphate needs may nearly double while nitrogen needs could rise even more (Hedlin, 1980, pp. 23–24), although where farmers introduce a forage or green manure crop (such as lentils, which are also nitrogen-fixing) as part of their rotation program, the increase in use of chemical fertilizers will be less (Anderson and Associates, 1981, p. 70; Slinkard, 1984). The higher the price of nitrogen fertilizer and the greater the loss of organic content in the soil from standard farming methods, the greater the inducement to farmers to use nitrogen-fixing legumes in their crop rotation. Thus much additional research will be needed on such legumes and on developing nitrogen-fixing grains and grains with deeper root structures.

Even on irrigated lands (of which there are 1.2 million acres in southern Alberta) where summerfallowing is not normally practised, changes will have to be made to correct the salinity problem affecting over 20 percent of the acreage. Seventy percent of the salinity is the result of seepage from unlined irrigation canals, while the balance derives from poor surface drainage, wasting of water during irrigation, and groundwater movements (Birch, 1983). Subsurface drainage is an economically feasible way of countering salinity, but it is likely that lining canals, placing cut-off curtains around canals, and improving the efficiency of irrigation of fields will have to be considered too. Not only can the salinity be dealt with, but more efficient use of water throughout the total irrigation system (from the current 35 percent level) will mean that much more acreage can be irrigated with existing water and storage facilities (Sanderson, 1982e, p. 8).

The possibility of retrieving increased yields from their land through new and improved varieties of grains or other crops will also encourage farmers to move away from summerfallow in favour of farming techniques that preserve and restore land quality. This possibility applies particularly to wheat.

One of the grains that can be used in this way is winter wheat, which is seeded and germinates in the autumn, winters in the ground as a young plant, and comes to maturity the following year. With snow management, winter wheat can yield 25 percent more than spring wheat (Rennie, 1980, p. 3). In the markets, the spread in price between the top three grades has been less than that for the top three grades of red spring wheat (Fowler, 1984). The majority of world trade takes place in winter wheats.

Such wheats used to be grown only in the fairly mild climate of southern Alberta, but their popularity has been surging. In the autumn of 1983, Saskatchewan's plantings of winter wheat were in excess of 300,000 acres, more than twice that of the previous year and for the first time even greater than in Alberta (Bjarnason, 1984). Such wheat is now the largest cash crop produced in Montana. It is subject to winter kill if cold temperatures are extreme, but the technique of seeding it into stubble in the fall and retaining the stubble to trap 8 to 10 centimetres of snow greatly reduces this risk. Winter wheat requires careful farming practices pertaining to weed control, sufficient fertilizer, attention to fall moisture conditions, and adherence to recommended seeding dates. Its development is still at the early stages on the Canadian prairies; it stands at about "the stage that spring wheat and rapeseed [had reached] in the early 1900s and 1950s respectively" (Fowler 1984, p. 329). Much more research is necessary, but the potential for successful crops is certainly there.

Another incipient change is the development of high-yielding, semi-dwarf wheats of the "3-M" type (medium hard kernel, medium gluten strength, and medium protein content). These wheats are the best quality for satisfying much of the world's demand for wheat. They are used by themselves or as a filler for wet and dry noodles, chapatis, steamed bread, Arabic-style breads, French-style breads, Brazilian breads and North American-style breads (Canadian Wheat Board, 1984). Traditional hard red spring wheat varieties account for only about 20 percent of world wheat sales. Some nations such as Japan (Canada's third-largest market) insist on "Canadian wheat red spring" (CWRS) No. 1 wheat and are willing to pay a premium for it. The United Kingdom also wants the CWRS Nos. 1 and 2 for blending with other wheats in the milling process. Because of its capability to produce this wheat, Canada has a special place in such world markets. Yet there are some indications that as the technology of gluten substitution is developed, the United Kingdom may rely less on Canadian high-protein hard wheat for blending. In general, future growth in demand for hard red spring wheat is not anticipated. The most vigorous expansion of world demand is going to be for the triple-M quality. Thus Canada must develop its production of such wheat if it expects to share in this expanding world market.

So far Canada has been ultra-conservative in this respect. A variety of triple-M wheat, HY320 (high-yielding 320), was developed in 1977 at Swift Current, Saskatchewan. It consistently outyields the most popular hard red spring wheat, Neepawa, by 30 percent when raised by dryland farming in years of either drought or adequate rainfall, and by 39 percent on irrigated land (De Pauw, 1984). Still it is not licensed by the Canadian Grains Commission. Only now is it being grown under contract for the Canadian Wheat Board in sufficient amounts (nearly 200,000 acres in 1984) to be market tested in a variety of countries (Canadian Wheat Board, 1984).

It is argued on occasion that Canada has had to be very conservative in its acceptance of different quality wheats in order to protect its market niche in very high-protein hard wheats. If seasonal conditions are adverse so that lower grades of these latter wheats result, they are still quite marketable. But if frost or excess moisture occurs before and during harvest, when triple-M wheats are being produced, the resulting grades may be more difficult to dispose of in world markets at anything better than feed-wheat prices. Thus farmers who have produced the grain may not be any better off, even though they are enjoying higher yields.

The rapidity with which plant breeders can usefully improve a grain variety depends on their degree of assurance that the variety is or will be licensed for production. It only slows improvements to delay the licensing until the "perfect" variety is developed; in fact, such delays will probably ensure that the desired characteristics will not be produced. If, many decades ago, Canada had not been willing to begin growing hard red spring wheat of the Selkirk variety, we should probably not have the greatly improved Neepawa variety today. And if we had delayed growing canola until Tobin or Westar were derived, such superior strains would likely not yet be in existence (De Pauw. n. d.(b)). (On this point, it is worth noting that developments in canola have been particularly well coordinated as a consequence of the close communication and cooperation of all participants in the industry, from plant breeders to exporters.)

A high probability exists that HY320 will be licensed as a separate grade of wheat in the near future (Bjarnason, 1984). Much research will still be required, however, to improve its resistance to loose smut and common bunt, to enhance further its dormancy qualities while it is in the swath awaiting final harvest — it is presently equal to Neepawa, but not as good as some other CWRS wheats such as Columbus–so that it can be more readily grown in the black- and grey-soil zones, and to determine the best farm-management practices using zero or minimum tillage, herbicides, fertilizers, and the like (De Pauw, n.d. (b)).

Another plant-breeding development similar to the growth of demand for wheat in world markets, and one which will augment the competitive position of western wheat growers, is the adaptation of white wheats to Canadian growing conditions. Many foreign markets wish to use wheat kernels to form up to 90 percent of the ingredients for flour as compared to about 70 percent in Canada. To use red wheats in this proportion leaves tiny red flecks in the flour, and consumers deem these flecks undesirable. Hence, Canadian producers must also offer white wheats. Development of a triple-M quality white wheat (lesprout) with dormancy characteristics equal to Neepawa is already well under way (De Pauw, 1984), and the new variety will be ready for test growing and marketing by 1988–89. Here again, of course, licensing by the Canadian Grains Council will be a vital step if additional improvements are to be made in this type of wheat.

Farmers must receive higher returns for their produce so that they can afford to adopt practices that preserve and improve the quality of farm land. This necessity requires the development of other practices beyond providing farmers with the possibility of growing higher-yielding grains. Among these additional practices is increased efficiency in the grading, handling, storing and transporting of agricultural output; the benefits of this improvement will be reflected in higher net returns to farmers. By and large, although some adjustments have been made in Canadian practices over time, such as the adoption of hopper cars for grain transportation and some very modest changes in grading, the rate of change has generally been glacial at best. While the number of elevators in the country has been reduced, and their average size has been increased, the country elevator system is little different from what it was 70 or more years ago. Recommendations have been made to reduce the number of grades of grain so as to minimize the separate categories that have to be stored in country elevators, to speed up the filling of hopper cars, and thus generally to increase the efficiency of the elevator and transportation systems. Such changes would also allow farmers to be more flexible, for if elevator-bin space were freed up, farmers would have greater opportunities to grow and sell other products through the elevator system (Thomas and De Pauw, n.d.). This recommendation along with other proposals — for example, a proposal to simplify the grading system according to end-use requirements for grain and to move away from the visual distinguishability requirement for all grades — were also made as a consequence of a major study completed in 1982 (Canada Grains Council, 1982b; see also Bushak, 1984). As yet, however, major changes have not been forthcoming.

Other characteristics of the grain-handling system, such as shrinkage charges, also give an impression of being written in stone. These shrinkage charges, which are charged to the farmers, are for leakages of grain occurring between the producer and the final sale at the terminals or ships. Because the grain-handling companies do not have to bear the charges themselves, they have little incentive to become more efficient. Thus the shrinkage charges have not been altered for over 40 years. As Loyns and Carter (1984, p. 64) have observed, "That these losses would remain constant . . . raises an interesting question on technological development in grain handling in Canada." The point is clear: there is immense room for reorganization of the entire system of grading, handling and transportation of grains to reduce the costs per tonne of grading, mixing and moving grain from farmers' fields to ocean-going ships and to increase the capacity of the system to cope with the augmented farm output that will be possible as yields rise on existing seeded acreage, and as the amount of summerfallow is minimized.[2]

Substantial new investments, possibly of a revolutionary nature, may be necessary in handling and grading grain prior to rail transport, and in rail transportation to the terminal or ocean-loading facilities. Farmers will be required to make changes, as well: to invest in new, possibly larger, equipment to handle cropping of land that is presently fallow, and to undertake new tillage and harvesting practices associated with zero tillage, to plow deeper and to grow green manure, forage and other crops.

In addition, further changes are necessary in the administration of the revised Crow Rate rail-transportation structure and in the subsidies to be given thereunder, so that the efficiency of Western Canadian agriculture is increased. This paper need not devote space to this major issue, for it is comprehensively examined in the recent Economic Council of Canada document, *Western Transition* (Economic Council, 1984, pp. 125–45).

Other changes may also be desirable if farmers' returns are to be enlarged and stabilized. Canada heavily depends on exports to relatively few buyers, of which the two largest are the centrally planned economies of the U.S.S.R. and mainland China with their rather unpredictable buying patterns. If Soviet agriculture were reorganized, the imports of the U.S.S.R. could be reduced substantially, and similarly, if China continues to improve its incentives to farmers, her demand for grain imports might be reduced or shifted from wheat to feed grains. Hence, Canada must diversify her markets for wheat, especially. Developing the triple-M red and white wheats will make this outcome more likely, for it is these wheats that other countries usually buy.

Concurrently, competition from the heavily subsidized exports of the European Community, along with U.S. retaliation, may reduce future markets for Canadian grain or require Canadian sales abroad to be subsidized, unless Canada in combination with the United States, has some success in GATT in bringing agricultural trade and the Common Agricultural Policy of the EC under GATT rules. This is particularly important if sales to developing lands are to be expanded to meet these nations' long-term food deficits and medium-term needs as internal structural changes are made, or to compensate for year-to-year fluctuations in harvests. Many of these nations lack the ability to pay for current or expanded food imports and so may require subsidies or more foreign aid, no matter what the EC or the United States does in the future (Cole and Horton, 1983).

Because of these uncertainties in world grain markets, it would make good sense for Canada to work more actively for a return to International Wheat Agreements among the main producing and importing nations such as existed from 1949 to 1968. Under these agreements, each exporting and importing nation could make a commitment concerning the minimum or maximum amount of grain it would buy or supply each year. In addition, Canada will likely have to be open, where necessary, to opportunities for bilateral trade involving agricultural, as well as other, products.[3]

As changes are made and efficiency is increased in the grain-handling and transportation systems, there is also good reason to move away from the grain-quota system as it now exists. The Canadian system often discourages additional output on highly productive land and encourages summerfallowing of such land because delivery quotas are allowed even on the land summerfallowed. A removal or revamping of quotas would increase specialization and continuous cropping.

All of the various areas mentioned — soil quality, grain varieties, farming techniques and grading and handling techniques — demand large, new research programs. The amount of study required is almost overwhelming.[4] Yet the step is long overdue.

The evidence strongly suggests that large net social benefits accrue from agricultural research: "Canola research undertaken in Canada between 1960 and 1975 reportedly yielded a *95–110 percent return per annum*.[5] At least two dozen other studies on the return to agricultural research which all document relatively high payoffs have been catalogued" (Anderson and Associates, 1982, p. 9). It is appalling, therefore, that Canada has allowed its emphasis on such research to diminish relative to gross national product (GNP) and relative to what competitor countries are doing. Federal outlays now stand at about one-half the proportion of GNP that such research represents in both the United States and Japan, and there are major shortages of funds for agricultural research and professional agricultural researchers (Veeman and Veeman, 1984a). That more such research is necessary is unarguable. The only debatable points concern the order in which matters should be undertaken. It would be a sad day for agriculture and for Canada if the present obsession of federal and provincial governments with reducing their deficits should prevent this vital increase in research and adaptation from taking place.

Another dimension of improved agricultural performance is the financial position of producers themselves. Grain farming is now an expensive undertaking, requiring initial capital outlays in the order of $500,000 or more. The capital to value-added ratio in agriculture is 8:1, compared with a 2:1 ratio or less for much of construction, forestry, manufacturing and mining. High interest charges thus can become a weighty problem for new farmers introducing measures either to prevent the further deterioration of their land or to restore its quality. Moreover, from 1976 to 1982, costs of fertilizer, chemicals and petroleum products rose by between 200 and 300 percent, whereas gross farm revenues remained roughly constant (*Edmonton Journal*, October 27, 1984, p. D-1). In general, farm-product prices are not expected to increase as rapidly in the future as farm input prices or the rate of inflation. As Table 1-11 shows, this expectation applies particularly to grain prices.

It is not infrequently proposed that more subsidies, low-interest loans, and extensions of time in which to repay loans are the answers to the financial problems besetting the one-sixth of Canadian farmers who

TABLE 1-11 Projections of Farm-Related Price Indexes, 1984–2000

	1984–1988	1984–2000
	(annual percent changes)	
Farm product price index	4.2	4.0 – 5.0
Grain price index	2.9a	3.0 – 3.7
Farm input price index	4.6	5.2 – 5.4
Inflation rate (GNP)	5.0	5.2 – 5.4

Source: S. Borland and G. Robertson, "A Sectoral View of the Longer-Term: Agriculture," in *Long-Term Economic Prospects for Canada: A Symposium*, volume
23 of the research studies prepared for the Royal Commission on the Economic
Union and Development Prospects for Canada (Toronto: University of Toronto
Press, 1985).
a. Weighted average of wheat (0.85) and barley (0.15).

experience severe financial difficulties. Certainly, one would hope that
the financial community would show as much patience with farmers as
they do with other groups. On occasion, indeed, low-interest loans may
help farmers to modernize their operations or to restore land quality, but
they are not long-term solutions. The more lasting solution must be to
increase farm productivity. This achievement necessitates additional
research on the many factors that can enhance productivity and, further,
requires effective communication to the farm community of the results of
this research.

This last tenet makes evident another necessary change: the upgrading of farm managerial skills. Farming is no longer, if it ever was, a
business for the uneducated or the untrained. It requires much technical
knowledge of proper tilling techniques, as well as of the biological,
chemical and herbicidal requirements of particular crops in relation to
seed varieties, soil types, moisture and other weather and climatic
conditions. It also demands management skills: record-keeping, organization, time allocation, risk-spreading and financing. Canada may have
to move to more of a European-style approach, which requires that
before people are allowed to work the land or to receive any sort of
financial assistance, they must successfully complete appropriate training programs.

Red Meats

Canada is a net exporter of animals, red meats and red meat products. In
1983 it exported $1 billion worth, primarily to the United States, but also
to Japan and, in relatively much smaller quantities, to other countries.
For future growth and international competitiveness of this industry, the
improvement of the farm-management skills named above will be important. Other changes will prove valuable, too (Economic Council of
Canada, 1984, pp. 92–96). The Crow Rate subsidy payments, which
encourage the railways to move feed grains to places like Quebec, along

with Quebec's agricultural programs to develop their provincial self-sufficiency in red meats — the province is now a net exporter of pork products — have eroded the comparative advantage that Western Canada has traditionally enjoyed in producing such products. Greater efficiency within Canada could come about by letting comparative advantage operate (Cole and Horton, 1983). More flexibility in Canadian production, grading, handling and pricing systems, both at the farm and at government levels, may be desirable, too, if foreign tastes, such as the Japanese preference for beef with more fat throughout the meat, are to be satisfied. More aggressive pursuit of markets for beef in California might yield good results also, given that the meat deficit in that state is expected to increase. A more vertically integrated production, processing and marketing system, such as now exists for hogs in Quebec, might well be necessary for the entire industry. Supply-management systems should be avoided, for if they were introduced, the industry would likely become less responsive to international market conditions and less able to compete internationally. (I shall elaborate on this point in the next section.) Finally, even though the low Canadian dollar makes domestic industry more competitive, it must still be recognized that U.S. meat-processing workers have accepted lower wages than their Canadian counterparts. If Canadian workers are too aggressive in their wage demands, the Canadian competitive position can easily be eroded. The results could be more exports of live animals to the United States and more imports of beef products to Canada, with a consequent reduction in Canadian jobs.

Poultry, Eggs and Milk Products

Canada does not now produce these products at competitive world prices. Import restrictions prevent large inflows of them. Any exports are generally sold much below world prices so as to dispose of accumulated surpluses.

All of these commodities are produced in Canada under supply-management systems involving quotas that are assigned first to provinces and then to individual producers, with prices set to yield suitable returns to all producers (Kelly and Moreau, 1982; Forbes, Hughes, and Warley, 1982; Hoos, 1979). The quotas themselves take on a monetary value, for a farmer wishing to retire from the business can extract the discounted market value of the quota from the person or firm buying him or her out. As quotas become capitalized, product prices must rise over time to yield adequate returns to those who purchased them.

The adverse effects of supply-management systems do not stop here. Rigid controls over supplies and prices and the freedom of the producer associations to raise prices as desired leave farmers little incentive to become more efficient. Nor is there much opportunity for farmers who are superior progressive managers to expand. New entrants with innovative ideas, new technology, or advanced management skills cannot enter the industry, either, unless they can find someone's quota to purchase. The allocation of quotas among provinces is based not on the natural comparative advantages of different regions, but on previous production patterns, such as production subsidies, which are themselves the result of market interventions by governments (Whalley, 1980). Hence specialization among provinces and improvements in efficiency derivable therefrom are not being achieved. Nor do provisions usually exist for declines in domestic prices as means of disposing of excess supplies. Storage costs mount. In addition, processors are less able to cope with international competition unless they are protected, for they have to rely on the high-priced inputs and are limited in their scale of operation and location because of provincial limits on supplies. Consumers are the ultimate losers in all of this because they must pay the higher production and storage costs for the products. The total costs of these supply-management systems were estimated at between $1 billion and $1.5 billion per year during the mid- to late-1970s. At today's prices the figures would likely be in the range of $2 billion to $2.5 billion annually. Another source of dissatisfaction is that the chief beneficiaries are the largest operators, who really do not need the assistance.

A variety of recommendations has been proposed that would reduce the exorbitant social waste of current policies, lower costs enormously for consumers, and make the industries more competitive internationally. These include such policies as reducing the prices that the marketing boards are allowed to set; disallowing any costs of obtaining quotas in the costs to be tabulated in setting product prices or allowing expense items for income tax purposes; and making quotas more easily transferable both between producers and across provincial boundaries so that economies of scale and the consequent lower production costs can be attained (Forbes, Hughes, and Warley, 1982, p. 101). So far, no federal or provincial government has had the courage to do much, if anything, along these lines. Yet this is the direction in which we must move if we are not to see the performance and competitiveness of this sector continue to fall further and further behind international standards. It is hardly appropriate for Canada to point its collective finger at the Common Agricultural Policy of the EC when it follows such policies within its own borders.

There seems to be an emotional attachment to the small family farm, and a feeling that everything possible must be done to keep it in operation. Yet there is nothing more sacred about the small family farm than there is about the small family corner grocery store, clothing store or restaurant. Many of these close down each year for one reason or another. It would be a woefully rigid and inefficient economy if price levels and other rules were established to keep all such small businesses in operation. Why should small, inefficient, family farms be treated any differently?

Fruits, Vegetables, and Other Horticultural Products

To some extent, Canada must rely on tropical fruit and vegetable products. But a wide range of imported horticultural products are directly competitive with domestic sources of supply. Table 1-12 summarizes the high significance of imports as a proportion of domestic consumption of fresh fruits and vegetables. For heavily consumed items such as tomatoes, celery and lettuce, the foreign share is over 80 percent. For field tomatoes (excluding greenhouse production), the foreign share is 96 percent. If all nontropical fresh fruits and vegetables are considered, the foreign share is well over 50 percent. When potatoes are excluded from this total, the foreign share rises to nearly two-thirds of domestic consumption of fresh produce. In addition, Canada imports large numbers of bedding plants, flowers and the like.

In the last decade or so, a substantial increase occurred in the per capita consumption of fresh produce: between 1971 and 1980, the increase was 95 pounds per capita (Kirsch, 1983). This increase was partly the result of a belief that unprocessed fruits and vegetables are more nourishing, and partly the result of the success of the promotional efforts of the Fresh for Flavour Foundation established in 1972.

On first glance it might appear that major opportunities for increased import-replacing promotion exist. Canada has vast supplies of land and water. Moreover, successful horticultural production does not require first-grade land. The technology is available to utilize inferior grades of soil such as the grade-five sandy soil in the southern Niagara Peninsula which has been used to grow tobacco, a crop now facing declining demand. Sand can be a quite satisfactory growth medium for many crops when modern hydroponics or other recently developed technologies are used. The technology also exists for proper storage of many fruits and vegetables to preserve freshness and quality so that supplies can be made available outside the usual field-crop growing season (Nonnecke and Ormrod, 1977). Finally, much waste heat from industrial sites could be used in greenhouses.

Yet any move toward import substitution will not be simple. Even leaving aside greenhouse production for the moment, capital costs of field-crop production are substantial. Because growing seasons are fairly short, suitable storage facilities are an essential part of the expansion of domestic output. To start up either a 300-acre potato operation or a 150-acre farm for growing and storing vegetables involves an investment of about $1 million (Schaupmeyer, 1977). This necessity makes this type of farming even more capital intensive than is grain farming. In contrast, in the southern United States, capital costs are lower, because of the longer

TABLE 1-12 Imports of Vegetables and Fruits for Fresh Consumption, 1983

Produce (vegetables)	Percent of Total[a]	Produce (fruits)	Percent of total
Field tomatoes	95.8	Plums	84.5
Tomatoes (all)	86.7	Cherries	65.9
Broccoli	84.3	Pears	64.8
Celery	83.9	Peaches	49.4
Lettuce	81.7	Apples	36.4
Beans	76.2		
Spinach	74.0		
Corn	67.8		
Cauliflower	66.0		
Radishes	64.3		
Cucumbers	55.5		
Onions	45.3		
Carrots	42.8		
Cabbage	32.4		
Potatoes	17.2		

Source: Canada, Department of Agriculture, Marketing and Economics Branch, *Annual Unload Report: Fresh Fruits and Vegetables on 12 Canadian Markets* (Ottawa: The Department, 1983).

Notes: A study of 12 major Canadian markets, Halifax, Saint John, Quebec City, Montreal, Ottawa, Toronto, Winnipeg, Regina, Saskatoon, Edmonton, Calgary and Vancouver.

All nontropical fruits and vegetables = 53.1 percent.

All nontropical fruits and vegetables, excluding potatoes = 64.4 percent.

a. Percentage, based on pounds not dollar values, of total domestic and import supplies for fresh consumption.

growing season, which allows greater utilization of land and equipment and necessitates fewer storage facilities. Cheap labour often lowers labour costs there, as well. Difficulties exist on the marketing side, too. Local growers must be able to break into supply channels of wholesalers (and accompanying retail chains) that have long-established contacts in areas like Florida, California and Arizona. To do so, they have to be able to provide guaranteed quantities of a clearly defined quality at specified times.

Some factors may, of course, favour Canadian over U.S. production. These include lower outlays for insecticides because of cooler climate; smaller transportation costs to market; the lower value of the Canadian dollar, which is now worth less than three-quarters of the U.S. dollar; and in the future, cheaper water in Canada as the United States is forced to raise its water prices to cover more closely the costs of supplying that resource, in order to deal with its declining water table.

Detailed costing studies weighing these and all the other factors that influence costs and returns are not readily available. There is some evidence, however, that Canadian producers, by and large, are not yet making the best of their situation. Lack of attention to reliability and, more especially, to quality are frequently cited weaknesses of Canadian growers (Wiebe, 1980, p. 86; Hole, 1980). Nor are the latest developments in storage always being utilized, even though some provincial governments have loan programs to encourage producers to develop suitable storage facilities. Scale economies exist in this industry, too; yet often Canadian farms are small-scale operations. Provincial policies involving subsidies, loans or guaranteed minimum prices to support small growers only defer the attainment of available scale economies and do little to improve the efficiency of the industry.

In greenhouse production more room exists for improvement, as well. Few greenhouses in Canada are as yet using the most modern technology for retaining heat or for temperature and humidity control, or the most efficient methods of space utilization, hydroponics and the like.[6] And apart from two complexes comprising seven acres of greenhouses and using the waste heat from a large gas-compressor station and gas ethylene plant, almost no use is being made of excess industrial heat. These complexes have been established at Princess and Joffre in Alberta by Noval Enterprises, a subsidiary of Nova Corporation. Most greenhouses are small scale, too, although the evidence indicates that returns per square foot are higher in larger operations (Chaudhary, 1984).

In summary, although producers in the southern states may enjoy some cost advantages over those in Canadian locations, Canadian producers are far from making the best of their circumstances. Provincial governments should encourage growers to be more efficient, and they should work together much more closely in developing policies that will improve the performance of the whole industry across the country. Marketing boards that simply provide quotas and guaranteed prices to producers should be abolished for the reasons given in the previous section of this paper. Larger-scale operations are worth encouraging both to attain economies of scale and to support growers sufficiently large enough and diversified that the short-term failure of one crop or the challenge of cheap imports in another crop does not send the company into bankruptcy. Greater vertical integration of producers, wholesalers and retailers may be a useful step to consider, as well. Additional research on improved seed varieties, better insect and disease control by means of biotechnology or other techniques, improved use of space, new uses of vegetable products, and new vegetable products are all likely to yield good returns (Tanner, 1983). If steps of these sorts are taken, there is little doubt that the efficiency and competitiveness of the Canadian horticultural industry will be improved, and that consumers, in turn, will benefit.

Agriculture: Conclusions

With the Canadian dollar now well below parity with the U.S. dollar, the potential exists for the continuing expansion of Canada's exports of grains, oilseeds and red meats. There may even be opportunities for a higher degree of import substitution in horticultural products if appropriate measures are taken to improve efficiency. Whatever the product, trade improvement will not be entirely clear sailing. Major uncertainties exist about the course of developments in world markets. Although some of these are not within Canada's control, a number of measures that are within Canada's control can be undertaken to enhance our competitive position. We might, for example, expand research programs (and communication of the research results to farmers) to cope with the problem of the deterioration of soil quality, and to develop improved varieties of plans adapted to Canadian conditions and productive of higher yields. We might extensively revamp and rationalize the internal gathering, grading, mixing and transportation systems for grains and oilseeds, many of which were in place at or near the beginning of the twentieth century; and we might provide financial assistance to farmers, where necessary, not to preserve the status quo, but to help them bring their operations into the twenty-first century.

Some of the problems faced today by Canadian agriculture, such as soil quality, are different from the scourges of cutworms, rust and smut of earlier decades. Others, such as the possibility of drought or grasshoppers, the need to improve yields, and the instability of farm incomes, still remain. Continuous adjustments to new problems and new situations are going to be necessary. The greatest danger that Canadian agriculture faces is the sort of attitude that dominates the supply-management systems of the marketing boards for poultry and milk products. The type of legislation placed before Parliament in the spring of 1984, which fortunately was never acted upon, but which would have guaranteed farmers a profit on their domestic sales, should be avoided. It would only increase the inflexibility of the food-supply system.

Economists are unanimous that one of the greatest contributors to real per capita income growth in this nation since World War II has been the combination of technological improvements and structural changes that took place as farming was rationalized. In Western Canada, instead of one family on every 160 acres as resulted so frequently from the original homestead allocations, farms grew in size to 640 acres and often much more; new sophisticated machinery was employed; improved varieties of plants were developed; and simultaneously, the proportion of the labour force in agriculture dropped from 25 percent to below today's 5 percent. It would be unfortunate if we were now to allow our agricultural system to become ossified and thus deprive ourselves of future improvements in productivity.

Energy

Energy forecasting is a risky business in which the chances of being "right" are virtually nil.

Jeanne Anderer (1983)

The World Situation

Because of the higher energy prices that resulted from success of the Organization of Petroleum Export Countries (OPEC) at raising oil prices, the growth rate of energy consumption has been declining in the world as a whole. During the 1960s, consumption expanded at an annual average rate of 6.0 percent, whereas for the 1970s the rate was only 3.1 percent (World Bank, 1984). It is expected to grow more slowly again, during the remainder of this century and into the next. Generally speaking, the more recent the projections, the lower the anticipated growth rates (Reddy, 1984). Table 1-13 illustrates this situation. Some believe that the projections of the International Institute for Applied Systems Analysis (IIASA) are too high because a number of the assumptions used in relation to energy conservation are already outdated. Efficiency standards for automobiles, households (through insulation measures), and even for wood-burning stoves, which were originally expected to be achieved by 2030, have already been achieved or exceeded (ibid., 1984, pp. 36–37).

Three other important trends are expected to develop as time progresses to reduce other nations' vulnerability to the policies of OPEC: nations will continue to move toward greater self-sufficiency in energy; nations and regions will increasingly diversify their energy-supply sources, and will rely less on oil and more on other types of energy; and a greater proportion of oil supplies will come from non-conventional sources (Foster, 1983). The projected relative importance of the various energy supplies is shown in Figure 1-2. The expected growth in coal and nuclear energy may, however, be exaggerated, for environmental concerns may deter such growth for years to come.

To achieve such growth in energy production, direct and indirect energy investment will have to increase in developed countries to 3 or 3.5 percent of gross domestic product (GDP) from 1975 levels of about 2.4 percent. In developing lands, investments will have to reach 6 percent of GDP or even more (McDonald, 1981, pp. 48–49). Massive financial assistance to the oil-importing developing countries will be necessary.

Forecasts of energy-resource use virtually ignore many pressing problems, or implicitly assume that they will be resolved by appropriate technological or institutional developments. These problems include acid rain from burning coal that has a high sulphur content; radioactive wastes that require safe disposal; the build-up of CO_2 in the atmosphere and its potentially serious implications for temperature and precipitation patterns; the possible surreptitious use of nuclear discharge for nuclear weaponry; and the implications for increased global inequalities of living standards. We shall not treat these issues here, but we must emphasize that to solve global energy problems without simultaneously resolving these issues will not leave us with a sustainable world economy (Reddy, 1984).

TABLE 1-13 Projections of World Energy Consumption: Annual Growth Rates to 2000 and 2030

	to 2000		2000–2030	
	High	**Low**	**High**	**Low**
IIASA: 1981: 1975–2000	3.0	2.1	2.2	1.4
IIASA: 1983: 1980–2000		2.2		1.2

Sources: International Institute for Applied Systems Analysis, *Options* (March 1983). Alan McDonald, *Energy in a Finite World: Executive Summary* (Laxenberg, Austria: International Institute for Applied Systems Analysis, 1983).

FIGURE 1–2 Global Primary Energy Consumption, 1980–2030 (in watt years per year)[1]

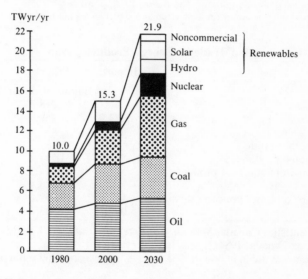

Source: H.H. Rogner *IIASA '83 Scenario of Energy Development: Summary.* (Laxenberg, Austria: International Institute for Applied Systems Analysis, 1984).

Note: 1 Terrawatt = 10^{12} watts = 1 petajoule of energy.

Canada

Unlike many countries, Canada is relatively well endowed with all of the major natural resources required for energy production: oil, natural gas, coal, uranium, and actual and potential hydro sites. Projected shares of different fuels for Canada in 1983 and 2005 are given in Table 1-14.

The major change expected over the next years is a decline in the relative importance of oil and an increase in primary electricity, particularly from hydro and nuclear sources, although coal-fired electricity, too, is expected to expand. This change is largely because these other energy sources are cheaper than oil. Canada is now a net exporter of

TABLE 1-14 Projected Fuel Shares in Primary Energy Demand and Production in Canada

	Primary Energy Demand[a]		Primary Energy Production[a]	
	1983	2005	1983	2005
	(percent)			
Oil	44	29	37	27
Gas	24	29	27	26
Coal	12	14	13	18
Nuclear	2	5	2	5
Hydro	11	15	11	14
Other	7	8	10	10
Total	100	100	100	100

Source: National Energy Board, *Canadian Energy: Supply and Demand 1983–2005: Technical Report* (Ottawa: The Board, 1984), p. 101.
a. Hydro and nuclear power are converted at 3.6 petajoules per terawatt hour.

TABLE 1-15 Canadian Trade in Energy Products, 1983

	Imports	Exports	Balance
	(millions of dollars)		
Natural gas	—	3,958.2	3,958.2
Crude petroleum	3,273.9	3,456.9	183.0
Fuel oil	405.4	—	−405.4
Coal and other crude bituminous substances	841.8	1,312.8	471.0
Other petroleum and coal products	572.6	2,814.9	2,242.3
Electricity	—	1,228.4	1,228.4
Radioactive ores and concentrates	—	62.6[a]	62.6
Total	5,093.7	12,833.8	7,740.1

Source: Statistics Canada, *Summary of External Trade, 1983.* (Ottawa, Statistics Canada, 1984).
a. This item was much higher in 1981 and 1982, averaging $269 million for those years.

energy in all of its main forms and is expected to remain so for the next two decades. Current figures are summarized in Table 1-15.

As the issues regarding each of the energy sources are different, it is worth considering them individually.

Petroleum

Historical View

We must review the recent history of the oil and gas industry before we can properly consider the industry's future prospects. Until late 1980, the oil and gas industry was a leading sector in the Canadian economy. Then, in October of that year, came the National Energy Program (NEP). Its declared objectives were threefold:

- to give Canada security of oil supply;
- to redistribute the benefits from Western Canada's oil and gas resources to all Canadians; and
- to increase domestic ownership of the industry.

An undeclared purpose of the program seems also to have been to move control and concentration of the oil and gas industry away from Western Canada. The NEP involved a series of new taxes on the oil industry, incentives to the industry to relocate away from the western sedimentary basin to frontier lands owned by the federal goverment, and restrictions on oil and gas prices to keep them below world levels. (An exception was made for oil found after 1980, which was to receive the new oil reference price, or NORP.)

The NEP is now in almost complete disarray. The incremental oil revenue tax (IORT), introduced in 1981 to take effect January 1, 1982, is no longer operative. The natural gas and gas-liquids tax (NGGLT), too, is no longer operative for conventional production. The petroleum and gas-revenue tax (PGRT) has been removed for small producers, reduced for *in situ* oil sands recovery (Wilkinson, 1984), and modified again for the recent Husky Oil heavy oil-upgrader project. Recent work by the Economic Council of Canada has demonstrated that the PGRT is much inferior to a profits tax because of its deleterious effects on exploration and development of oil reserves (Economic Council, 1984d). The petroleum incentive-payments plan (PIP), which gives much more generous benefits to oil companies for drilling on frontier lands than in Western Canada, has also been questioned because of its wasteful use of society's resources (Scarfe, 1984; Waverman, 1984). The NORP has been made retroactive to cover oil found since 1974. It was reduced a few percentage points for foreign owners, but at the expense of several Canadian firms — Dome, for example — going deep into debt. The major U.S. companies continue to prosper, while many small Canadian service companies have collapsed.

Although the levelling out of world oil prices certainly had an adverse effect on the activity in the oil industry (Helliwell, MacGregor, and Plourde, 1983), it remains true that because of the NEP, oil and gas development in Western Canada was set back considerably, particularly in 1981 and 1982, at great economic and social cost to all of Canada; that development is only now beginning to recover (Scarfe, 1984). It has become increasingly clear that Canada would benefit in terms of oil self-sufficiency, higher employment and economic growth, and lower inflation, by allowing both oil and natural gas prices to reflect the world market situation. Oil prices would rise somewhat, on average, while natural gas prices might well decline below the 65-percent oil British thermal unit (Btu) equivalent, at which they are currently set (Economic Council, 1984d).

The lesson is clear: when federal and provincial governments battle for control over the economic rents from the nation's resources, the entire nation may suffer. Canada experienced a similar, though much less widely felt struggle in the mid-1970s, when federal and provincial governments severally attempted to increase their share of rents from the metal-mining industry to the point where aggregate marginal tax rates were greater than 100 percent. We must hope that future oil and gas scenarios will avoid arbitrary, ill-devised, inefficient, growth-reducing, federal government policies that are proclaimed without consultations with other governments or with the industry which they are going intimately to affect.

Consider next the future prospects for the oil and gas industry.

Oil Prices

Along with the projected growth rates of energy consumption in general, estimates of growth rates of future oil prices have been moderating as time passes.[7] Thus, in September 1984, the National Energy Board (NEB) provided in its low-price scenario for no real world oil-price increases until 2005. Its high-priced scenario, deemed to allow for such developments as an escalation of the war between Iran and Iraq, was for real price increases, from 1983 to 1990, of 2.5 percent annually and, from 1990 to 2005 of only 2.4 percent per year. Dependence on OPEC is much lower than it was a decade ago. Energy developments have to be planned with these modest price changes in mind.

Domestic Supply and Demand for Oil

Future demand for oil in Canada depends on a host of considerations. Among them are: the rate of economic growth; the extent of the continuation of conservation measures in response to the oil-price increases of the late 1970s; the extent to which the levelling out of prices will reduce the move to smaller, fuel-efficient automobiles or the conversion from fuel oil in industry and home heating to other energy sources; the amount of substitution that may occur between gasoline and other possible motor-vehicle fuels; the extent of excess capacity of hydro, nuclear and thermal electricity industries, and their pricing policies; and the effect of changes in industrial structure and in technology on energy usage and its efficiency. Some of these forces or trends may cancel one another out. At this time it is difficult to be adamant about detailed outcomes (National Energy Board, 1983a).

However uncertain the demand projections may be, even less confidence can be held in future oil-supply projections. Nevertheless, one aspect of future supplies is certain. Reliance on conventional oil from the Western sedimentary basin, even including tertiary or enhanced recovery projects, will diminish (Waverman, 1984; Canada, Department of Energy, Mines and Resources, 1983; Nelles, 1984). More oil has already

TABLE 1-16 Predicted Sources of Crude Oil Production

	1983	1990	2005
	(thousands of cubic metres per day)		
Conventional light and pentanes plus	174.1	117.5	49.9
Oil sands synthetic (including upgrading heavy)	23.5	42.5	63.5
Frontier	—	1.9	44.0
Total light	197.6	161.9	157.4
Blended heavy crude and bitumen	43.9	39.1	59.2
Total	241.5	201.0	216.6

Source: National Energy Board, *Canadian Energy: Supply and Demand 1983–2005: Summary Report* (Ottawa: The Board, 1984).

been produced from this basin than is expected to be recovered from remaining and still-to-be-discovered reserves. Non-conventional sources of supply will have increasing significance. This trend is already in evidence. Suncor and Syncrude oil-sands production already exists, and large extensions to capacity are both under way and planned; Norman Wells production on the Mackenzie River is being increased; smaller *in situ* bitumen plants are in production or under construction by Esso Resources at Cold Lake, and by British Petroleums and Petrocan at Wolfe Lake, and more are in the planning stages; a heavy-oil upgrading plant and an increased drilling program at Lloydminster have been announced by Husky Oil; and exploratory drilling continues in Hibernia off the East Coast and in the Beaufort Sea in the Arctic.

Although frontier oil is expected to be very important by the turn of the century, the greatest potential in terms of known reserves lies with the oil sands of northern Alberta and Saskatchewan. Estimates of reserves recoverable by open-pit mining techniques range from about 25 billion barrels to 85 billion barrels, with another 200 billion barrels or more recoverable by *in situ* techniques. Compared with current recoverable reserves of conventional oil in Alberta of about 5 billion barrels, these oil-sands reserves are immense.

Table 1-16 summarizes the National Energy Board's assessment of the changing relative importance of the different sources of oil supply for the next two decades. Synthetic and frontier light crude oil plus blended heavy crude and bitumen are expected to advance from representing only 28 percent of the total supply in 1983, to representing 77 percent in 2005.

As production is forthcoming from these new supplies, Canada will be able to enjoy a continued excess supply of heavy crude oil so that exports to the United States could be expanded. Concomitantly, the

FIGURE 1-3 Supply and Demand Balance for Domestic Light Crude Oil, Canada

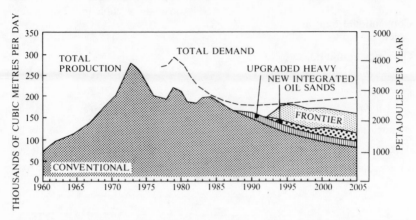

Source: National Energy Board, *NEB Update of Energy Supply and Demand, 1983-2005: Summary Report* (Ottawa: NEB, 1983).

FIGURE 1-4 Supply and Demand Balance for Domestic Heavy Crude Oil, Canada

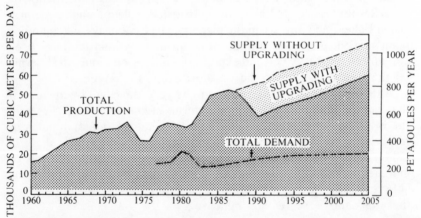

Source: National Energy Board, *NEB Update of Energy Supply and Demand, 1983-2005: Summary Report* (Ottawa: NEB, 1983).

nation's recent self-sufficiency in light crude oil — involving some exports to the United States from Western Canada, accompanied by roughly equivalent imports to Quebec and the Atlantic provinces from OPEC — would be sustainable. These possibilities are portrayed in Figures 1-3 to 1-5. If new sources of supply do not meet expectations, large future imports of light crude will be necessary, and the ramifications for

FIGURE 1–5 Plausible Ranges for Crude Oil Supply & Demand

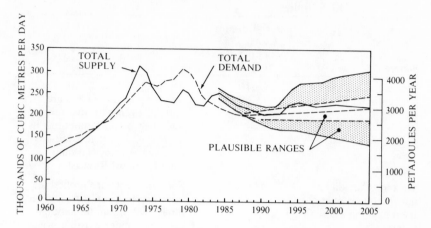

Source: National Energy Board, *NEB Update of Energy Supply and Demand, 1983–2005: Summary Report* (Ottawa: NEB, 1983).

oil distribution and refining within Canada, as well as for the national macroeconomic situation, would be enormous (Haughey and Bruton, 1983).

Economic assessments of oil-recovery costs from alternate supply sources have recently been made by the Economic Council of Canada (Eglington and Uffelman, 1984a, 1984b, 1984c, 1984d). These are summarized in Table 1-17.

The reader is cautioned against a superficial reading of this table. A look only at the dollar figures suggests that Hibernia or Beaufort Sea oil is expected to be quite competitive with Western Canadian conventional or tertiary-recovery oil. But the numbers alone are misleading. As the accompanying comments suggest, the existence of commercial reserves in the Beaufort Sea is still uncertain, and the technological and environmental risks of production from there, as well as from Hibernia, are much greater than in the Western sedimentary basin. Again, the reported costs exclude the immense exploration costs, greatly subsidized by society, that have gone into frontier work. Neither should the high $47 per barrel cost for surface mining of oil sands be accepted uncritically as a good reason against further such developments. The economics of new, smaller oil-sands plants, involving lower initial investment and hence lower total financial burden, seem to be much better. Alternatively, lower financial outlays are possible by constructing plants that produce only bitumen rather than high-grade petroleum so that the time before payout begins may be shorter. Other investors may take on the upgrading process as a separate project. In addition, with over one-third of the construction industry unemployed in Alberta (Sta-

TABLE 1-17 Summary of Social Supply Costs for Alternative Oil Supplies

Source	Social Supply Costs, 1983 Dollars per Barrel 10% Rate	Comments
Western Canadian conventional light oil.	$16	Although risk and costs are relatively low, supplies are limited, even with the new oil reference price. Reductions in taxes could expand additions to reserves beyond National Energy Board forecasts.
Western Canada enhanced oil recovery from existing known reserves.	$13–25	Some projects are profitable; recovery from existing known others will be quite marginal reserves. under existing price and tax regimes. Lower taxes would enlarge the number of profitable projects.
Large-scale surface mining of oilsands to produce synthetic high-quality oil.	$47	Based on Alsands data. High financial risk.
In situ oilsands production of bitumen (without upgrading)	$28	Wolfe Lake data; still at experimental stage.
East Coast Hibernia oil	$15	Delivered to Montreal. Costs count only the development and production stages and so are not fully comparable to other sources of supply because exploration costs are not included. High technological risk (including iceberg problems, for example).
Beaufort Sea Oil (assuming a commercial discovery	$15–40	Delivered to Montreal. Costs count only the development and production stages and so are not fully comparable to other no frontier supply sources. Considerable environmental risk.

Source: Adapted from Economic Council of Canada, *Submission by the Chairman of the Economic Council of Canada to the Standing Senate Committee on Energy and Natural Resources* (Ottawa, 1984).

Note: Social supply costs equal the total experienced by industry, excluding all taxes and royalties.

tistics Canada, 1985) the real social cost of employing construction workers in building new plants is virtually zero. Moreover, if cheaper, often more productive, non-union labour is used, the actual dollar outlays on labour can be substantially below the Alsands estimates. Extensions to capacity are already under way or planned by Syncrude and Suncor. Although these will naturally be cheaper than starting an entirely new project, the fact that they are in progress suggests that the economics of surface oil-sands mining does not make for a product as much above current world oil prices as the Economic Council's figures indicate.

The Council's work also intimates that the *in situ* bitumen plant in progress at Wolfe Lake will be extremely marginal. Yet, since Esso Resources is proceeding with a similar, 19,000-barrel-per-day plant at Cold Lake, since it has plans for another 19,000-barrel-per-day unit to be commenced this summer and a third within a year, and since other companies have various pilot projects under way, one is inclined to believe that the economics may be much better than the Council's work suggests, particularly if non-union labour can be used in the construction programs.

Finally, observe that the figures in Table 1-17 represent social costs. Private costs, which would include taxes and royalties, could be higher. Hence, regardless of the method used to increase Canadian oil production, government taxation regimes are going to have to be flexible enough to keep marginal projects virtually free of taxes while only the more profitable ventures bear the burden of taxes (Economic Council, 1984d). Economic rents cannot be extracted if there are none to extract. Yet even projects that yield no economic rents can be of immense benefit to the economy if, while yielding a reasonable return to the operators, they provide employment, on the one hand, and, on the other hand, produce oil at a price competitive with world supplies, thus reducing the reliance on unnecessary imports.

These statements deserve some elaboration. First, the importance of developing and preserving a stable, cooperative, federal-provincial environment cannot be overestimated. When federal and provincial governments cannot agree on how economic rents from resources are to be divided among themselves, they tend to try to take more than are being generated, with the result that the industry — and thus the entire economy — is adversely affected. To minimize this source of conflict, a new fiscal equalization system is needed to replace the one that will expire in the spring of 1987. A full discussion of the ingredients of such a system cannot be entered into here, but a few, desirable, key characteristics can be outlined (Wilkinson, 1984 and references cited therein).

The present equalization system is designed "to provide reasonably comparable levels of public service at reasonably comparable levels of taxation" (*Canada Act*, 1981, s. 36 (2)). It is a representative five-province standard whereby the five provinces — British Columbia, Saskatchewan, Manitoba, Ontario, and Quebec — are used to determine the average revenues per person that would be acquired from applying national average tax rates. The federal government employs this average in making equalization payments to individual provinces. All provincial revenues, including resource revenue (except for interest earned by entities such as the Alberta Heritage Savings Trust Fund) are counted, as are municipal property taxes and local receipts from sales of goods and services. Because Alberta is excluded from the five-province standard and yet is the province with the largest resource revenue, the equalization payments to the other provinces are not nearly as high as they would be if Alberta revenues were involved in the setting of the average standard for provincial revenues. Also excluded from the equalization system are the economic rents that go to residents of particular provinces because they have been able to buy their oil or gas below the world price or, as with hydro-electricity in Quebec, below long-run marginal cost price. Currently, it is to the advantage of provincial governments to underprice these energy services to their residents.

A new net equalization scheme for resource rents could be initiated, using a national average of revenues, not a mere five-province standard. Those provinces with below-average resource revenues per capita would receive payments, whereas — and this would be a radical change — those provinces with above-average resource receipts would pay into the system.

The process would be more complicated than the present one for a variety of reasons. Any net fiscal benefits in provinces with high economic rents that are capitalized into land and house values would have to be excluded in determining net provincial revenues per capita. Similarly, if residents of a province benefited because energy or other resource prices were below market or long-run marginal cost price, the benefits they received would have to be counted. Again, if a province sold resources to other provinces below market or long-run marginal cost price, it would have to get a credit for its low sales price in the equalization payments. All explicit and implicit rents would have to be counted whether they arose with respect to oil and gas, hydro-electricity, forest stumpage or any other resource, even though provinces like Quebec or Manitoba might not be pleased with the arrangement because their equalization entitlements would be less than they would otherwise be.

To give provinces an incentive to develop their resources, some proportion of the economic rents — possibly 50 percent — would have to be left out of the equalization calculations. In return for agreeing to such a system, Alberta would probably require a federal commitment to include all non-oil-and-gas economic rents being earned by other provinces and not to raise taxes levied on the oil industry in the future without careful consultation if prices should once more increase substantially.

Certain other specific changes in the taxation of the oil industry would also be desirable. The incremental oil-revenue tax (IORT), which has been suspended for conventional oil, and the natural gas and gas-liquids tax (NGGLT), which disappeared in February 1984, might well be cancelled entirely to remove uncertainty for the oil industry in the event that conditions improve in the future. The petroleum- and gas-revenue tax (PGRT) could be revised in favour of a tax that is more flexible with respect to the net profit position of the companies themselves. Possibly a royalty could be adopted that is levied after costs have been recovered and that is based on a percentage which varies positively with the productivity of the well or other installation. If new oil sands ventures or *in situ* bitumen plants were undertaken, government participation would be a useful way for governments to obtain detailed access to cost and revenue figures and to receive a share of any rents generated, both through profits and through any revised PGRT.

The petroleum incentive-payments (PIP) grants, which artificially distort exploration activity away from the Western sedimentary basin in favour of frontier areas owned by the federal government, warrant revision too, for they make little economic sense. When the present PIP program expires at the end of 1986, it could be amended so that the incentives offered to frontier work would not be significantly different from those provided for activity in Western Canada.

Natural Gas

The situation respecting natural gas is quite different from that for oil. Exports of natural gas to the United States remain substantial, although they have been diminishing in recent years. They totalled a little over $3 billion in 1984. In 1983, they amounted to $4 billion or about 700 billion cubic feet and represented less than 24 percent of the maximum permitted under approved export licences. (During the 1970s, exports averaged about 950 billion cubic feet annually.) The real questions have to do with how much natural gas will be exported annually, at what price, and for how long. Before considering these matters, a very brief overview of Canada's position in a world context is appropriate.

Tables 1-18 and 1-19 summarize world natural gas reserves and consumption. Viewed in isolation, Canada's proven gas reserves of about 123 trillion cubic feet (tcf) seem immense, but they are small by world standards: only 4 percent of proved world reserves. Canadian consumption at 3 percent of world consumption is also relatively tiny. Current prices and costs of transportation mean that many of these world reserves are not yet marketable at long distances from the source of

TABLE 1-18 World Natural Gas Reserves, January 1, 1982

	Proven Reserves		Percentage of World Reserves
	(trillions of cubic feet)		
OPEC		1,017.9	33.3
North America		295.1	9.6
(Canada)	(123.0)		(4.0)
Western Europe		149.8	4.9
Eastern Europe		1,241.5	40.6
(U.S.S.R.)	(1,218.4)		(39.8)
Other		356.5	11.6
Total world		3,060.8	100.0

Source: B. Mossavar-Rahmani, "The OPEC Natural Gas Dilemma," in *Proceedings of the International Gas Markets Conference* (Calgary: Canadian Energy Research Institute, 1983). Canadian reserves are from National Energy Board estimates.

TABLE 1-19 World Natural Gas Consumption, January 1, 1982

	Consumption		Percentage of World Consumption
	(trillions of cubic feet)		
OPEC	2.45		4.5
North America		20.31	37.5
(Canada)	(1.79)		(3.3)
Western Europe		7.31	13.5
Eastern Europe		19.10	35.2
(U.S.S.R.)	(15.73)		(29.0)
Other		5.05	9.3
Total world		54.20	100.0

Source: B. Mossavar-Rahmani, "The OPEC Natural Gas Dilemma," in *Proceedings of the International Gas Markets Conference* (Calgary: Canadian Energy Research Institute, 1983). Canadian reserves are from National Energy Board estimates.

supply (Mossavar-Rahmani, 1983). The only options for nations such as those in OPEC, with their massive reserves and minute consumptions, are to divert their consumption to gas from oil, thus freeing more oil for export or, possibly, to try to attract heavy energy-using industries such as aluminum (ibid.). After the turn of the century, if gas prices rise considerably, they might export to Europe, Africa or beyond. Whatever happens, the huge world-reserve figures do suggest that even after the year 2000, when gas prices might be considerably higher than they will be for the next decade or two, Canadian gas from the Arctic or other frontier areas is not likely to have any market power in countries other than, possibly, the United States. Our focus, therefore, must be primarily on Canadian exports to the United States, in competition with both U.S. gas and alternate sources of energy.

Exports to the United States

Canadian gas supplies about 4 percent of U.S. demand. The United States presently has a sizeable gas surplus — about 16 to 20 percent of capacity is shut in (Sharp, 1983, p. 96) — which is expected to last until 1986. (The exception is the northeastern U.S. market, such as New England, where gas is in fairly tight supply.) At that time, gas markets will firm up as reserves decline quite rapidly (Eck, 1983, p. 104). The current surplus stems from increases in proven reserves of gas as prices were allowed to rise, particularly after 1978, and from declines in demand for gas (11 percent between 1979 and 1982) that have occurred as a result of general conservation measures in response to higher energy prices throughout the 1970s. More recently, the levelling out of world oil prices has, in some regions, made fuel oil cheaper than natural gas. In 1982, the U.S. switch to fuel oil from gas amounted to the equivalent of 258,000 barrels per day, although some observers believe that users have now shifted back to gas again (ibid., p. 107). About 65 percent of gas consumed in the United States is taken by industrial users (ibid., 104).

Prior to April 1983, Canadian gas-export prices to the United States were US$4.94 per mm Btus. At that time they were reduced to US$4.40 per mm Btus or US$3.40 if more than 50 percent of authorized exports were taken. In July 1984, greater flexibility in gas-export pricing was permitted, effective November 1, 1984: prices could be set as necessary to meet market conditions in the various segments of the U.S. market, provided that they were not below the Toronto city-gate price of US$3.15 per mm Btus, or approximately Cdn. $4.20 per mm Btus.

Since that date, existing export contracts have been renegotiated and new ones made, with prices mostly in the US$3.15 to US$3.40 range, which represents an approximate price reduction of 25 percent from previous rates. This means that export volumes for 1985 will have to rise by at least 25 percent if total revenues to producers are not to be lower than in 1984.

Over the longer run, it is expected that gas exports will continue to increase so that by 1987, deliveries will reach 68 percent of committed volumes. By 1990, they will rise up to 90 percent of authorized sales of about 1760 billion cubic feet (Bcf), an increase of 130 percent from the 1982–84 average of 760 Bcf (National Energy Board, 1984b).

Export revenues could be in the $7 billion to $8 billion range in the peak years, more than double current levels. Until the U.S. gas surplus is worked off, however, tensions may arise with the United States because of the extra Canadian exports. Although the new Canadian pricing flexibility was in accord with U.S. desires when it was established, the enlarged exports to the United States, at a time when U.S. demand for gas is not increasing, have raised concerns in that country about Canadian competition.

The estimates of longer-term exports are of course subject to several conditions: modifications in gas-pricing policies that may occur in the United States (and that have, indeed, been under consideration for one time); the degree to which U.S. legislation will enforce clean air requirements; the extent of new reserves being discovered there; and the extent to which other exporters to the United States, such as Mexico and perhaps Alberta, are willing to reduce prices to serve the U.S. market (National Energy Board, 1984b, pp. 62–65).

Two final points regarding gas trade with the United States deserve mention. First, it now appears unlikely that Alaskan gas will be shipped to the rest of the U.S. mainland during this century. This unlikelihood also implies that the prebuilt Canadian portion of the Alaska Natural Gas Transportation System (ANGTS) will probably not be used for Alaskan exports during this century, in spite of assurances by successive U.S. presidents that the entire project would be completed.

Secondly, it will be important to Canadian producers that the Canadian dollar remain at its current level of about US$0.73, since this factor will affect the net returns after taxes (i.e. netbacks) from export sales. It has been shown that in constant 1981 dollars these netbacks do not approach those of 1978 (Scarfe, 1984). If they were to be lowered more on exports by an increase in value of the Canadian dollar, net returns to the gas industry of Canada would be less again.

Canadian Supply

Future exports also depend on the Canadian supply situation. For several reasons — the difficulty of increasing exports to the United States; the slowdown in demand in Canada because of the recession, mild winters, and fierce competition from electricity utilities; and lower netbacks to gas producers because of the National Energy Program — drilling for gas in Canada has dropped off substantially since the last half of the 1970s. In 1983–84, the estimated gas-well drilling for exploration and development was only 40 percent of the 1976–80 average.

Projections made by the NEB in January 1983 suggested that there would be little exportable surplus (beyond licences existing at that time) from 1990 onward, and that 1997 would be the year when exports based on conventional supplies would have to cease. Beyond that date, frontier gas was expected to be necessary. The estimates made in early 1984 by the Canadian Energy Research Institute (CERI) are more optimistic than those of the NEB. In their scenario, demand for natural gas is expected to be lower than those NEB estimates because of continuing conservation measures. Exports under current licences are anticipated to be lower and additions to reserves somewhat higher. The CERI estimates predict that there will be as much as 7,600 Bcf of surplus gas from non-frontier sources available to export, beyond that committed under extant licences and required to meet expected domestic needs, up to the years 2002 to 2005, depending on whether high or low oil prices prevail. Between 1990 and 1997, in contrast to 1983 NEB estimates, between 500 and 1000 Bcf per year of extra shipments to the United States are forecast (Haughey and Coad, 1984). These additions naturally depend on taxes being low enough — and thus netbacks to the industry high enough — to stimulate additional drilling.

In its most recent projections of September 1984, the NEB is more optimistic than it was in January 1983, about the adequacy of supply relative to demand. At the beginning of 1983, non-frontier remaining reserves were estimated to amount to 77.3 trillion cubic feet (tcf). Reserve additions from non-frontier sources expected to the year 2005 amount to another 43.2 tcf, representing an increase of 56 percent. Thus, the NEB now foresees that exports will be sustained from conventional supply sources until at least the year 2000 and perhaps longer. With the inclusion of non-conventional sources, the time could be extended a little more as Figures 1-6 and 1-7 show.

Exportable supplies are sensitive to the application of the current reserves-protection formula (Haughey and Coad, 1984). New export licences are granted only if current reserves exceed the sum of commitments under existing export licences plus 25 times the present year's gas demand. Because the year used for comparison can be affected by weather and economic conditions, variations can occur in the quantity of reserves deemed available for export. Accordingly, surplus reserve estimates have to be made with this in mind.

Some observers argue that the requirement of 25 years' worth of domestic supply unduly inhibits exports. Yet given that even under generous assumptions, supply from conventional sources if forecast to be adequate to meet domestic demands and existing export contracts for only 20 years or less, that alternative supplies from the Arctic will be substantially higher priced, and finally that gas is a clean fuel compared with coal and does not involve the actual or potential safety problems of nuclear power, it would seem wise not to alter significantly the 25-year reserves requirement.

Currently, development is proceeding on the Venture gas field off the coast of Nova Scotia. Gas from this field will be high priced. Excluding exploration costs, which have been substantial, social supply costs are estimated to be, at a minimum, about five times greater than those for Western Canadian gas (Eglington and Uffelman, 1984c). Exports to the U.S. Northeast will have to be substantial, particularly in the earlier years of production, if the project is to be feasible. Although some sales have already been tentatively arranged,[8] it is far from clear that such exports will be competitive with other energy sources in that market.

One final possibility needs to be mentioned: the export of Canadian Arctic gas in liquified form to Japan. Japan expects liquified natural gas to make up about 13 percent of her total energy demand by 1990–95 and

FIGURE 1-6 Plausible Ranges for Natural Gas Supply and Demand, Conventional Producing Areas

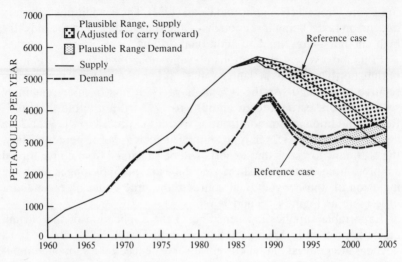

Source: National Energy Board, *Canadian Energy Supply and Demand, 1983-2005: Summary Report* (Ottawa: NEB, 1984).

FIGURE 1-7 Plausible Ranges of Natural Gas Supply and Demand, Canada

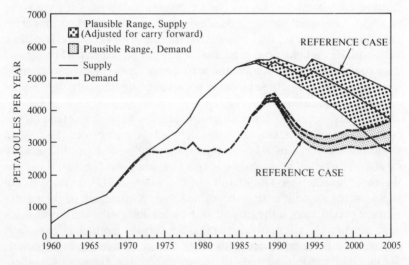

Source: National Energy Board, *Canadian Energy Supply and Demand, 1983-2005: Summary Report* (Ottawa: NEB, 1984).

is moving ahead with plans to import it from a variety of countries. Canada is only one of many possible sources, perhaps supplying 6–8 percent of the Japanese gas market from 1990 to 1995 (Shimizu, 1983). There were plans to export about 140 Bcf to Japan beginning in 1986, but doubts exist as to whether this will occur, at least within the original time frame.

In conclusion, whether gas is to be exported to Japan or the United States or used at home, a supportive, predictable taxation regime will be necessary on both federal and provincial fronts if gas resources are to be found and developed in a reasonably orderly and efficient manner. Consequently, the remarks made about taxation of the oil industry and federal-provincial resource-rent distribution are applicable here. One need only add that the Natural Gas and Gas Liquids Tax (NGGLT) imposed under the 1980 NEP and reduced to zero in February 1984 should be cancelled permanently, to remove the apprehension of the oil industry that when gas sales or prices again improve, the industry will once again be hit with this tax. Taxes that are responsive to profit levels are more suitable.

Coal

Canada, with about one percent both of the world's recoverable coal reserves and of world production, ranks twelfth in the world in reserves and tenth in production, far behind the three leading nations — the U.S.S.R., the United States and China — which among them have 57 percent of the economically recoverable world reserves and about 58 percent of total world production. As an exporter of coal, Canada ranks sixth, well behind the United States, Australia, South Africa, and the U.S.S.R. and nearly on a par with Poland. In 1980–81, the nation's exports accounted for about 6.3 percent of world exports from the major producing nations and 10 percent of world exports of metallurgical coal (Dyack, 1983).

Coal reserves are concentrated in the three Western provinces, Saskatchewan, Alberta and British Columbia, which together account for 98 percent of Canada's endowments and 93 percent of recoverable reserves. Nova Scotia has most of the remainder (primarily in Cape Breton), but its coal has a high sulphur content (about 1.2 percent).

The quality of coal in Western Canada improves as one moves farther west. Saskatchewan's reserves are lignite, which has the lowest heating value of any coal deposits. Alberta has both sub-bituminous and bituminous coal. The former, used almost entirely for thermal electricity generation within the province, is found in the plains, while the latter is found in the foothills and mountain regions. The foothills bituminous coal is also used for thermal purposes; the mountain reserves are pri-

TABLE 1-20 Growth in Production of Western Canadian Coal, 1972-1981

	Annual Compound Growth Rate Percentage			
	By Volume	By Total Sales	By Average Value/Tonne	Total Dollar Value, 1981
				($000)
Saskatchewan	8.5	20.4	13.6	42,061
Alberta	8.5	25.7	15.7	481,830
British Columbia	8.0	23.7	14.6	554,271
Total	25.0	69.8	43.9	1,078,162

Source: Adapted from Brenda L. Dyack, "Western Canada's Minerals–Coal" (Ottawa: Economic Council of Canada, 1983), Tables 21, 24 and 25.

marily exported to supply metallurgical needs. Although British Columbia has all types of coal, its anthracite is not yet being mined, and its thermal coal is of a lower quality than that of many other world sources of supply. Most of its coal exports are for metallurgical purposes (Dyack, 1983). Generally, the sulphur content of Western coal is low — about 0.3 percent in Alberta coal, which means that it produces less of an acid rain problem than the type of thermal coal that Ontario Hydro imports from the United States; the U.S. coal has a sulphur content as high as 3 percent (Haessel, 1983).

The annual compound growth rate of production of Western Canadian coal over the decade 1972–81 has been higher than 8 percent in volume terms and nearly 25 percent in value terms, with nominal prices rising at about 15 percent annually (Table 1-20). Exports over this same period expanded at an annual compound rate of 26.8 percent in value terms, which is roughly equivalent to the growth in value of total production. Thus, although Canada had been a net importer of coal, the rapid growth of exports over the 1970s reversed that situation by 1981.

Canadian exports of coal are summarized in Table 1-21. Japan is the dominant market (taking 67 percent of exports) although nations such as South Korea have become increasingly important buyers. Japan is by far the largest importer of coal in the world, taking 60 percent of OECD imports and about 45 percent of world imports of metallurgical coal. Although at this time she accounts for only 3–4 percent of world thermal coal imports, because such trade is still small relative to metallurgical trade, her share of total world coal imports is about one-third. Japan thus has considerable market power, and because her importing firms act in concert with one another and often have direct investments in supplying countries, this power is even more weighty (Dyack, 1983).

Canada is Japan's third-largest supplier of metallurgical coal; our import share averages about 15 percent in terms of both tonnage and

TABLE 1-21 Canadian Coal Exports, 1983

	Value ($ millions)	Percentage
Japan	829.9	67.3
South Korea	160.6	13.1
Brazil	54.0	4.4
West Germany	51.0	4.1
Taiwan	39.2	3.2
Others	97.6	7.9
Total	1,232.3	100.0

Source: Statistics Canada, *Trade of Canada, Exports* (Ottawa: Statistics Canada, 1984).

dollar value. (It was as high as 22 percent in 1978.) Australia and the United States together supply about 75 percent of Japanese needs.

Future Prospects for Canadian Coal Exports
Although metallurgical coal has been the main world coal export in past years, thermal coal trade has been rising more rapidly. On the one hand, nations have been striving to diversify their energy-supply sources and reduce their dependence on oil imports from the OPEC nations. On the other hand, more efficient steel production has reduced the demand for metallurgical coal. At the same time, reductions in the demand for steel itself have been taking place; for instance, the amount of steel used in North American cars has been halved. These trends are expected to continue, particularly those relating to the expanded use of thermal coal. In September 1984, the World Bank projected that world coal demand would rise at a rate of only 2.7 percent per annum from 1985 to 1995. (This figure is substantially lower than the 4.1 percent growth rate projected in the 1982 World Bank report.) Eighty-three percent of the extra demand from 1982 to 1995 is for thermal coal (World Bank, 1984, pp. 104, 115).

Real price increases in the years ahead are expected to be small. As with forecasts of other energy prices, the more recent the projection, the smaller the anticipated price growth. In early 1984, the World Bank placed the real thermal coal price in 1995 at US$56 per tonne, less than $1 per tonne more than in 1978 (although at least $10 more than the prices expected to prevail in 1984–85). In their September 1984 report, the 1995 real price was expected to be only US$50 per tonne, which implies an annual increase between expected 1985 prices and 1995 prices of 1.3 percent (World Bank, 1984, pp. 114, 121). This lower rate of increase is based on anticipated smaller increases in petroleum prices and on pro-ductivity improvements in the mining of coal. There was improvement of as much as 30 percent between 1980 and 1983 in some U.S. mines. Detailed price projections were not made for metallurgical coal, but the

1981 constant-dollar difference between traded thermal and metal-lurgical coal of about US$10 per tonne is expected to remain. In brief, only small changes in real prices of any coal are expected to develop in the next decade or so.

A number of these points are relevant to the Canadian situation. First, although Canadian coal costs at the minehead are generally in line with those in other producing countries, transportation costs tend to raise Canadian prices somewhat more than they do prices elsewhere. This is not because of inefficiency in internal transportation, for Canadian costs per kilometre are the least in the world; nor is it because transportation bottlenecks within Canada or at Canadian seaports will be a concern when exports expand. The revisions to the Crow Rate and government support to the railways are expected to enable the railroad companies to improve their lines to the west coast wherever necessary. Port-facility expansions currently under way at Roberts Bank, Vancouver will nearly double existing capacity, and the potential is there to triple this new capacity. The Ridley Island terminal at Prince Rupert will have a capacity of 55 percent of the expanded Roberts Bank facility, or 12 million tonnes (Dyack, 1983). Rather, the Canadian transportation-cost disadvantage occurs because the overland distances to be travelled are often greater than those in other lands (ibid.). Canadian thermal coal, in spite of its low sulphur content, is thus often at a noticeable cost disadvantage, in terms of dollars per Btu, in European markets, compared with supplies from places such as the eastern United States, South Africa and even Australia. In Japanese markets, Canada is also a much higher-cost source than Australia, South Africa and Poland; it is on a par with western U.S. coal suppliers and only a trifle cheaper than eastern U.S. coal suppliers (World Bank, 1984).

Secondly, thermal coal from British Columbia is less acceptable to important nations such as Japan because of its low volatility. Future Canadian thermal coal exports are likely to have to come from farther inland in Alberta (Varangu, 1983, p. 91).

Thirdly, Canada, like the world, now has substantial excess capacity of metallurgical coal (which accounts for about 85 percent of its exports), and this excess capacity is likely to last well into the future. For example, at the same time as huge new developments came on stream in north-eastern British Columbia in 1984, other producers in southeastern British Columbia were having to shut down some of their production temporarily or possibly permanently (*Globe and Mail*, June 6, 1984, p. B3). The new northeastern B.C. coal was initially priced at about Cdn. $28 per tonne higher than a similar quality of coal mined in southeastern British Columbia. Given this difference, plus the fact that the coal now appears to be of lower quality than initially expected, and the current softness of world markets, it is not surprising that some renegotiation of prices downward has had to occur.

TABLE 1-22 Canadian Coal Export Forecasts and Capacity

Date	Region	Total Exports
		(millions of metric tonnes)
1982	Western Canada (actual)	15.0
	All Canada (actual)	16.0
1985	All Canada	20–31
1990	All Canada	25–46
1995	All Canada	35.0
2000	All Canada	34.0
		Producing Capacity
		(millions of metric tonnes)
1983	Western Canada	25.0
1985	Western Canada	46.0

Source: The particular original sources are shown in Brenda Dyack, "Western Canada's Minerals–Coal" (Ottawa: Economic Council of Canada, 1983), from which this table is adapted.

A summary of recent Canadian projections of exports and Canadian capacity is provided in Table 1-22. Because projections made in earlier years tended to be overly optimistic, only forecasts made since 1982 are presented. Even these look rather enthusiastic in view of the excess capacity in the world coal industry, the levelling out of oil prices, and the fewer environmental concerns provided by oil and gas. Thus the projected doubling of exports as the 1990s approach may not come to pass, or at least not that soon. The table also suggests that the Canadian capacity to meet such exports is not likely to be a constraint, and that little new capacity will need to be developed beyond what will be made available during the mid-1980s. Nevertheless, the NEB projects that exports will expand sufficiently to comprise 38 percent of total demand for Canadian coal in 2005, compared with 29 percent in 1983 (National Energy Board, 1984b, p. 95).

Opinions differ about whether the Japanese share of Canadian exports will grow or diminish. While some observers forecast expanded sales to the burgeoning economies of Korea and Taiwan, they nevertheless suggest that Japanese efforts to lower their dependence on their most important suppliers, Australia and the United States, may keep the Japanese share of Canadian exports at or even above current levels (Dyack, 1983). Even this diversification argument may not augment Canada's share. Japan may decide, instead, to diversify more fully, buying from China with its vast resources as China improves its supporting infrastructure appropriately. Alternatively, Japan might acquire suppliers in a variety of poor nations that have significant reserves and that are hungry for foreign exchange. It is not inconceivable that coal exports could be subsidized by developing nations to earn foreign exchange just as metal ores and concentrate exports have been subsidized in recent years.

In any event, because Japan is the dominant world coal importer and her industries act as a unit in negotiations with supplying firms, it may well be necessary for Canadian producing firms to develop a united front and to combine with their respective provincial governments, as well as with the federal government, in negotiating with Japan — as Australia is now doing — if they are to maximize discounted present values of the return from coal. As it is now, new mines coming on stream with Japanese encouragement and minority-share participation, such as those in northeastern British Columbia and various other places throughout the world, are depressing the prices that all producers can get for their exports to Japan. Within Canada, as provinces compete with one another to promote economic development by providing an infra-structure to support new coal mines, they may simply find themselves subsidizing the Japanese steel industry at the expense of Canadian taxpayers (Dyack, 1983). Simultaneously, the implications of measures such as the restriction on car imports from Japan should be assessed not only for their effects on domestic car production and consumer prices, but also for their effects on Canadian exports of other products, such as coal.

Even with a comprehensive approach, however, coal prices will rise, at best, very little. Increased revenues will have to come from expanded volumes from existing or incipient mines.

Domestic Coal Consumption
Between 1983 and 2005, domestic demand for coal is expected to grow, on average, by about 1.95 percent annually. The mix of demand will remain about the same as it was in 1983, with industrial use accounting for about 23 percent, electrical generation about 74 percent, and other uses approximately 2 percent (National Energy Board, 1984b, p. 95). Although Ontario is currently the largest user of coal for electrical production, its plans are to place increased reliance on nuclear energy. By 2005, coal will provide only 10 percent and nuclear energy production about 66 percent of Ontario's needs, compared with 31 and 33 percent, respectively, for these two electricity sources today. Alberta will become the largest user of coal for electricity generation, and nearly three-quarters of its electricity will continue to come from this source.

Other provinces that will be using coal in increasing amounts are Prince Edward Island (98 percent of energy production by 2005), Nova Scotia (90 percent), Saskatchewan (66 percent), and New Brunswick (20 percent). Thus, by 2005, although the share of coal in electricity genera-tion is projected to be reduced to 14.3 percent of energy production in that year dropping from 17.3 percent in 1983, the total use of coal in terms of petajoules of energy provided for electricity generation and all other uses is expected to increase by 53 percent over the period 1985–2005. Accordingly, although the growth in demand for coal for domestic and export purposes will not match the pace of the 1960s and 1970s, coal production should be able to continue to expand.

This statement, of course, assumes that the taxation regime for coal production will be supportive, not punitive. This assumption, in turn, implies that taxes and royalties should be based on profits, as in Alberta, and not be inflexible as the British Columbian tax system has been (Marshall, 1984, p. 10).

One final issue deserves brief mention. It has occasionally been asked whether the market for domestic coal could be expanded if Ontario Hydro were to shift more of its purchases of thermal coal from the United States to Alberta. (Currently, of 13 million tonnes used by Ontario Hydro per year, about one-quarter is from Canadian sources.) If only private costs of delivered coal are considered, this move would not pay. The greater distance that the Alberta coal must travel makes it much more expensive — $107 per tonne compared to $66 per tonne for the U.S. product. In addition, the U.S. coal has nearly 20 percent higher Btu value per tonne than Albertan coal. However, if the social costs of the acid rain produced by the higher-sulphur-content U.S. coal are considered, the differential is not nearly as great. The sulphur emissions can be reduced either by using a larger proportion of low-sulphur-content coal, or by installing expensive scrubbers, which will remove 90 percent of the sulphur. But even if the acid rain problem is addressed, only if the capacity utilization of the coal-burning plants is less than 40 percent does it become more attractive to Ontario Hydro to use more Canadian coal than to install scrubbers with their large depreciation costs per unit of electricity produced. By the early 1990s, however, because nuclear plants provide cheaper electricity in Canada than does coal (providing that the annual capacity utilization of plants is above about 20 percent), Ontario Hydro expects to use only about 4 million tonnes of coal (less than one-third of what is used now), of which about one-half will come from Canada. Thus the scope for greater use in Ontario of Western coal does not appear to be very large (Youston, 1980; Ontario Hydro, 1982). Only if the environment ministers of Canada were to advance the date when sulphur emissions must be reduced by 50 percent from the present date of 1994 would Ontario Hydro be forced to use more Western coal. The reason is that it probably would not pay Ontario Hydro to install the capital-intensive scrubbers for the interim period until more nuclear capacity could be installed.

Electricity

Electricity exports to the United States have been growing rapidly since the early 1970s (with the exception of 1974, when they declined), and since 1971, Canada has had a trade surplus in electricity. This surplus rose to over $1.2 billion in 1983. Most of these sales have been in the market for interruptible energy, displacing high-cost U.S. sources. They help to use more fully the excess generating capacity now existing in Canada.

Future Export Prospects

As the United States moves to replace existing oil-fired electricity generation capacity, particularly in New England, New York, the mid-Atlantic area, and the California-Nevada regions, there will be considerable opportunity for Canada to meet the energy need thus created. The U.S. market open to capacity additions of coal- and nuclear-fired electricity is ten times that for oil-fired displacement, and so there will be opportunities there, as well. But, because the electricity produced by U.S. coal-fired and nuclear facilities will be much closer in cost to Canadian electricity, the total share of this market that Canada might hope to capture will be not as great as that in the oil-fired market (Battle, Gislason, and Douglas, 1983).

Apart from competitive prices, Canadian electricity may be increasingly acceptable in the United States because its use is consistent with the U.S. objective of reducing reliance on imported oil. In addition, the U.S. electricity-generation industry, particularly its nuclear segment, has been plagued with more onerous regulatory difficulties than has the Canadian industry, so that many plans for new nuclear plants have been delayed or dropped entirely.

There may be some constraints on Canadian exports, however. These include:

- lack of transmission capability. Financial and regulatory hurdles, particularly in the United States, will need to be overcome, although the record for Hydro-Quebec exports to New England and New York shows that they can be overcome;[9]
- regulatory constraints in Canada by federal and provincial governments including, but not limited to, concern about nuclear waste disposal, acid rain problems from coal-fired plants, and flooding from hydro-site development;
- political resistance in the United States to a reliance on imported electricity, particularly if there is surplus capacity in the United States, or if buying from Canada is seen to reduce jobs in the United States; and
- Canadian concerns about whether the export of electricity by Canada is reducing the opportunities for attracting energy-intensive industries to Canada.

Estimates of future exports of electrical power vary considerably. A study for the Canadian Energy Research Institute (Battle, Gislason, and

Douglas, 1983) projected that exports to the United States would expand, by the year 2000, to about $4 billion annually, and that all provinces except Prince Edward Island would participate in this growth. Quebec, Newfoundland, British Columbia, Manitoba and Ontario would expand their production of hydro-electricity; New Brunswick and Ontario would increase their nuclear generation; Nova Scotia, Saskatchewan and Alberta would generate more coal-fired power and Nova Scotia, conceivably, would generate tidal power.

More recent projections by the National Energy Board are much less optimistic about continued growth of exports in the longer run. They envisage exports peaking in 1987, at about 36 percent above the 1984 levels and 67 percent above 1983 levels (in terms of gigawatt hours), and then declining to slightly less than the 1983 level by the year 2000 and to about two-thirds of the 1983 level in 2005. The NEB, for instance, forecasts that Quebec, the province with the biggest exports, will double its electricity sales to the United States to 21,000 gigawatt hours by 1987, but will have no exports by 2005. In other words, their assumption seems to be that the United States will take increased amounts of Canadian electricity only as an interim measure until their own generation capacity is expanded — probably by the development of more nuclear facilities. Such projections, however, do not seem to take fully into account Quebec's plans for continuously growing, competitive, hydro-electric exports to the United States (Bérubé, 1984).[10]

Canada will need to give attention to the possibility of greater interprovincial power linkages and transfers so as to use resources as efficiently as possible. This achievement will lower the total excess capacity required for domestic needs, thereby freeing more energy for export (Battle, Gislason, and Douglas, 1983). Greater coordination among provinces and among the different utility exporters should be considered in order to minimize competition among Canadian producers for exports. Such competition gives away a larger than necessary share of economic benefits to U.S. buyers able to play one Canadian supplier off against another, and thus reduce unnecessarily the present discounted value of the net income streams to Canada.

To the extent, too, that there are economic rents involved, particularly with hydro-electric power generation, we must determine whether U.S. buyers, Canadian producers or all Canadians are going to share in these rents. To argue, as the electricity industry does, that "electricity is a manufactured product, not a primary energy source and, as such, should not be subject to resource taxes" (Canadian Electrical Association, 1983a, p. 7) seems to ignore the basic fact that if there are economic rents involved in electricity generation, they should be treated the same way as economic rents from other energy-producing sectors such as oil and gas (Wilkinson, 1984). Within Canada as much as 30 percent of the natural gas price represents government revenue, whereas electricity, because it is produced by Crown corporations, is not subject to such taxes. This lack of taxation, including the corporate profit tax, also means that exports to the United States are essentially subsidized more than are other energy exports. U.S. consumers are benefitting from these subsidies at the expense of Canadians. These issues relating to economic rents from electricity generation and taxation of Crown corporations must be resolved.

Uranium

To forecast uranium requirements for the world outside the centrally planned economies (WOCA) is complicated. It depends not only on expectations of future energy demands and the relative prices of electricity produced from nuclear plants as compared with coal-fired or other plants, but also on estimates of what reactor types will be employed, the capacity utilization of plants, the efficiency of enrichment plants, the gestation periods for new plants, and the amount of reprocessing and recycling done (Owen, 1983). Because of rapidly changing circumstances, the anticipated future world demand for uranium is less today than it was in the mid-1970s. The main reason is that, particularly in the United States, the pace at which nuclear installations are now being planned and installed has decreased during the past decade because of safety and environmental concerns. One hundred projects have been cancelled since 1972, no new nuclear plants have been ordered since 1978, and gestation periods have increased from six to about twelve years because of licensing hurdles and revised requirements for equipment. Other reasons include the reduction in the rate of expansion of electricity demand as a consequence both of the great slowdown in economic growth and of higher energy prices, as well as greater efficiency in the use of energy. Projections of installed nuclear capacity for the world outside the centrally planned economies which the OECD made in 1982 for the year 2000, are only 30 percent of projections made for that year in 1976 (ibid.).

Another change from 1976 is the reduction in the proportion of nuclear capacity that is expected of fast-breeder reactors by the year 2000; that proportion has dropped from 10 percent to about 3 percent. This shift occurred primarily because of the 1977 U.S. decision to delay production of such reactors for commercial purposes (Owen, 1983). But the situation may change again. The U.S.S.R. has demonstrated the commercial application of fast-breeder reactors; a new experimental machine will be available in 1986, and it is hoped that a fusion reactor able to produce electrical power will be available in 10 years. France which, along with Japan, the United Kingdom, the United States, and West Germany, has prototypes in operation now is planning to commence commercial development this year (Blix, 1983). Fast-breeder reactors are far more efficient in the use of uranium, and their widespread adoption in the 21st century would mean that known uranium reserves, which might otherwise become in short supply by 2030 or thereabouts, would be virtually inexhaustible. Heavy-water reactors are also more efficient in the use of uranium than are light-water reactors (although not nearly as efficient as fast-breeder reactors), but they are not expected to make up a very large portion of the market even by the year 2000.

At present, although there is some uncertainty about exact stocks, inventories of uranium are believed to be quite high: about quadruple the 1981 output of uranium by WOCA and eight times the consumption of WOCA in that year (Owen, 1983, p. 111). Current production is about twice the extent of present consumption, and this situation is expected to prevail until well into the 1990s at least (ibid., p. 120). Nevertheless, recent work indicates that nuclear power is less expensive than coal-based power in all major OECD countries, with the major exception of the United States. Such findings, if concerns about safety and waste disposal can be overcome, may once again spur a somewhat more rapid adoption of nuclear power. In the United States, however, the situation is unlikely to be reversed in the foreseeable future. Various studies show that new nuclear-generated electricity will cost anywhere from 25 to 80 percent more than electricity from new coal-fired plants (*Globe and Mail*, September 8, 1984). This discrepancy is the result of the much higher capital costs accruing from the long arduous process of licensing and the stringent equipment requirements. Total costs of a new plant have more than quadrupled since the late 1970s.

Canadian Supplies and Trade Possibilities
Although the Elliot Lake area of Ontario has been dominant in the production of uranium — in 1980, for example, about 60 percent of Canada's reserves were in this region — Saskatchewan's role has been growing rapidly. In 1980, only about one-third of the nation's reserves and production were from Saskatchewan. But the high (60 percent) share of the national exploration expenditures being made in that province have resulted in new, extremely high-quality finds (Campbell, 1984, chap. 3). The most recent find, at Cigar Lake, is estimated to contain as much as 230 million pounds of ore with a spectacular 8.5 to 10 percent grade (compared with a grade of 0.1 percent uranium for Elliot Lake and many southwest U.S. mines, and 2.5 percent for the new Key Lake, Saskatchewan mine, which has recently been developed and is now the largest open-pit uranium producer in the world). The other area in Canada receiving substantial exploration outlays is the Northwest Territories, which was the object of 23 percent of total expenditures in 1980. New finds have been made there, but the ore quality is much below that of the Saskatchewan reserves (0.4 to 0.8 percent uranium oxide) so that

development is not likely to occur until the uranium market improves significantly (*Globe and Mail*, November 8, 1984). Almost no exploration — only 1 percent of the total in 1980 — is occurring in Ontario. Production in Ontario will be sustained, however, because much of it is under long-term contract by Ontario Hydro (until 2011 for Denison Mines and 2020 for Rio Algom (Campbell, 1984), which has agreed to pay prices that may continue to be above current market levels.[11] Clearly, Saskatchewan will increasingly dominate the Canadian uranium industry in the years ahead.

In relation to WOCA, Canada produced about 20 percent of the world output of uranium in 1982. For 1984, this share will be closer to 25 percent (about 10,000 tonnes) so that Canada may replace the United States as the world's number-one producer.

At present Canada generates only 11 percent of its electricity by means of nuclear power, but this proportion is expected to increase to 19 percent in 1990, and to 22 percent in 2005 (National Energy Board, 1984b). Domestic use of uranium will, therefore, increase. Still, Canada will require only about 15 percent of its uranium production for its own use. Thus, it will have to negotiate new export contracts if its growing productive capacity is to be utilized.

During the next decade WOCA nuclear power production will double. This is true even in the United States, where many cancellations and delays have occurred. Since the United States accounts for about 50 percent of unfilled uranium requirements in the WOCA market, new sales to that nation are important. Yet, considerable pessimism exists about the opportunities in the U.S. market. Although Saskatchewan production will continue to be much cheaper than internal U.S. sources of supply, the expectation is that the United States may restrict imports so as to preserve the domestic industry: the old security-of-supply argument. This action can be taken more readily with uranium than with many minerals because the price of uranium, whether it is $15 or $75, is not a major factor in the costs of electricity generation. Rather it is the capital cost of the plants themselves that is the main determinant of the cost of electricity produced.

New export contracts also are likely to be negotiated with other nations besides the United States. France, Japan, West Germany and the United Kingdom in that order, are the next-largest producers of nuclear power. (France, for example, generates 55 percent of its electricity from nuclear energy.) About 35 percent of as-yet-unfilled uranium needs projected to 1992 are in Western Europe. Hence new contracts there seem reasonable possibilities. Developing countries may also be promising customers if they switch to nuclear power generation at the rate currently estimated (Economic Council, 1984d). Canada, however, is likely to want assurances that the importing nations will use the uranium only for peaceful purposes. This requirement may restrict sales to some of these nations.

Wherever the sales are made, projections are for substantial increases in Canadian production to the year 2000 and beyond. Campbell (1984), for example, estimates that production will be 19,000 tonnes in 2000 and 35,000 tonnes in 2020. These numbers imply growth rates of over 4.25 percent to the year 2000 and a little over 3 percent thereafter. These projections may be only wishful thinking, for there is little solid information to support them. Still, they are as reasonable as any.

It is equally difficult to make firm statements about prices relating to export sales. Such prices have been volatile in the past: US$5.50 per pound in 1972; as high as US$44 per pound in 1979 (with the help of the uranium cartel, of which Canada was a member); down again to US$17 per pound in 1982 (Campbell, 1984, pp. 3–11); US$24 per pound at the end of 1983; and US$17 in the autumn of 1984. Australia has now set a floor price on exported uranium of US$30 per pound. Campbell uses prices of US$27 per pound to the year 2000 and US$39 per pound thereafter (in 1980 dollars).

In general, although Canada is likely to be the low-cost uranium supplier in WOCA for years to come, export volumes and prices are difficult to forecast with any degree of confidence. Canada may find it necessary not to price her exports as low as she might profitably be able to do, for if she did, producers in other nations that use uranium, such as the United States, might be pushed out of business. Rather than see that happen, those nations might restrict imports from Canada in order to preserve their own domestic industries. Thus Canada may have to show considerable restraint in setting pricing policies. It is probable, however, that the value of uranium exports will rise considerably in future years. Still, the value of exports is expected to remain small relative to exports of other energy materials.

Energy: Conclusions

Energy and energy-product exports now make a sizeable contribution to Canada's balance of international trade. Oil self-sufficiency on a continuing basis may be sustainable in the 1990s, but it will require the fairly rapid development of more non-conventional sources of oil supply. If these developments are to occur, and if industry is to be encouraged to undertake the required investments, federal and provincial taxation regimes will have to be supportive and predictable. A new equalization scheme that would take careful account of revenues from all resources, including hydro-electricity and non-energy products, would be desirable.

Natural gas exports to the United States from existing and anticipated reserves in the Western sedimentary basin will continue at least until the turn of the century. Export prices may have to remain in the range of US$3.15 to US$3.40. It will also be important for the Canadian dollar to remain at about US$0.73 or less and for no additional taxes to be imposed if netbacks to the industry are to be high enough to stimulate increased drilling activity. Although Arctic gas may eventually go to Japan, and East-coast gas to the U.S. Northeast, thus providing some additional export revenues, little, if any, economic rent will be involved in this segment of the industry.

Real coal prices up to 1995 and beyond are unlikely to be much different from what they were in 1981 because of the world's excess capacity. Competition in world markets will be intensive, but because Western Canadian coal is low in sulphur, exports of coal may double by the 1990s — though, then again, they may not — and then level out. It might be worthwhile for Canadian interests to take a unified position in bargaining with Japan. Taxation regimes on coal production should be based on profits, not merely on volume of output. A decision to reduce sulphur emissions more rapidly might expand the market for Western coal in Ontario.

Electricity exports to the United States may continue to grow until the late 1980s. If the United States is amenable to importing Canadian-produced electricity on a long-term basis, exports could well be sustained beyond this point. Otherwise, as new U.S. capacity is created, they will diminish again. Canada as a whole will have to decide if it wishes to make electricity exports a major thrust of trade and energy policy. (Quebec already seems to have a positive decision in this matter.) In the process, greater interprovincial cooperation will be desirable so that domestic capacity may be more efficiently used and potential benefits to Canada not be lost unnecessarily in the competitive scramble for U.S. markets. Issues such as economic rents will have to be resolved, particularly on hydro-electricity generation and absence of a corporate-profits tax on Crown corporations that produce and export electricity. As things stand now, Canadians are simply subsidizing U.S. consumers.

Current annual uranium production is about double the existing free-world consumption so that excess inventories are expected to prevail until well into the 1990s. Because of the new high-quality reserves found in Saskatchewan, Canada will probably continue to be the cheapest source of supply in WOCA. Thus exports are likely to increase substantially in the years ahead, although prices and volumes are difficult to forecast. The value of exports will, however, likely be less than that of other energy-product exports.

Fisheries

The problems in the industry boggle the mind. On every hand there is a crisis and a fundamental problem that must be solved.

Pacific Coast Salmon Seiners Association (1981)

The widespread emergence of aquaculture as the growth segment of the

world's fisheries and as an important means of food diversification . . . warrants greater attention.

G. Ian Pritchard (1984c)

The World Situation

The world fishing industry has experienced a dramatic decline in the
growth rate of its output over the last decade or so. The total saltwater
and fresh-water catch expanded, throughout the 1950s and 1960s, at an
annual rate of almost 6 percent, rising from 22 to 71 million tonnes. From
1970 onward, however, the marine catch has been growing at less than 1
percent per year. The freshwater harvest in 1981 of 8.1 million tonnes
was, in fact, 12 percent lower than it had been in 1970 (FAO, 1983b).

The prime reason for this decline is simply that fish stocks are limited;
some species are overfished already, and others are nearing that point. In
addition, higher energy prices have raised considerably the costs for
fishing boats. The world recession of the 1970s and early 1980s has also
had a negative influence on the fishing industry. Finally, in 1973, the
annual 13-million-tonne Peruvian anchoveta harvest plummetted to 1.7
million tonnes, both because of some overfishing and because of the
great drop in plankton food supplies that occurred in 1972. It has
remained ever since at least 80 percent below the 1970 volume (Revelle,
1984).

In 1970, the Food and Agriculture Organization (FAO) projected that
the world demand for fish products used directly for human food would
reach 113 million tonnes by the year 2000, compared with 50 million
tonnes used for this purpose in 1980. By far the most rapid expansion —
well over 100 percent for the 20-year period — was expected to derive
from the demand of the developing-market economies and the centrally
planned economies. If the fish reduced to fish meal (for poultry and
livestock feed) and fish oil were added to this estimate, the tonnage
required could be as much as one-third more. However, if the rate of
growth of world catch during the last decade is any indication of future
supplies, by the year 2000, that catch would be only about 100 million
tonnes (Revelle, 1984).

The difference between expected demand and supplies could
undoubtedly be narrowed if prices of fish used as food were increased
substantially, thereby discouraging future consumption. Unfortunately,
demand would be reduced the most in the developing countries, where
the food need is greatest. On the supply side, the shortfall might be made
up through the reduction of fish wastage in both the fishing and processing stages; through both technological developments and economic
adjustments to increase the proportion of fish used directly for consumption rather than as animal feed where only about one-third of the fish
protein becomes consumable protein in meat, dairy or poultry products;

and through greatly expanded aquaculture production. Aquaculture output has already been growing rapidly, at a rate of over 7 percent annually for the years 1975 to 1980, and it will comprise more than one-twelfth of the total marine and freshwater catch by 1980. It is now practised by over 70 countries (Revelle, 1984, pp. 12, 19).

Canadian Fisheries

Issues and Concerns

Canada's fisheries are composed of three main divisions: the Atlantic fisheries, the Pacific fisheries, and the freshwater industry. The relative importance of these is summarized in Table 1-23. The Atlantic industry is by far the largest in terms of both tonnage and dollar value. But because over 84 percent of the tonnage caught in this area, representing 70 percent of the total Canadian catch, consists of groundfish and other cheaper types of fish, the dollar-value share is substantially lower than the tonnage share. By contrast, on the Pacific Coast the large proportion of the total catch that consists of high-value salmon and herring (70 percent) means that the value share of fish caught there accounts for well over double the volume share in the national industry. Freshwater species, although relatively high in value, nevertheless form only a small proportion of the entire industry output, even in value terms.

Canada's 1977 extension of sovereignty over her resources to 200 miles offshore was a stimulus to the domestic fishing and fish-processing industries. Both in anticipation of this event and subsequently, capital investment and employment increased substantially, with government encouragement and financial assistance. Between 1974 and 1982,

TABLE 1-23 Major Components of Canada's Fisheries, 1981

	In Quantity Terms	In Value Terms
	(percent)	
Atlantic Coast	84.7	66.0
Groundfish	55.3	30.8
Shellfish	13.4	28.2
Other	16.0	7.0
Pacific Coast	11.8	27.4
Salmon	5.6	18.5
Herring	2.7	4.1
Other	3.5	4.8
Freshwater	3.5	6.7
Total	100.0	100.0

Source: Canada, Department of Fisheries and Oceans, Annual Statistical Review of Fisheries, 1981 (Ottawa: The Department, 1983).

Canada's Share of the World	1976	1977	1979	1980
Percent of world fish catch	1.5	1.7	2.0	1.9
Rank	16th	17th	15th	16th
Percent of world production of preserved and processed products	1.8	2.1	2.2	2.1
Rank	9th	7th	9th	9th
Percent of world exports	7.7	8.2	7.9	7.2
Rank	3rd	2nd	1st	1st

Source: Canada, Department of Fisheries and Oceans, *Annual Statistical Review of Fisheries, 1978 and 1981* (Ottawa: The Department, 1980 and 1983 respectively).

licensed fishermen on the Atlantic Coast increased in numbers by 45 percent, and freezing capacity was more than doubled (Canada, Task Force on Atlantic Fisheries, 1982, p. 13). On the Pacific Coast, between 1977 and 1981, total numbers in the fishing sector expanded by 37 percent (Canada, Department of Fisheries and Oceans, 1980, 1983). During this period, Canada advanced to become the world's largest exporter of fish products. Yet, as Table 1-24 indicates, its share of both world production and world exports is still relatively tiny and reflects little market power for Canadian exporters.

The consequences of this enthusiastic expansion are sad. Over-capacity abounds in both the Atlantic and the Pacific fishing fleets and processing industries. The common-property nature of the resource has encouraged this development. Even though governments have set maximum quotas in an attempt to preserve or to rebuild fish stocks, the incentive remains for individual fishermen to have larger, more efficient boats so that they can bring in as large a share of the total available catch as they are able before someone else does. When all or many of the fishers are following the same strategy, no one makes a larger catch, but each is saddled with greater capital investment and debt and much underutilized capacity. The rise in interest rates during the 1970s and into the 1980s, as well as the higher fuel oil costs since 1973, have augmented operating costs and reduced the financial circumstances of those in the industry.

Other difficulties have also arisen. On the Pacific Coast, salmon and roe-herring prices rose dramatically during the 1970s (by 400 and 500 percent, respectively). But during the 1980s, Alaskan shipments of salmon were quintupled, and this occurrence greatly reduced world market prices. The world recession and the higher value of the Canadian dollar in markets outside the United States also had adverse consequences for West Coast products. In addition, serious declines in

TABLE 1-25 The Importance of Fishing and Fish Processing for the Major Producing Provinces

	Share of Provincial Employment 1981	Share of Gross Provincial Product 1980
	(percent)	
Newfoundland	20.6	15.5
Prince Edward Island	8.3	13.1
Nova Scotia	5.1	15.3
New Brunswick	2.8	5.5
British Columbia	1.8	1.8

Source: Canada, Department of Fisheries and Oceans, *Annual Statistical Review of Fisheries, 1981* (Ottawa: The Department, 1983).

stocks of some salmon, such as chinook and coho, and long-standing low stocks for chum salmon — all as a consequence of overfishing — mean that catches must be reduced in order to rebuild these stocks (Canada, Department of Fisheries and Oceans, 1984e). Attention must also be paid to restoring and improving the inland productive habitats where the salmon come to spawn; these waters have been damaged by pollution and other consequences of economic development.

On the Atlantic Coast there are similar massive problems of excess and underutilized capacity in both the fishing fleets and the processing facilities. The problems are, if anything, even worse than on the Pacific Coast because a larger proportion of the population depends on the fisheries for employment and income. This is evident from Table 1-25. Newfoundland, where over 20 percent of the labour force works in the fishing sector, is particularly vulnerable. Several hundred small communities, primarily in this province, but to some extent in the other Atlantic provinces too, have no other form of employment. Moreover, many of those in the industry cannot easily take on other work because they lack the education and skills to do so and would find it extremely difficult to acquire new skills.

That there are, essentially, three categories of fishing fleet makes resolution of overcapacity and other problems even more difficult. The inshore fleet, consisting of smaller boats unable to venture as far from the coast and more vulnerable to adverse weather conditions, has a shorter fishing season (usually lasting from May to September). Thus, not only these boats, but the processing plants, as well, relying primarily on the catch of inshore fisheries, are able to function during only a portion of each year, or at least must operate at much less than full capacity during the off-season. The resulting idleness of capacity raises average unit costs of fish products. Moreover, the groundfish (mostly cod) that is caught inshore tends to be smaller and to have softer flesh. Hence the fish, per pound, costs more to process and yet must be processed into blocks rather than into fillets, which command a higher market price (Weeks and Mazany, 1983). Newfoundland has yet another problem: because inshore cod is frequently caught in traps, merely reducing the number of vessels will not readily increase the catch per vessel.

The midshore fishery, which consists of somewhat larger boats, has a longer season, while the offshore fishery, which is made up of trawlers and other bigger vessels, operates year round. The more capital-intensive, offshore fleet provides much less employment than does the inshore fleet, but the employment it does provide is for a much longer period of the year. There is a trade-off here. The processing plants serving the midshore and offshore fleets can operate for longer periods and can accordingly spread their capital costs over more output. But even here, because there are so many of them (although over 50 percent of their total processing capacity is owned by just two or three companies), they frequently operate at less than full-capacity output. The year 1984 saw considerable governmental financial assistance given to assist in the reorganization of some of the large firms.[11]

Other issues, too, are of concern. The attempts of inshore fishermen to handle large numbers of fish during the peak season often lower the quality of fish brought to processors. Moreover, because processors are anxious to maximize their throughput during this time, they have, in the past, been reluctant, individually, to offer lower prices for poorer quality fish. Fishermen thus have lacked the financial incentive to take greater care of the fish they catch.

Generous unemployment-insurance benefits encourage workers to remain in the industry. Fishermen, who may collect benefits based on their average income during the time they do work, are sometimes inclined to work only during the peak of the inshore season, when their catch is highest, and only long enough to qualify for sufficient unemployment insurance benefits to cover the remainder of the year. Incentives for efficiency-improving measures are reduced in this environment.

Government policy has tended to focus on encouraging the inshore fisheries because they provide employment for more people, and has allocated allowable catches accordingly. In general, that policy has been to use the fisheries as an instrument of social policy (employment, preservation of communities, and so on) rather than to attempt to achieve the most efficient production. To complicate matters even more, the provinces and federal government have long disputed the division of responsibility for fisheries problems and resource management (Wildsmith, 1985).

Overall, Atlantic Canada is not as vulnerable to a shortfall in stocks of fish as is the world in general. Yields of some types of fish, such as Gulf redfish and salmon, have dropped significantly and are going to take considerable time to rebuild. But the cod catch, particularly off the northeast corner of Newfoundland and Labrador, is expected to be 75 percent greater in 1987 than it was in 1982, a rare development in world fishing today. The flatfish catch is anticipated to be higher, too (Canada, Task Force on Atlantic Fisheries, 1982, pp. 5, 9, 15).

A greater problem for the East Coast fisheries at this time is the sale of its growing supplies of fish and fish products at a profit. Canadian consumption takes only a relatively small proportion, 10 to 15 percent, of national production. The balance must be exported. On a per capita basis, domestic consumption was still only about 17.5 pounds of fish products per year in 1980–81. That per capita consumption has been growing at all — it was only 12 pounds per person in 1971 — is perhaps surprising, since over the decade 1971–81, when food prices were rising at a yearly rate of 2.9 times as compared with prices of other consumer products, rising at a rate of 2.2 times, fish prices rose even faster (by 3.6 times). They also rose 26 percent more than beef and 20 percent more than poultry.[12] As for many products, income and price elasticities and cross-price elasticities for fish products are notoriously difficult to estimate. (The Task Force on Atlantic Fisheries (1982); the Commission on Pacific Fisheries Policy (1982); and Weeks and Mazany (1983) do not even mention them.) But the casual evidence presented suggests that lower prices certainly have not been the reason for the modest rise in fish consumption in Canadian diets. In any event, there is no hope that realistic future expansion of Canadian fish-products consumption can put much of a dent in the expanding national fisheries' output. Larger exports are the only alternative.

As with most products that Canada exports, the United States is the dominant market for fish products, although the European Community and Japan are also significant purchasers (Table 1-26). Particularly noteworthy is Japan's increasing take of Canadian fish-product exports; Japan's purchases rose to nearly 13 percent in 1982–83, from less than 2 percent in 1975–76.

A major concern relating to the United States is the propensity of U.S. fishing interests to charge that Canadian government financial support to beleaguered fish-processing companies or to the fisheries directly are export subsidies against which U.S. countervailing duties ought to be applied. These same interests like also to link such matters with the settlement of the boundary disputes over Canada-U.S. fishing rights.[13]

Another problem has been the mediocre quality of Canadian products; only one-fifth of Canada's East Coast groundfish meets the standards of the highest-quality U.S. markets. The U.S. market tapped has had to be the price-sensitive middle one, between the high-quality restaurants and that segment of the retail market content with lowest quality and price (Canada, Task Force on Atlantic Fisheries, 1982). We shall return to these problems in the following section.

Canada hoped that when European fishing vessels were excluded

TABLE 1-26 Canadian Fish Products Trade, 1975–1983

	Exports	
	1975–76	1982–83
Average annual value	$459,000,000	$1,565,000,000
Percentage of total Canadian exports	1.4	1.8
Distribution of Trade	**1976**	**1983**
	(percent)	
United States	67.9	61.6
European Community	18.3	15.7
Japan	1.7	12.7
Other	12.1	10.0
Total	100.0	100.0

Source: Statistics Canada, *Summary of External Trade, 1976 and 1983* (Ottawa: Statistics Canada, 1977 and 1984 respectively).

from the waters within the Canadian 200-mile limit, sales of Canadian fish would develop in the EC. Up to now, however, this development has not occurred. The EC countries seem to have been able to satisfy their fish needs from other sources, such as the Scandinavian countries, which have privileged access to their markets, and have moved rapidly ahead not only with conventional fish harvesting, but also with aquaculture techniques; these techniques have resulted, to take one example, in the new challenge to Canada by Norwegian fjord-grown salmon. The EC also applies to Canadian products much higher tariffs than does the United States: 15 percent on frozen cod fillets and 12 percent on fresh, chilled or frozen cod.[14] Quotas are involved, as well.

A final concern is the relatively undeveloped state of aquaculture (this term includes mariculture) in Canada. Increasingly, in the future, world supplies of fish products, including shellfish, will come from this source. Already some nations have moved into aquaculture in a big way. Even by 1982, Norway and Denmark were each producing annually about 20,000 metric tonnes of salmon and trout. By 1986, Norway expects to be producing 40,000 tonnes of salmon alone (*Globe and Mail*, October 15, 1984). In contrast, Canada's 1982 production by aquaculture of these two types of fish amounted to less than 800 tonnes. Oyster farming by Japan in 1982 amounted to about 250,000 tonnes, compared with Canada's 2,000 tonnes (Science Council, 1984).[15]

The greatest advantage of aquaculture production of fish is that it enables producers to provide the market, on order, with a regular supply of fresh fish that is of a uniform high quality. Expensive product inventories and considerable handling can be eliminated. From this perspective, standard fish-boat harvesting, subject to seasonal and year-to-year variations in catch, is second best. Aquaculture is also a means of providing alternative employment to workers who must be withdrawn gradually from traditional fishing as excess capacity is reduced. Much of the work it provides is in keeping with their fishing experience and interests. The Norwegian example of moving strongly into European markets, on the one hand and, on the other, providing direct employment (of about 2,000 person-years in 1983) in their small seaside communities has demonstrated both these features of aquaculture (Gordon, 1984).

Norway has had a sustained research and development program since at least 1970, in such matters as developing superior-quality fish using genetic methodology similar to that used with farm animals; testing types of feed to use; disease treatment; and production, harvesting, and packaging procedures. In addition, sales for small farmers are coordinated through a non-profit farmers' sales organization, which also does market research, and provides education and training to farmers (Gordon, 1984).

Canada is well behind Norway in these matters. Considerable interest has been generated in the country, as was reflected by the National Aquaculture Conference held in 1983, sponsored by both the Department of Fisheries and Oceans (DFO) and the Science Council. Nevertheless, there have been more failures than successes in aquaculture ventures, particularly in British Columbia. Research focussed specifically on aquaculture is still relatively rare. In the Pacific Region, an immense amount of sheltered coastline exists, and water temperatures are suitable for aquaculture. Yet current operating expenditures by the federal government on R&D relating to salmon have actually diminished from a not-very-large average of $120,000 per year for the period 1973–76 to a miniscule $20,000 per year for 1980–83 (Bourne and Brett, 1983). The Salmonid Enhancement Program (SEP), which was begun in 1977, and which involves measures to augment traditional supplies of salmon, seems to have diverted attention and resources from aquaculture per se. Some work on rainbow trout, funded by the provincial government, and on herring, funded by the federal government, has begun since 1980 and totalled about $100,000 in 1983 (Bourne and Brett, 1983). These amounts are still small, considering the magnitude of work that could be done. Other amounts are, of course, spent on R&D throughout the country at DFO laboratories and by provincial governments directly through their agencies and through the commissioning of individual projects. These entail several millions of dollars. But there is no overall coordination of R&D programs in this country. Within many universities, too, a wide range of research projects are carried out that could have applicability to aquaculture, but at this point, the expertise is neither focussed nor mobilized to support the development of this industry. The preoccupation tends to be more with academic biological research or aquaculture technologies too expensive for actual use, than with resolving practical aquaculture problems (MacCrimmon, 1983). Weaknesses exist in the availability of teaching and research expertise on the actual production and marketing side, as well.

Finally, jurisdictional issues arise between the federal and provincial governments concerning responsibility for aquaculture. Federal provisions that do exist for aquaculture are scattered among a variety of statutes. This only makes the federal role more difficult to comprehend and complicates attempts to move systematically forward to resolve jurisdictional difficulties (Wildsmith, 1984).

In conclusion, the issues facing the fisheries sector are numerous and diverse. They suggest that new policies are required. Fortunately, some of these are already under way. Others remain to be instituted. The next section reviews what the more important of these policies are and might be.

Policies

As a consequence of the major studies undertaken in recent years on the Atlantic and Pacific fisheries, a number of policy changes are under consideration. These will be outlined in the context of the other policy possibilities that deserve attention at this time.

The overcapacity in the fisheries sector is clearly the key economic problem to be faced. In mid-1984, the federal Department of Fisheries and Oceans announced a new policy to reduce this capacity, within the Pacific Coast industry, to increase the profitability of that industry, and to contribute to the rebuilding of fish stocks. At the time of writing, the new policy has not been instituted, but its main components are worth noting. A Buy-Back Corporation, in which the federal government and the financial institutions that have lent to fishermen would be the shareholders, would purchase boats and equipment from fishermen, with the aim of reducing fleet size by 35 to 45 percent. Over the years 1985–87, the Department of Fisheries and Oceans (DFO) would institute a new licensing arrangement whereby fishermen would be given the right to take a certain percentage of the total allowable catch (TAC) by area and by type of fishing gear to be used. This would prevent competition among fishermen who might otherwise try to take a larger share of the TAC in any given area, by investing in larger vessels or in more sophisticated finding equipment. When all fishermen do this, no one is better off. Fishermen would be permitted to buy up others' fishing allocations to increase their own catch, and to utilize more fully their own capacity and thereby improve their returns. More precise management of stocks in this way will leave more fish to migrate to spawning areas for the rebuilding of stocks. This tactic, along with policies to restore spawning habitat that has been allowed to deteriorate, to increase access to unused habitat, and to alter patterns of interceptions (by agreement with the United States) are expected to increase the total catch, in the early 1990s, by nearly 40 percent, and in the year 2000, by nearly 65 percent, over 1980–83 levels (Canada, Department of Fisheries and Oceans, 1984a–1984i).

Steps are being considered under the same program to preserve and strengthen the participation of Native peoples in the salmon-fishing industry, on which many small coastal communities depend for food and employment. To support communities, both Native and non-Native, where employment opportunities may be adversely affected by the decline in the number of fishing vessels, measures to encourage sport fishing and mariculture may be instituted, although it is not clear what these measures are to be. Continuation of the Salmonid Enhancement Program is supposed to help the employment situation, too.

On the Atlantic Coast measures are also beginning to be taken to lower the capacity for commercial fishing of declining stocks of salmon and herring by means of licence buy-back schemes and transferable fishing rights among fishermen. The agreement struck in the autumn of 1984 between Ottawa and New Brunswick on this matter is one example. If this approach is taken more widely, as it clearly should be, the average catch for offshore fishermen remaining in the industry can be enhanced, and unit costs of fish production reduced accordingly.

Painful as it may be, there would also appear to be a need for the federal government to move away from its existing unemployment-insurance benefits program, which encourages fishermen to work for less than the entire season, to a program like that applicable to all other workers. There is good reason, too, for the government to ease off on its traditional encouragement of the inshore fishing sector at the expense of the offshore sector and not to use fishing merely as an employment-creating device. If fish of poorer quality and higher cost are the result, and they cannot be marketed, or when marketed, if they face U.S. countervailing duties because of subsidization, such a policy is hardly appropriate. At the same time, rationalization of the processing sector is also necessary, since in Atlantic Canada there are about 700 fish-processing plants in operation (Weeks and Mazany, 1983).

Some jobs lost from rationalization of the fisheries might be replaced with new opportunities in aquaculture, but if the Norwegian experience is any example, we may be talking only of 1,000 or 2,000 jobs after considerable development occurs, not of many thousands. Different work possibilities will have to be found in other sectors, such as, perhaps, in much greater encouragement of the tourism industry in the Atlantic provinces, or in development of the incipient oil and gas sector.

The second major problem facing the fisheries, particularly those in Atlantic Canada which concentrate on finfish such as cod (as distinct from shellfish) is that of marketing within Canada and, to an even greater extent, abroad. Expansion here involves matters of marketing organization; marketing strategy; product variety, quality and price relative to other protein products; and foreign tariffs or other restrictions on imports. Let us consider these matters briefly in relation to the nation's major markets.

The Canadian fish-processing industry is highly concentrated; the largest firm is more than twice as big as any rival firm among the North

Atlantic countries (Canada, Task Force on Atlantic Fisheries, 1982, p. 53). Hence, although competition in the U.S. market is severe and Canadian firms must face large U.S. retail buyers and compete with much bigger U.S. food corporations, lack of size is not likely to be Canada's major concern. Given the recent financial reorganization of National Sea Products Ltd. and much government assistance, we can expect that with capable management, the fisheries will survive and be internationally competitive.

At present, of total U.S. consumption of meat and fish protein, fish comprises only 5.5 percent, and groundfish (like cod, the product in which the major growth in supply will be occurring up to 1987) accounts for only 1.7 percent. For the expansion in cod output to be totally absorbed by the United States that nation would have to increase its consumption of fish by one pound per capita, or about 7 percent. The continued development of new fish products may help to attract new buyers. In addition, a substantial and sustained generic advertising program, such as the one just begun by DFO, is desirable in order to shift consumer demand from red meats to fish products; this development occurred some years ago with respect to poultry products (Canada, Task Force on Atlantic Fisheries, 1982).

Another objective might be to so improve efficiency in the fishing sector that the price of good-quality fish to consumers could be lowered noticeably relative to other forms of protein. This move would require that the potential gains that might come from rationalization and consequent reduction of excess capacity of the fishing and fish-processing industries not go entirely either to the industries themselves in the form of higher profits or to society as economic rents from its natural resource of fish, but be used, in part, to lower the prices of fish products. Such a possibility is one that was not addressed by the Task Force on the Atlantic Fisheries, nor by the Pearse Commission on the Pacific Fisheries, nor by the Institute for Research on Public Policy (Weeks and Mazany, 1983). The Task Force, for example, limits its price objective for the East Coast industry simply to maintaining "present real prices." This limited objective, even supported by a generic advertising program, which has been begun both in the United States and in Canada to raise consumer awareness of fish products and how to prepare them, may not be sufficient to dispose of the growing Canadian fish supplies. Lower nominal and real prices may be necessary.

Although it is not the only consideration (Macdonald and Mazany, 1984), much greater attention to quality improvement is essential, too, if the quality and consistency of fish blocks and other exports are to be improved and inroads made on Iceland's hold on the U.S. quality fish-markets, such as white-table restaurants. The voluntary fish-grading system being instituted in 1985 and possibly to be made mandatory in 1986 is important to pursue. Monetary incentives, such as substantially lower prices for, or outright rejection of, carelessly handled fish brought to dockside, would appear to be vital to the success of any quality-improvement program. As quality is improved (for example, by prompter bleeding and gutting), the yield from a given volume of raw fish will also improve; this gain will permit lower prices to consumers as well as higher profits.

Since the European nations still desire access to Canadian fishing waters, there would seem to be room for continued bargaining. The approach that Canada is now taking of offering access to its fishing grounds only in return for increased quotas or lower tariffs in Europe, along the lines of the tentative December 1983 agreement between Canada and the European Community (Schrank, Tsoa, and Roy, 1984), is worth sustaining. More arrangements might also be made such as the modest one negotiated with the U.S.S.R. in May 1984, whereby access to fish stocks not usually desired in North America is given in return for a commitment to purchase processed Canadian fish. A similar type of strategy might also be used with Japan, Canada's third-largest market, whose post-Tokyo Round tariffs remain fairly high, standing between those of the United States and the EC.

Earlier in this paper we noted that the FAO projections suggested that the most rapidly growing markets for fish products were the developing nations and countries with centrally planned economies. None of these markets are as yet very well exploited by Canadian fish-products merchandisers. Accordingly, much remains to be done in this respect. Clearly, there is a continuing role for government in working for a more liberalized, multilateral trading environment and, where necessary, adding authority to intercountry bargaining processes where, for instance, countertrade is involved. But it is up to the industry itself, either as individual firms, or through a marketing corporation such as that used by the potash industry, to develop its own world sales program.

The future of aquaculture in Canada must also be considered. If the Canadian policy focus remains too exclusively on revamping and making more efficient the traditional fishing industry, Canada may well find itself badly behind in future world fish-products markets. Awareness of the importance of moving forward in this industry is growing, but much remains to be done (Pritchard, 1984a, 1984b, 1984c; Bourne and Brett, 1983; Aiken, 1983; MacCrimmon, 1983).

Research and development (R&D) opportunities and challenges abound. These relate to the planning and design of facilities, including choice of location, water and other environmental factors; fish health as affected by disease, parasites, fish immunity systems, vaccines and so on; stock selection and improvement to develop larger, faster-maturing, superior-quality fish by means of breeding, genetic and other techniques; development of cost-efficient feed supplies and nutrition for each stage of growth; improvement of handling, sampling and harvesting technology; and the establishment of pilot-scale systems to test and enhance research findings that relate not only to the biological aspects of fish growth, but also to other aspects of the aquaculture industry, including organization, administration and marketing (Pritchard, 1984c).

It is clear that many more dollars must be devoted to aquaculture research. Yet because the extent of the research task is so great, more resources will also have to be devoted to acquiring and absorbing, and where necessary, adapting and disseminating technology from abroad. This implies tapping more effectively into the aquaculture-related knowledge and research that already exists and that is going on in universities (MacCrimmon, 1983), so that these institutions can make a more effective contribution to the industry. It will also require further development of training programs and extension services to aquaculturalists such as have existed in and been so successful in improving the technological and administrative productivity of the agricultural sector. Centralized, possibly producer-owned, and at least producer-oriented marketing agencies to keep abreast of the changing world market situation and to find markets for products are also a necessity. If the same type of coordination could exist among the various components of the aquaculture industry as has been developed among university researchers, producer organizations and marketing agencies for an agricultural product such as canola, the advancement of the industry would be greatly furthered.

Successful aquaculture depends simultaneously on adequate supplies of inputs such as disease-free fish eggs, reliable quality of fish feeds appropriate for the progressive stages of fish growth, available veterinary services, and the like. Gradually, the industry may integrate backward to include some of these functions as some firms in Norway have done. By and large, however, supplies of eggs produced from superior fish by means of selected breeding programs will likely have to remain a function of government research stations.[17] Aquaculture ventures will also require financing arrangements with banks that recognize the nature of this industry, since returns may not be forthcoming for three to five years after start-up (see also Science Council, 1984). Adequate record-keeping for the industry in disease problems and fish-survival rates, productivity, financial matters, reasons for operational failures, and the like will also help to improve success ratios of firms.

A final observation: if the fishing sector as a whole is to compete effectively in world markets, it must be aware of the importance of developing a spirit of cooperation among its various components. New research findings, new administrative structures or changes in strategy will be of little avail by themselves unless fishermen, fish boat owners, processors, aquaculturalists and governments make a concerted effort to work together to improve their common lot. This ingredient of success seems to have been lacking in some segments of the industry. Its lack can only be rectified if each interested party recognizes and accepts the need for improvement in this respect. This implies, too, that the jurisdictional disputes that have occurred between the federal and provincial governments must to be resolved through negotiation and, where necessary, through legislation that clarifies the respective roles of the various governments (Wildsmith, 1984, 1985).

Forest Products

Forestry today is experiencing a transition similar to that which occurred in agriculture much earlier in human history.

Roger Sedjo (1983b)

The forest products sector, which consists of both logging and manufacturing activities, is a major component of the Canadian economy. Logging shipments, mostly roundwood used for domestic processing into wood and paper products, amounted to $4.6 billion in 1980, while processed products totalled $23 billion in that year, or 13 percent of all manufacturing shipments and 10 percent of manufacturing value-added. Although most of the provinces have some forest-products industry, the overwhelming amount of activity takes place in British Columbia, Ontario and Quebec. British Columbia dominates the logging industry with about 45 percent of logging employment. It also produces about one-half the value-added in the wood industries. Pulp and paper activities are more heavily concentrated in Ontario and Quebec, which together account for nearly two-thirds of Canadian value-added in pulp and paper manufacture. Total employment in the sector represents about 300,000 workers, of which about 44,000 are in logging, and the remainder are in manufacturing. Details of the provincial distribution of total employment are given in Table 1-27.

There are really three segments in the forest products manufacturing sector, and they are defined by the products they produce (Canada, Department of External Affairs, 1983, p. 73):

- lumber, woodpulp and newsprint. These three categories account for approximately 60 percent of shipments and about 85 percent of forest-products sales abroad. The domestic and world environments for such products have been relatively duty free.
- plywood, waferboard and a few paper grades sold in both internal and external markets, but quantitatively much less significant as exports than the three products in the first group.
- other products including millwork, kitchen cabinets and converted paper products, which rely on protection to supply the Canadian market and are not exported to any significant extent.

TABLE 1-27 Provincial Distribution in Canada's Forest Products Industry

| | Employment 1979 | | | | 1981 Forest Products Processing As Percentage of | |
| | Logging (000s) | Processing (000s) | Total Nos. (000s) | Total % | | |
Province					Provincial Employment	GPP
British Columbia	23.4	73.9	97.3	32.0	6.8	21.1
Alberta	1.1	8.9	10.0	3.3	0.9	1.8
Saskatchewan	0.6	2.4	3.0	1.0	0.5	2.0
Manitoba	0.6	4.2	4.8	1.6	1.0	3.2
Ontario	9.8	68.8	78.6	25.9	1.7	3.8
Quebec	12.2	72.5	84.7	27.9	2.8	8.5
New Brunswick	3.8	9.9	13.7	4.5	4.7	22.1
Nova Scotia	1.3	6.1	7.4	2.4	1.7	7.7
Prince Edward Island	0.0	0.2	0.2	0.0	2.0	1.0
Newfoundland	1.2	3.1	4.3	1.4	2.2	9.4
Totals	54.0	250.0	304.0	100.0	2.9	7.1

Sources: Statistics Canada, *Historical Labour Force Statistics* (Ottawa: Statistics Canada, 1985); Canadian Forest Congress, *The Forest Imperative* (Montreal: Canadian Pulp and Paper Association, 1980), p. 161.

Forest Products Trade

The changing relative importance of the major export items in total forest-products exports is summarized in Table 1-28. Particularly noticeable are the substantial decline in the significance of newsprint and the gradual growth of the lumber and residual category. The drop in relative significance of newsprint exports and the rise in that of lumber is also plain when one examines Canadian production as a share of world production and Canadian exports as a percentage of world exports (Tables 1-29 and 1-30). As for woodpulp, Canada as the world's largest producer has maintained its share of world exports, but as a proportion of world production the Canadian role has been diminishing.

TABLE 1-28 Canadian Forest Products Exports, Selected Years, 1950–1983

	Percent				Total Value	
	Softwood Lumber	Woodpulp	Newsprint	Other	Percent	$ millions
1950	24.3	19.0	44.3	12.4	100.0	1,102
1960	20.4	20.5	47.8	11.4	100.0	1,587
1970	21.8	26.8	37.9	13.5	100.0	2,929
1980	25.7	30.5	29.0	14.8	100.0	12,697
1983	29.7	28.3	30.5	16.6	100.0	13,148

Source: Bank of Canada, *Bank of Canada Review* (various years).

TABLE 1-29 Canadian Volume Shares of World Production, Selected Years

	Softwood Lumber	Woodpulp	Newsprint
	(annual average percentages)		
1951–55	9	22	53
1961–65	8	17	41
1971–75	9	16	36
1980–81	13	14	32

Source: FAO, *1981 Yearbook of Forest Products* (Rome: FAO, 1983).

TABLE 1-30 Canadian Volume Shares of World Exports

	Softwood Lumber	Woodpulp	Newsprint
	(annual average percentages)		
1970–71	37	32	69
1980–81	44[a]	33	61

Source: FAO, *1981 Yearbook of Forest Products* (Rome: FAO, 1983).
a. The Canadian share of softwood lumber exports reached a peak of 49.7 percent in 1978 and it has been declining gradually since then.

TABLE 1-31 Major Forest Products Export Markets, 1983

	Softwood Lumber	Woodpulp	Newsprint	Total
	(percent)			
United States	76.5	52.6	82.0	72.5
EC	7.5	24.0	8.6	12.7
Japan	8.8	11.1	0.2	5.7
Other	7.2	12.2	9.2	9.1

Source: Statistics Canada, *Summary of External Trade, 1983* (Ottawa: Statistics Canada, 1984).

Canadian exports comprise nearly 25 percent of world exports of forest products. Our main markets and their relative significance for the major export products are listed in Table 1-31. Clearly the United States dominates, particularly for lumber and newsprint. In turn, Canada is the dominant supplier for the United States, accounting, for example, for over 95 percent of U.S. lumber imports.

World Projections

Paper and paperboard Although projections of world consumption vary considerably, one point seems to be clear: that the growth rate in the coming decades will be slower than it was in earlier decades. This trend has already become apparent in that the growth rate of paper and paperboard for the 1960s averaged 5.6 percent, whereas for the 1970s it was down to 3.0 percent (Canadian Pulp and Paper Association, 1983, p. 17). The prime reasons for this shift are the lower anticipated future rate of growth of income and the increased competition from paper and paperboard substitutes. Technological developments, particularly with respect to computer applications and the electronic transmission of information, have the potential for altering both the nature and the volume of paper usage. On the one hand, electronic bill paying and shopping may greatly reduce the use of paper by the mid-1990s; the yellow pages of phone books, for example, might be reduced or eliminated (Haas, 1982). On the other hand, the greater amount of data that can be processed, prepared in report form and printed allows greater efficiency of printing and publishing processes, thus stimulating the continued use of paper. In some instances, as paper prices have risen, shifts to lower-quality paper have occurred. In other instances, the adoption of better-quality paper has expanded advertising in newspapers (O'Donoghue, 1982; Udell, 1983). The net effects of these and many other types of forces are hard to predict. Recent forecasts for the world are summarized in Table 1-32. Those by the FAO were made in the mid-1970s, when anticipations of future economic growth were much more buoyant than they are today. Hence these projections look high

TABLE 1-32 Projected Growth Rates of World Consumption of Paperboard and Paper

	Period	
Forecaster	1985–90	1990–95
	(% average annual growth rates)	
1977 FAO industry working party (medium forecast)	3.5	
FAO 1977	4.6	
Valmet 1982	3.0	2.7
Poyry 1982	3.2	3.2
Graff 1983	1.9	0.9

Source: Peter Graff, "Paper Consumption — A Global Forecast," *Pulp and Paper International* (May 1983), p. 58.

from today's perspective. If we take a simple average of the three more recent forecasts by Valmet, Poyry, and Graff (Graff, 1983), the growth rate for 1985–90 would be 2.7 percent, substantially below the outstanding 5.6 percent rate of the 1960s.

Lumber

Over the past 25 years, global demand for lumber has grown at a rate of about 2 percent annually. For the years to 2000, demand is projected to expand, at most, about one-half as rapidly as that for paper products over the same period (cited in Farrell et al., 1984, pp. 51–52).

Projection for Canada

Demand

Projections of market growth for Canada's logging, wood and paper industries are difficult to make, given the range of domestic and world influences that have the potential to influence the results. The slowdown in world growth will naturally tend to reduce Canadian exports. Other more particular developments must be considered too, especially in the United States, Canada's largest market. Recent investigation suggests that intensive forest management in the United States, particularly in the southern states, could stabilize wood-product prices by the year 2000, so that they would not continue to rise at their historical rate of about 1.5 percent per year in real terms. This development could in turn mean that the rate at which substitutes replace wood and paper products would be reduced, a plus for market demand for forest products. But it could also mean that while softwood imports from Canada would remain at approximately current levels to the year 2000, they could be eliminated by 2030 (Adams et al., 1982).

Other recent U.S. estimates also give little basis for great optimism. Up to 2000, annual total U.S. imports of softwood forest products are projected to be no greater than they were in 1980, and by 2010 are expected to be 9 percent lower, although they will probably rise again by nearly 2 percent per year over the subsequent 10 years. Total U.S. hardwood forest-product imports, of which Canada supplies relatively little, are expected to double between 1980 and 1990, but to remain constant thereafter for the subsequent three decades (cited in Farrel et al., 1984, p. 57).

A variety of changes taking place in other parts of the world are significant, too. Even a decade ago there were as many as 90 million hectares of plantation forests in the world (Sedjo, 1983a, p. 5). (Only a negligible amount of these are in Canada.) The higher-quality ones can produce 15 to 10 cubic metres of timber growth per hectare per year. (In Brazil, timber growth is as great as 40 to 60 cubic metres per hectare per year (Hall, 1984). With a yield of even 10 cubic metres per hectare per year on all plantation forests, it would take only about 4.7 percent of existing world forest lands to satisfy the world's demand for timber (Sedjo, 1983a, p. 81). As countries, both developed and developing, move forward rapidly in afforestation and plantation programs, the demand for Canadian natural forest products exports will be adversely affected. The nations with the most rapid increases in lumber production in recent years have been Japan, Brazil and India. For newsprint, the leaders have been the United States, Finland, China, South Africa, Korea, Norway and Germany.

Concerning developing countries one author has aptly stated:

> It is not logical for developing countries or zones of the world to continue to buy large volumes of primary forest products from highly industrialized countries. . . . they have the potential to become the major supplier to world markets in the long term. (Macdonald, 1983)

The success stories in nations such as Brazil, Chile and Zambia suggest that new industrial plantations can be financially successful, eventually reducing imports of forest products by developing countries from developed nations by as much as US$10 billion a year (Spears and Ayensu, 1984, p. 70).

Note, however, another dimension of this issue. The continued and expanded success of the efforts of developing countries depends on substantial investments in the years ahead, not only in intensive forest management of existing plantations, but in the expansion by fivefold of the planting of trees for fuelwood, to about 5 billion trees per year, at a cost of about US$1 billion a year for the next 15 years (Spears and Ayensu, 1984). This advance is essential, for over 80 percent of the wood resources in developing countries are used for fuel in contrast to about 11 percent in developed countries (Bowonder, 1983). Without such extended effort, by the year 2000, about 2.4 billion people in 57 different developing nations might be experiencing extreme difficulties in finding fuelwood. Consequently there would be increasing pressure on the remaining industrial forest resources of these lands (Spears and Ayensu, 1984). Of course, Canada should neither hope for nor count on dire problems in the impoverished lands of the world to maintain the continued marketability of its own products, but Canadians should be aware of this aspect of world demand for wood.

Other factors affecting the future demand for Canadian forest products in world markets include changes in trade barriers on the one hand, and technological advances, on the other. Since January 1, 1984, the Scandinavian countries have had unrestricted tariff-free access to the European Community, Canada's second largest market and no longer are restricted by the 1.5 million tonne tariff-free quota on imports that they previously had to share with Canada. (Sweden also benefits from the devaluation of the Swedish krona by over 40 percent as compared to the Canadian dollar in the last three or four years.) Conversely, the EC initially saw fit to impose a quota on Canadian imports of 500,000 tonnes, substantially below the 700,000 tonne average that Canada has shipped to the EC in recent years. As a result of a Canadian appeal, the GATT recommended that Canada and the EC reopen negotiations. At the time of writing (February 1985), no issue has yet been resolved in this dispute.

Again, U.S. lumber interests in the Pacific Northwest are much concerned about the increased imports of lumber from Canada, particularly British Columbia. In 1982–83, Canada successfully staved off an attempt by U.S. producers to have limits placed on imports of Canadian lumber. But in late 1984 and early 1985, pressures are once more building up in the United States to find means of limiting the entry of Canadian products. A problem facing U.S. firms is that the amounts they paid or committed themselves to pay for harvesting timber are now too high, given the rather depressed state of the lumber market. One of their ways of coping with this difficulty is to attempt to have Canadian imports restricted to a given share of the U.S. market.

As for technological change, the effects are diverse. New technology allows the production of low-cost pulp for fine papers made from hardwoods, the major forest reserve of many tropical and southern temperate-zone nations. This development, plus the fact that wood costs for hardwood are much cheaper in these areas than in the northern temperate zone, amounting to US$50 per tonne in Brazil as compared to US$105 in Canada (Hall, 1984), adds an additional negative element to the situation. However, Domtar's work on fast-growing poplar (hardwood) in eastern Ontario, which matures in 10–12 years for use in their fine-paper mill, suggests that the Canadian disadvantage in hardwoods may be greatly exaggerated. On the other side, the new chemical/

TABLE 1-33 Canadian Projections of Annual Growth in Forest Industries, 1980–1995

	Total Shipments	Domestic Shipments	Export
	(percent)		
Logging	2.0	2.0	—
Lumber and other wood products	2.4	2.7	2.2
Paper and allied products (including woodpulp)	2.2	2.4	2.0

Sources: Interim Report of the Forest Industries Advisory Committee (Ottawa: Minister of Supply and Services Canada, 1983); also John Wansbrough, "Sectional View of the Longer Term: Forest Products," in *Long-Term Prospects for Canada: A Symposium*, volume 23 of the research studies prepared for the Royal Commission on the Economic Union and Development Prospects for Canada (Toronto: University of Toronto Press, 1985).

mechanical technology for producing softwood pulp makes it cheaper (Canadian Pulp and Paper Association, 1983), although the southeastern United States is at present, and is expected to continue to be, a lower-cost producer of softwood market pulp, as well as of newsprint and lumber, than the northwestern United States or Canada.

With such a diverse range of influences operating in world markets, any projections of Canadian production and exports must be considered highly tenuous. Table 1-33 summarizes one set of these projections. Exports are expected to experience somewhat slower growth than domestic shipments; that growth will probably be in the range of 2 percent for woodpulp, paper and allied products, and 2.2 percent for lumber and other wood products.[18]

If the U.S. projections of domestic supply growth mentioned earlier are realized, these estimates will probably have to be viewed as overly optimistic.[19] Huge new markets would have to be found in the rest of the world to compensate for a lack of growth in the U.S. market. Given the current and prospective developments of plantation forestry, particularly in the southern hemisphere, this would be difficult. Employment in the forest sector, which, as we shall see later on, may well decline even with market growth, would diminish even more under this scenario.

Rather than taking this particular possibility any further, let us accept these projections and examine some of their other implications for the Canadian forest industries and the economy as a whole. Although the forecast-growth rates are lower than actual rates experienced in earlier years, they nevertheless represent a substantial expansion of potential consumption of Canadian forest products.

A 2.0 percent annual compound growth rate indicates that the need for Canadian products will grow by more than 37 percent by the year 2000 and by over 67 percent by 2010. A 2.5 percent growth rate would mean necessary increases in output of nearly 50 percent and 90 percent respectively. These figures suggest, therefore, that Canada's primary concern probably should not be about the fact that growth rates of world needs for Canadian products will be lower in the future than in the past, but concerning whether Canada will be able to meet these needs from its resource base at prices competitive with alternative sources of world supply.

Canadian Supply

Canada's timber supply is not nearly as large relative to annual harvests as was once thought. The last peak in harvest levels occurred in 1979. The difference between the harvest that year and the annual allowable cut (AAC), "the regulated yearly harvest for a managed forest unit under sustained yield or the annual harvest authorized by a licence over its term" (Percy, 1984, pp. 2–14)) is the theoretical physical timber reserve, or the amount by which the industry could theoretically expand the annual harvest. For the nation as a whole, the size of the theoretical reserve of softwood timber (37 percent above the AAC) suggests that a 2 percent growth rate in annual harvest could be readily achieved (Reed and Associates, 1980).

But a host of factors reduce the amount of this reserve that would be worth harvesting, given existing and anticipated price and cost factors. These include inaccessibility; small size, poor quality, or inappropriate mix of trees in relation to the available processing facilities; and inferior land base, which makes reforestation uneconomic. In some areas the AAC estimates are gross figures, ignoring losses caused by forest fire, disease or insect destruction (Percy, 1984). Such losses are substantial; taken together and reckoned on an annual basis, they equalled, in the latter part of the 1970s, about 80 percent of the annual harvest (Canadian Pulp and Paper Association, 1983, pp. 67–69). In Quebec, over the past four years, the spruce budworm has ruined half as much wood as was harvested (Pinard, 1984). The jackpine budworm is of rising concern in Ontario, where it affected 1.2 million hectares in 1983. Acid rain is a growing problem, too.

If realistic reserves are specified, then only Alberta has much scope for expanding softwood production using existing forest stands. For the nation as a whole, at a 2 percent growth rate of harvesting, a deficit would exist by 1995 (Reed and Associates, 1980). For hardwoods there would still be a sizable surplus at that time, equal to nearly 160 percent of requirements. But even by 1995, it is anticipated that hardwood, used primarily for fine papers, will still be a little less than 10 percent of the total softwood and hardwood harvest requirement (Canadian Pulp and Paper Association, 1983, p. 51).

In the short term there probably would not be a problem in meeting supply needs, at least for British Columbia, the largest timber-producer. About 55 percent of the existing productive forest reserve is mature timber, 40 percent is immature, and the remainder is brush, unreforested land and the like. Hence there could even be some increase in annual harvests for a time. If too much timber is harvested too soon, however, there could be a sizeable decline in future annual harvests below what might otherwise be possible (Percy, 1984). The consequence would be an interruption in the ability of Canada to meet its customary market commitments.

In the longer term, even with some increase in utilization of hardwood forest reserves, Canada will face a major challenge in sustaining, let alone increasing, her forest harvests. Much can be done to reduce the enormous losses to forest fires, disease and insect infestation. Steps can also be taken, as they are now on occasion, to reduce the quantity of highly productive forest land that is being diverted to other uses. Intensive forest management involving genetic improvements in trees used for reforestation, proper site preparation, prompt reforestation, fertilization, removing of brush and weeds, commercial thinning, and so on can produce average annual timber growth several times greater than the current average AAC per hectare for all Canada.[20]

Continued improvement in the efficient utilization of timber stands is essential, too, including the harvesting of branches and of less-desirable species, expanding the proportion of wood from a given log (the proportion of lumber that Japanese firms are obtaining from a tree, for instance, is about 70 percent compared to 40 to 50 percent obtained by Canadian firms) and using residues for other pulp and paper products.

Softwood timber stands in Canada take from 50 to 80 years or more to grow to harvestable size, compared with about 20 years or less for pine in the U.S. South and 15 years for Brazilian pine (Hall, 1984). Some reductions in this length of time might be possible if the criteria for cutting were shifted from physical requirements focussed only on achieving the greatest volume of wood output, to economic requirements that focus on cutting to achieve the best social returns from the resource. This change would involve, in addition to the faster harvesting of existing mature timber mentioned earlier, the rapid replanting and earlier harvesting of second-growth timber (Percy, 1984; Economic Council, 1984). It could mean, quite conceivably, a greater volume of wood harvested over time than if purely physical criteria were applied. Yet even allowing for shorter rotation periods, any major reforestation and accompanying intensive management programs commenced in the near future would not result in enhanced yields until well into the 21st century. Improved forest management of existing natural stands may help, in the meantime, quickly and effectively to reduce the possibility of a longer-run decline in forest yields.

A number of other features of the Canadian situation need to be highlighted in this context. First, even though the forestry industry is heavily regulated, up to the present, industry and governments have not been ensuring that reforestation of harvested lands was adequate. Less than one-third of these lands are replanted or seeded. In Quebec, where the industry has been expanding at only one-half the rate of the entire Canadian industry, only 8 percent of timbered lands are artificially replanted (Pinard, 1984). A second one-third is supposedly being regenerated by nature, but much of this growth consists of brush or of the less-desirable hardwood varieties, such as aspen poplar, rather than the softwood that forested the land originally. The final one-third is neither being reforested nor experiencing natural regeneration at all.

It appears that absence of silviculture by industry stems to a large degree from the fact that 94 percent of Canadian forest land is owned by the government, compared with only 27 percent in the United States and 24 percent in Sweden. Thus, the incentives for silviculture by privately owned forest-products companies have been lacking. Generally, too, the leases that companies have on leased lands are shorter than the time required to reap rewards from reforestation and accompanying forest-management work. And to the extent that forest yields are enhanced, stumpage charges by the Crown tend to be raised so that the major benefits from silviculture would not accrue to the companies that undertook them even if their tenure were long enough (Economic Council, 1984). Governments have not compensated for this lack of forest management by industries. It is perhaps not surprising, therefore, that the Canadian record on intensive forest management is inferior to that of other important producing nations. In both Scandinavia and the United States, there is one professional forester for every 380,000 hectares of productive forest land. For 1981–82, although spending by Canada's industry and governments on silviculture amounted to about $240 to $270 million, if the nation were to have matched the Swedish intensity, it would have had to spend an additional $450 million (Science Council, 1983).

Research will also have to be increased. That additional research is worthwhile can be seen from the U.S. Forestry Service estimate that the average benefit-cost ratio for their forestry research is 50: 1 (Science Council, 1983).

Secondly, because the southern hemisphere and southern U.S. forests grow much more rapidly than do those in Canada, investments in silviculture in Canada, at least for softwoods (the major resource) will take much longer to pay for themselves, and accordingly the rate of return will be lower. Recent work on the economics of plantation forestry throughout the world bears out this statement (Sedjo, 1983a).[21] Estimates indicate that even with the Canadian dollar at US$0.73, current Canadian wood costs for newsprint are nearly 40 percent above U.S. costs (Pinard, 1984). On the encouraging side, however, is the contemporary finding that the net economic returns to intensive forest management in British Columbia are expected to be sufficient to yield profits, even at real interest rates of 10 percent (Heaps, 1984).

Thirdly, labour costs are an important part of industry costs, amounting to about one-half the cost of wood delivered to mills for example, and Canadian labour costs are higher than those in the southern United States and higher still than those in tropical zones. For newsprint, labour costs are currently nearly 20 percent above those in the United States, in equivalent U.S. dollars (Pinard, 1984). Moreover, Canada has had an unenviable record of labour strife, which only aggravates supply and marketing problems (ibid. 1984). The most recent example of this dissension was the stoppage of production in the British Columbia pulp and paper industry for some months during the early part of 1984, just at a time when the expanding U.S. market would have been able to absorb virtually all the additional output that Canada could have supplied.

In the fourth place, even in British Columbia, which has the most sophisticated stumpage-charge system of all the provinces, the method employed is seriously deficient. It reduces the incentives for new capital investment in the industry, the incentives for firms that could be more efficient in the use of labour to hold down labour costs, and the incentives to harvest all the available wood in a timber stand (Percy, 1984).

Fifthly, the largest timber-producing province, British Columbia, has been cutting back on its forest management during the recession of the 1980s at a time when such programs should be being expanded. It is encouraging to note, however, that Quebec is expanding its forest management programs.

In the sixth place, although major new investments have been made in recent years, because returns to Canadian forestry were relatively low, investment in the Canadian pulp and paper industry was sluggish throughout most of the 1970s in comparison with what was occurring in the rest of the world, particularly in Canada's major market, the United States. This situation has contributed to the decline in Canada's market share for newsprint that was noted earlier. While the U.S. newsprint market doubled during the last 30 years, imports from Canada rose by only one-quarter, and the U.S. producers' share of their own market increased to 43 percent from only 18 percent (Pinard, 1984). More important, existing machines in Canada are, on average, older, often smaller and technologically obsolete, and hence less productive than those of major competitors. Over 50 percent of the paper-making machines in this country were built before 1950, whereas in the United States, only 25 percent are in this category and in Scandinavia a mere 5 percent. In terms of person-hours required per tonne of newsprint, the average for all of Canada is 50 percent above that in Scandinavia and about 25 percent greater than in the United States. For fine papers and other specialized products, too, Canadian plants are smaller and less efficient, geared to producing just for the protected Canadian market. Large investments will be required to bring the industry up to a world competitive level (Wansbrough, 1985; Pinard, 1984).

Employment projections for the forest-products manufacturing sectors are somewhat mixed. One estimate suggests that if new investment in and modernization of the industry occurs, then employment cuts may only be 10 percent, but if such investment is not undertaken, they could approach 20 percent. The pulp and paper industry, however, projects that employment to 1995 could increase by about one-sixth and will necessitate a significant upgrading of worker skills (Canadian Pulp and Paper Association, 1984a).

Probably the major industry subdivision for which the future is the most promising will be that of producing market pulp. Although the world trend is toward the construction of large integrated mills that produce their own pulp as well as its finished products, there is nevertheless expected to be considerable investment of foreign firms in pulp-producing facilities in Canada, to supply pulp to their homeland paper and allied products industries; the value-added and employment opportunities are much greater in the latter industries than in pulp production.

An area of dispute, especially in British Columbia, has been the extent to which the export of raw logs should be permitted. Such exports amounted to 2.3 percent of total B.C. cut in 1982 and about 4 percent in 1984. Opponents of such a policy see a possible loss of jobs in the sawmill and processing sectors. At the same time, nations such as Japan can build up inventories of logs while prices are depressed. Advocates suggest that under current market conditions no more sales of processed lumber would occur even if all log exports were banned, and that, in fact, lumber sales to countries like China increase as sales of logs rise. They also see the export of raw logs as a means of increasing employment in, and cash flow for, the logging sector in periods such as the present, when demand for lumber products is slack. In addition, the provincial government gains stumpage and other tax revenues from the extra logging activity made possible by log exports.

Finally, Canada is still not recycling its waste paper as completely as it might. The consequence is that on average, over the last few years, the 43 mills in Canada that are able to use this input have had to import about 30 percent of their waste-paper needs (Canadian Pulp and Paper Association, 1983, pp. 78–83).

One possibly encouraging factor is that energy costs, a large factor in the pulp and paper industry, are much lower in Canada. In Quebec, for example, with its cheap hydro-electricity, such costs are about 40 to 45 percent of those in the United States (Pinard, 1984). But if the United States begins to interpret Canada's cheap electricity as a government export subsidy, as they have been threatening to do for aluminum processing, this advantage could be short-lived.

Forestry: Conclusions

A host of recommendations has been made in recent years with respect to improving the performance and competitive position of the forestry and forest-products sector. They include the need:

- to educate the Canadian public about the great importance of the forest industries to the Canadian economy and to the nation's export trade;
- to improve the factual base relating to the international competitiveness of Canadian forest industries;
- to arrange investment incentives and government assistance that would expand intensive forest-management programs, put new investment into the processing industries, and support additional research and development;
- to train (or retrain) workers to meet the changing demands of the entire sector;
- to clarify federal, provincial and industry responsibilities for new investments and training;
- to revise administration of economic rent collection by means of governmental stumpage charges, in a way that would actually encourage new capital investment and the efficient use of all the wood in the timber stands being harvested; and
- to work for an open world-trading environment involving a minimum of tariff and non-tariff barriers (Canadian Pulp and Paper Association, 1983, 1984a; Armson, 1983; Forest Industries Advisory Committee, 1983; Percy, 1984; Economic Council, 1984).

The reader is referred to these other documents for examination of these various recommendations. Only a few of them need to be elaborated here. Consider log exports. Canada is only a marginal supplier of logs to Asian countries and thus has little or no monopoly power in these markets. Other nations such as the United States, Chile and New Zealand are increasing their log exports, so that even if Canada were to prohibit them, it would not necessarily mean increased sales of sawn lumber or other processed wood. Canada would thus appear to have little choice but to participate in such sales.

Instead of trying to prohibit log exports, the wood-processing industries might take a more positive three-fold response. They might update their own production systems, including the use of technology to improve their utilization of each log and thereby to lower their costs of production. They might do more research to develop new products using wood. Finally, they might undertake more research into what the Asian markets want and then make more effort to adapt their own processing to meet such demands as those for six-foot plywood or other types of board as distinct from the traditional, North American eight-foot lengths.

Next, consider the current land-ownership and -tenure system and the past lack of adequate reforestation and application of other forest-management technology. The agreements between the federal government and most provincial governments on forest management that have been negotiated in recent years have been important steps forward in sorting out jurisdictional issues relating to this subject. Nevertheless, although it is known that the incentives to private companies to undertake silviculture are weak, as their tenure agreements are for limited and often uncertain duration, there has been a reluctance to advocate selling of public lands to forestry companies or other private companies or individuals. The Economic Council 1984 report is an example of this reluctance. Yet to permit industry to buy forestry lands under competitive bidding programs may well be the simplest way of stimulating the essential increase in silviculture that this nation needs, without increasing — perhaps even decreasing — the regulatory government bureaucracy (Haley, 1984). One need only consider, for instance, what would happen to agricultural land and the amount of regulatory policing that would be necessary, if all the farmland were owned by the government, and farmers were not certain of leases long enough to benefit from the positive effects of crop rotation and other soil-maintenance programs. Possibly one-quarter to one-third of usable forestry lands could be offered to the industry on sufficiently long leases to allow the industry to generate or negotiate suitable financing. These arrangements would enable firms to submit bids that would reflect the market values of the lands leased. Scenic, recreational, and environmentally sensitive lands would of course be excluded (ibid. 1984).

Since hardwoods grow so much more rapidly than softwoods — the hybrid poplar, for example can be harvested in about 12 years, compared with 50 to 80 years for softwoods — it would be an enormous step forward for the Canadian forest-products sector if technology could be developed to manufacture newsprint from hardwoods. Because hardwoods have a short fibre, they are currently only usable for fine papers, and not for newsprint. It does not appear that any research is currently addressing this possibility. Yet the returns to the industry and to Canada could be enormous; they warrant substantial outlays by both industry and governments.

In addition Canadians need to be educated not only about the importance of the forest-products industry, but also about the serious situation facing the industry in the years ahead, and the great need for Canada to be competitive. A central aspect of this competitiveness is labour cost. Even if the necessary research and development, silviculture, modernization, and other new investment take place and all the other recommendations are put into effect, unless restraint is exercised in paying both executives' salaries and workers' wages, Canada cannot hope to preserve its position in world forest-products trade. The initial improvement in the Swedish situation following the devaluation of the krona by over 40 percent in relation to the Canadian dollar was only possible because wages were not allowed to rise to offset the adverse effects of the devaluation on real incomes. Controls at first prevented wage increases from exceeding 2.5 percent in 1983, even though unemployment was only 3.2 percent (*The Economist*, April 7, 1984, p. 101), although wages have since increased somewhat more than this. A decline of the Canadian dollar will make little improvement in the national situation if Canadians are generally unwilling to accept lower real incomes.

Employment in the forestry and forest-products sector should recover somewhat if world prosperity returns, although, as we have indicated, it will probably not reach previous peak levels. Such measures as improved management of our forests by means of increased fire protection, fighting of insect infestation and disease, and the host of intensive reforestation techniques (thinning, fertilizing and so on) can provide much employment for young Canadians now and in the future. Concern has been expressed on occasion that such work is often labour intensive. We should see this circumstance not as a problem, but as an opportunity. With the unemployment rate at 10.5 percent overall and the rate for young people at over 20 percent, we need not reject labour-intensive jobs. Since welfare payments must be paid to the unemployed, the real costs of intensive forest management can be interpreted as essentially zero. The returns to society would, accordingly, be high.

Minerals

> Strategies, policies and processes that were good in the sixties and adequate for the seventies are inappropriate in the present decade, and likely to be fatal in the next.
>
> Peter Richardson (1984)

The Canadian minerals industry has played a pivotal role in the economic and regional development of the country. Mines exist in every province of the country except Prince Edward Island, although 56 percent of them (excluding coal and uranium) are in the three leading mineral-producing provinces, Ontario, Quebec and British Columbia. Because of the major world recession in 1982, the Canadian mineral industry in aggregate experienced losses for the first time in many decades. These losses have meant lower exploration and development expenditures and reduced employment in the industry. Conditions have improved modestly since 1982, but continuous attention to efficiency-improving measures remains essential.

Although our concern will be with the longer-run prospects for the industry, we shall initially sketch the current production and trade situation. Subsequently, we shall consider key features of the altering world situation, global projections for the mineral industry, and implications of these for Canada and Canadian policy.

Because the focus of this paper is primarily on Canada's competitive position in a world economy, some minerals, such as cement, sand and gravel, and stone, although produced in substantial quantities, will be ignored, for they do not enter world trade to the degree that the other minerals do.

TABLE 1-34 Canadian Production and Rank for Major Minerals

Mineral	Canadian Production 1981 ($ millions)	Share of world Production in 1981 (share in 1975) (percent)	Producing Rank in 1981 (rank in 1975)	Other Major Producing Countries, 1981	
				Countries	Total Share of These Countries (percent)
Iron ore	1,748.1	5.8 (5.1)	6 (7)	U.S.S.R. Brazil Australia	49.9
Copper (Mine)	1,529.8	8.3 (10.0)	4 (4)	United States U.S.S.R. Chile	45.2
Nickel (Mine)	1,238.1	22.3 (32.3)	1 (1)	U.S.S.R. New Caledonia Australia	41.5
Zinc (Mine)	1,089.6	17.9 (19.9)	1 (1)	U.S.S.R. Australia Peru	33.1
Lead (Mine)	263.6	9.6 (9.8)	4 (4)	U.S.S.R. United States Australia	39.2
Gold (Mine)	922.1	4.1 (4.3)	3 (3)	South Africa U.S.S.R. China	75.6
Silver	458.1	10.7 (13.9)	5 (2)	Mexico U.S.S.R. Peru	40.4

				United States	82.3
Molybdenum	288.5	3		Chile	
		(2)		U.S.S.R.	
				United States	48.8
Aluminum (Primary)	1,148.1[a]	3		U.S.S.R.	
		(4)		Japan	
				U.S.S.R.	58.1
Asbestos	548.4	2		China	
		(2)		Zimbabwe	
				U.S.S.R.	53.3
Potash (K$_2$O)	990.4	2		E. Germany	
		(2)		W. Germany	
				United States	57.1
Sulphur (Elemental)	647.7	2		Poland	
		(3)		U.S.S.R.	

Source: Canada, Department of Energy, Mines and Resources, Canadian Minerals Yearbook: 1981 (Ottawa: Minister of Supply and Services Canada, 1984).
a. Shipments rather than production.

Canadian Output and Trade

The most important minerals in Canadian output are listed in Table 1-34, along with Canada's share of world output and rank in 1981 compared with 1974–75, as well as the names of the three other main producing countries in the world for each mineral. Apart from ever-ubiquitous iron ore production (where she ranks sixth), Canada is among the top three or four producing nations in the world for a wide range of minerals. Little change has occurred in Canada's rank among producers since 1975. Only for silver has it altered (in this case, dropped) by more than one rank. Although it is known that over the past two decades or so, a reduction in both the geographic and corporate concentration of the world mineral industries has occurred, it is only with regard to nickel that Canada's share of world production has diminished dramatically in recent years, decreasing from about 33 to 22 percent. This is a continuation of a trend that has been going on for several decades, although the trend was undoubtedly augmented because Inco, which was accustomed to having substantial market power, failed to adjust its prices downward in response to worsening world economic conditions (Olewiler 1983). For some of the other metals — molybdenum, silver, copper and zinc — small decreases in the Canadian share have occurred, while for other minerals, such as potash and sulphur, Canada's role has enlarged significantly. Generally, apart from its past role as the predominant world nickel producer, Canada has not had for some time, and cannot expect to have, much market power in mineral resources. It is, by and large, a price taker and as such will be subject to the usual, and sometimes not-so-usual, market forces.

Canada is the world's largest exporter of minerals, selling abroad approximately 80 percent of its mineral production. The magnitude of these exports and the share going to the main nations of the Western industrial world are summarized in Table 1-35. The United States is the dominant buyer, even though, except for iron and steel, aluminum, and precious metals, its share of Canada's mineral exports is substantially less than the 70 percent average that it takes of total Canadian exports. Canadian mineral sales abroad are much more geographically disbursed than are its sales of most other products, for they go to over 100 countries.

This table shows, too, the relatively small role that Japan plays as a buyer of Canadian minerals compared to the United States and the European Community. Only for copper, precious metals and molybdenum is its share greater than 20 percent, and then its purchases are in the least-processed form possible, unlike purchases by the United States and the EC.

Past World Trends and Future Prospects

Trends over the past three decades in world output of major minerals and

TABLE 1-35 Canadian Mineral Exports, 1983

Mineral	Total export value $ millions (% of mineral in each form)	Country of Destination				
		U.S.A. %	EC %	Japan %	Other %	Total %
Metals						
Iron:						
Ores, concentrates, and scrap	$1,054 (39.2)	45.5	41.7	7.9	4.9	100.0
Iron alloys, primary iron, and steel	$ 291 (10.8)	75.2	12.5	6.7	5.6	100.0
Other iron- and steel-intensive materials	$1,342 (49.9)	89.3	1.3	0.1	9.2	100.0
Total	$2,688 (100.0)	70.6	18.4	3.9	7.1	100.0
Aluminum:						
Ores, concentrates, and scrap	$ 116 (6.2)	88.5	2.1	8.6	0.8	100.0
Aluminum including alloys	$1,744 (93.8)	67.4	2.1	12.6	17.9	100.0
Total	$1,860 (100.0)	68.7	2.1	12.3	16.9	100.0
Copper:						
Ores, concentrates, and scrap	$ 475 (40.6)	16.7	1.5	57.7	24.1	100.0
Copper and alloys	$ 695 (59.1)	40.3	36.4	0.5	22.7	100.0
Total	$1,171 (100.0)	30.7	22.3	23.7	23.2	100.0
Nickel:						
Ores, concentrates, and scrap	$ 336 (40.4)	15.7	40.7	0.3	43.3	100.0
Nickel and alloys	$ 496 (59.6)	62.7	20.3	7.3	9.7	100.0
Total	$ 833 (100.0)	43.7	28.6	4.5	23.2	100.0

in prices in the United States, the world's largest user of minerals, are presented in Tables 1-36 and 1-37 respectively. Average compound growth rates of output for the 1950s and 1960s were high. In contrast, prices on average diminished. Then for 1973–1981, growth rates of output

TABLE 1-35 (cont'd)

Mineral	Total export value in $ millions (% of mineral in each form)	Country of Destination				
		U.S.A. (%)	EC (%)	Japan (%)	Other (%)	Total (%)
Zinc:						
Ores, concentrates and scrap	$ 282 (35.9)	4.5	7.7	7.7	10.8	100.0
Zinc including alloys	$ 503 (64.1)	66.9	7.1	0.5	25.5	100.0
Total	$ 785 (100.0)	44.5	32.1	3.1	20.3	100.0
Lead:						
Ores, concentrates, and scrap	$ 19 (18.5)	22.7	75.5	0.07	1.7	100.0
Lead, including alloys	$ 83 (81.5)	50.2	32.2	2.1	15.5	100.0
Total	$ 102 (100.0)	45.1	40.2	1.7	12.9	100.0
Molybdenum[a]	$ 238	13.2	57.4	22.5	6.9	100.0
Precious metals:						
In ores, concentrates and scrap	$ 386 (17.5)	26.9	38.1	29.3	5.6	100.0
Precious metals including alloys	$1,828 (82.5)	96.3	0.6	1.6	1.5	100.0
Total	$2,214 (100.0)	84.2	7.2	6.4	2.2	100.0
Non metals						
Potash[a] (muriate)	$ 743	60.9	0.4	9.5	28.9	100.0
Sulphur	$ 571	13.3	9.0	0.05	77.4	100.0
Asbestos (unmanufactured)	$ 455	13.9	25.9	9.2	50.9	100.0

Source: Statistics Canada, *Summary of External Trade, 1983* and *Exports by Commodities, 1983* (Ottawa: Statistics Canada, 1984).
a. Figures for 1982.

of all minerals listed, especially the metals, dropped off dramatically, whereas for approximately the same period, U.S. metal prices reversed their long-term decline, which actually extended back for decades before 1950, and began to rise quite significantly.

TABLE 1-36 Growth of World Output of Major Minerals, 1953–1981

| Minerals | Average annual compound rate of growth | |
	1953–73	1973–81
	(percent)	
Iron ore	5.7	0.8
Copper	7.6	1.0
Nickel	9.7	0.3
Zinc	5.5	0.2
Lead	5.2	0.1
Molybdenum	5.5	3.5
Gold	4.0	0.2
Silver	5.8	1.9
Potash	6.6	3.0
Sulphur	7.5	1.1
Asbestos	8.7	4.0
Aluminum[a]	8.3	3.0

Sources: U.N. *Yearbook of Industrial Statistics: 1981 Edition*, Vol. 2, *Commodity Production Data: 1972–1981* (New York: United Nations, 1983).

U.N. *Yearbook of Industrial Statistics: 1974 Edition*, Vol. 1 (New York: United Nations, 1976).

U.N. *Growth of World Industry: 1967 Edition*, Vol. 1 (New York: United Nations, 1969).

U.N. *Growth of World Industry: 1967 Edition*, Vol. 2 (New York: United Nations, 1968).

U.N. *Growth of World Industry: 1969 Edition*, Vols. 1 and 2 (New York: United Nations, 1971).

U.N. *Growth of World Industry: 1972 Edition*, Vol. 2 (New York: United Nations, 1974).

a. Unwrought aluminum.

TABLE 1-37 Relative Real Price Changes of Minerals for the United States, 1950 to 1980

Ores and Metals	1950–70	1970–80
	(percent[a])	
Iron ore	−1.1	0.4
Steel	−0.3	4.5
Aluminum	−0.1	4.7
Copper	0.3	−1.3
Nickel	1.1	3.6
Zinc	−2.1	2.7
Lead	−2.8	6.0
All ores and metals[b]	−0.2	2.3

Source: H. Barnett and J. Myers, "Minerals and Economic Growth," in *Economics of the Mineral Industry*, 4th ed., edited by W.A. Vogely (New York: American Institute of Mining, Metallurgical and Petroleum Engineers, 1984).

a. Average annual rates of change.

b. Includes some not shown individually.

These contrasting trends of output and prices, and more particularly the secular decline in mineral prices, may be surprising to some readers. They certainly do not bear out the Club of Rome projections, now discredited, that mineral resources will be exhausted within decades, nor do they support other physical and mechanical theories and projections of resource use and exhaustion, such as those propounded by Ridker and Watson (1980) and Leontief et al. (1982). These theories assume a fixed stock of minerals, which will decrease as extraction expands so that prices will have to rise in the long term. In fact, however, not only has the long-run trend in prices been downward, but known reserves have been increasing (Tilton, 1977; U.S. Bureau of Mines, 1980).

Price rises, when they do occur, are a consequence of one or more of three influences:

- Market power exists and is exercised.
- Costs that were previously borne by society (such as environmental pollution) are shifted to firms and thus must be reflected in product prices.
- New technology fails to offset, by one means or another, the exhaustion of existing, known-producing deposits (Vogely, 1984).

The increases in prices that occurred in the 1970s were not the result of the failure of technology to provide new reserves, for reserves continued to swell. Rather they were the result, in part, as in the cases of aluminum and particularly steel, of OPEC's exercise of market power; this action raised the price of energy, which is a sizeable input into production. The effects of these price increases naturally spread to all sectors to a greater or lesser degree. In addition, increasing concern about the environmental and health hazards of pollution has resulted in higher production costs for mineral producers, who must internalize these costs.

What are the implications of these observations for future price and output possibilities? The expected levelling-out of energy costs in the years ahead plus the continuation of technological change that favours energy-efficient processes of production suggest that energy-cost increases probably will not be a significant reason for price increases in other minerals. Nor would it appear that there is much likelihood of effective cartels developing in the production of these minerals. Inadequacy of reserves, and resultant price increases, are not likely, either, to occur. In addition, considering the large excess reserves and unused capacity that exist world wide, much evidence supports the long-run adequacy-of-reserves view (e.g., Goeller and Weinberg 1978). Thus the only factor that might prevent real mineral prices from continuing to fall would be the costs of anti-pollution measures required of firms. Many of these costs are offset either by technological change or by the sale of the by-products from such measures, such as sulphuric acid produced from non-ferrous metal smelting. The pressure from this direction is unlikely to determine the trend, however, at least until about 1990 or even beyond, because of present excess capacity, the anticipated slow world economic growth in the years ahead, and the efficiency-improving measures that firms are continuing to take.

As with other resource products, the more recent the projections of demand growth and price increases, the more modest they tend to be. Forecasts such as those contained in *The Global 2000 Report to the President* (1980) and other studies completed before 1980 nearly all look unrealistically high. Even those published in 1982, before the full depth of the recent recession was understood, now appear high.

As Table 1-38 shows, more recent projections made by the World Bank in September 1984 suggest that growth rates of world demand to 1995 will generally be much below the rates typical of markets for the two decades prior to 1973, although they do tend to exceed, modestly, the rates for the particularly slow period 1973–1980. (Compare with Table 1-36.) The greatest growth is anticipated in the developing countries, but for two reasons this may not imply anything like as large an expansion of exports by the mining sector in developed countries such as Canada. First, many of these minerals are already produced by some of the developing countries themselves. Secondly, there is the continual problem of the inability of those developing countries that do require imports to pay for them without going increasingly into debt.

The future for prices is mixed. Rates of real price change are presented in the final column of Table 1-38. Only for zinc, lead and potash are prices to 1990 expected to rise from their 1983 levels, and of these products only zinc will have a rate of real price increase sufficient to bring its price in 1990 above that of 1981. All the other minerals shown are expected to face real prices in 1990 below those that existed in 1981. After 1990, some recovery in real prices is anticipated for all but iron ore and potash, but even of these by 1995, only copper, aluminum and zinc are expected to enjoy real prices that are modestly above 1981 levels. In general, then, the next decade promises a price record for minerals not much different, on average, from that which occurred in the decades prior to 1970.[22]

Challenges for the Canadian Mineral Sector

The foregoing projections of demand and price suggest that unless unforeseen changes occur in the world scene, the Canadian mineral sector is not likely to experience, at least within the next 10 or 15 years and probably never again, the buoyant conditions that it enjoyed in the 1950s or 1960s. For most minerals, gains will be slower in coming and harder to achieve than they were in earlier decades. If the Canadian industry is even to maintain its current world market shares, it will have to cope effectively with two types of challenges: those external to the industry, which come from having to sell in a competitive and changing

TABLE 1-38 Global Projections of Demand and Price Changes: Minerals

Minerals	Demand Growth Rate By Economies				Real Price Changes	
	Industrial Countries	Centrally Planned Economies	Developing Countries	World	(1983 /1981) × 100	1984 Projection % per Year
	(percent per year)					
Iron-ore[a]					102.5	
1983–90	0.1	1.1	5.3	1.0		−1.12
1990–95						0.00
1985–95						
Aluminum[b]					107.1	
1983–90	2.6	2.0	4.7	2.9		−0.75
1990–95						0.79
1985–95						
Copper					95.8	
1983–90	0.9	2.1	3.4	1.6		−0.14
1990–95						1.72
1985–95						
Nickel[c]					97.8	
1983–90	1.6	0.7	3.6	1.5		−0.22
1990–95						1.69
1985–95						
Zinc					94.6	
1983–90	2.2	1.9	3.1	2.3		2.25
1990–95						0.16
1985–95						

Lead					
1983–90	0.7	2.6	3.0	61.3	3.21
1990–95					0.63
1985–95	1.6	3.1	1.6		

Potash[d]					
1983–90	1.6	3.1	2.8	60.6	5.75
1990–95					0.00
1985–95		4.6		0.0	

Sources: World Bank, *Price Prospects for Major Primary Commodities* (Washington, D.C.: World Bank, 1984), Vols. I, II and IV.

a. Projected growth rates for gross imports (1985–95).
b. U.S. producers' list prices.
c. Merchant market prices — as published by *Metals Week*.
d. Potassium chloride, also known as muriate of potash.

world economy, and those that are, to a large degree, internal to the domestic industry itself.

World Marketing Issues

Recent investigation (Jewett, 1983) indicates that the leading advanced industrial countries, such as the United States and Japan, are concerned about reducing size, weight and final manufacturing costs of mineral production. This concern has certainly been evident in the automotive industry, where the building of smaller cars has resulted in diminished demands for iron and steel, zinc, copper, nickel and lead. The same concern affects defence-related production. The U.S. Department of Defense has a well-defined research objective of weight reduction for much of its equipment, to increase mobility, fuel efficiency and overall performance. Commercial applications often flow quickly from such mission-oriented research results. The U.S. Department of Energy aims to develop the use of materials, such as ceramics or plastics, which require less energy to produce than do metals. Materials experts from industry, academia and research institutions regard virtually all metals (apart perhaps from steel, particularly high-strength low-alloy (HSLA) steels) as expensive today, even at current depressed prices. They also envisage that over the next 15 years no material that is currently in use is exempt from the possibility of replacement by new substitute materials (ibid., 1983).

Substitutions of non-metals for metals have already been occurring: for instance, plastics have been substituted for copper in plumbing; fibre optics for copper in communications; and plastics for steel and associated metals such as zinc and nickel in automobiles, aircraft and appliances. Still other dramatic substitutions may appear in the future, such as the development of a ceramic automotive engine, although no one can say definitely if or when they might occur (Jewett, 1983).

Various substitutions to improve weight reduction and cost effectiveness have been taking place between metals too, such as the substitution of aluminum for copper in automobile radiators and power transmission lines. Recycling of metals such as copper and aluminum will also reduce demand for new supplies of these materials. The energy cost of recycling scrap aluminum is only 5 percent of the cost of smelting primary aluminum (Maule, 1985). One estimate suggests that about one-third of all existing wire systems will need to be renewed by 1995 (Jewett, 1983) and these systems are likely to be replaced by fibre optics. The amount of copper scrap that will thus become available means that even with some growth in demand, the need for expansion in output of newly mined copper will be minimal until after the year 2000. The development of new uses for copper will be essential even then. Finally, there is less demand for such minerals as lead and asbestos because of their threat to human health.

Another concern relates to the fact that most minerals are much more

ubiquitous than was once believed. Many of these more recently identified sources are in developing countries and have been exploited over the
last two decades with the aid of national and international aid or other
concessional financing from developed countries, their agencies, and
their banks, often with little regard for the total effect on world capacity
(Hendrick, 1984a; Buck, 1984). Many of the new facilities are state
owned,[23] and they involve huge fixed costs for the host nations. Repay-
ment provisions on the loans and even renegotiated provisions for
nations in financial difficulty have frequently had the effect of requiring
the developing nations involved to continue production, even in times of
slack demand, to meet payments on interest and principal. This effect
has been augmented by the aspirations of the backward nations to
acquire as much foreign exchange as they can to enhance their own
general development plans, to pay for energy imports, and to generate
domestic tax revenues. It has been complemented by the desire of
industrial consuming nations such as Japan and European countries to
diversify their sources of supply and reduce their dependence on single
supplier nations such as Canada. Sometimes the developing nations
have had cost advantages, as has Chile for copper, because of cheap
labour, higher-quality reserves, or less concern for environmental safety,
with the consequent avoidance of costly anti-pollution and safety equipment and precautions. Not infrequently, even higher-cost producers
have been unwilling, for the reasons mentioned, to lower production
during the recent serious recession. In fact, most of the paring-down of
production has had to take place in privately owned corporations. State-
owned companies have not been very responsive to market conditions
(Buck, 1984). Countries such as the U.S.S.R. and other COMECON
nations are also reputed to be following subsidized export strategies.

A third concern is that some markets are difficult to enter because of
special trade and aid links involving regional arrangements, such as
those made by the EC with former colonies around the Mediterranean
and Africa, under the Lomé convention, among the Andean nations of
South America, and so on. A related aspect of this problem is that
Europe and Japan, as well as the newly industrialized countries (NICs),
and less-advanced nations also maintain higher tariffs on processed and
fabricated mineral products so that the effective tariff rates they face are
escalated even more. Canadian export aims are accordingly thwarted.

Tariffs are not so much of a problem with respect to the United States,
but that nation repeatedly attempts other forms of protectionism, usually trundled out as "security-of-supply" considerations. Although such
measures are frequently aimed at offending countries other than Canada
(as with steel), Canada nevertheless is included. Sometimes, however,
the U.S. concern is directly with Canada, in matters such as whether
Canada's cheap hydro-electricity rates for smelting aluminum are an
export subsidy.

Countertrade, or barter trade, is another commercial policy of growing importance. Some estimates place the proportion of world trade in this category as high as 30 percent (Barclays Bank 1984). Others say that it amounts only to about 12 percent (Parsons 1984). Whatever the true figure, to the extent that countertrade arrangements are used, pure market and price considerations lose much of their significance. This was very plain a few years ago when, although Saskatchewan had (and still has) the cheapest and largest supplies of potash in the world, its share of Brazil's potash supply fell from 40 to 2 percent as a consequence of countertrade and special credit arrangements by Soviet and East German interests that enabled them to take over the market (Parsons, 1984).

These conditions facing the mineral sector demand new responses and new initiatives, as well as improvements in initiatives already undertaken. Before examining what these might be, let us consider a number of important domestic and internal challenges that face the Canadian industry.

Internal and Domestic Challenges

One of the biggest difficulties presently facing many mining companies in Canada is their financial predicament, or more specifically, their high ratio of debt to equity and hence their high interest costs. Although this situation has been evolving since the late 1960s, it reached crisis proportions in 1982, with the advent of extremely high interest rates and the serious world recession provoked by tight monetary policies. Their debt-to-equity ratio rose from 0.60 for 1979–1980, to 1.04 for 1982, and their cash-flow-to-debt ratio dropped during the same period from 0.54 to 0.04. This debt-equity-high-interest-rate bind that the companies now find themselves in was, however, largely a result of their own choice to move from reliance on equity and long-term bonds to bank loans with floating interest rates, apparently in the erroneous belief that this would prevent dilution of shareholders' equity and raise the return on this equity (Sultan, 1984). This course was not forced on them because the mining industry had become more capital intensive. The ratio of capital to value-added actually diminished over the 35-year period, 1941–1976 (Ryba, 1983). Nor was it purely a consequence of economic recession, for the trend to greater dependence on debt financing has continued over several business cycles (Sultan, 1984). It was simply an unfortunate and mistaken management strategy.

Other criticisms of mining management are also coming to the fore. These include an inadequate and short-range view of corporate planning which has led to rapid reversals of policy, erosion of longer-run cost and efficiency improvements, and weakened employee morale; failure to develop appropriate relationships between corporate human resources and employees, substituting instead higher pay, so that efficiency and productivity of the workforce have not met their potential; and finally, slowness in developing and sustaining open communications and effective relations with governments and the public (Richardson, 1984).

Another aspect of management performance that has been weak has been the lack of importance assigned to market and product research and development. Much of the metals sector has confined itself simply to mining, smelting and refining metal to meet market demands, whatever they happen to be. It has been very self-focussed (Buck, 1984), paying little attention to monitoring technological changes in other material sectors that would eliminate or alter the nature of demand for certain metals. Nor has it given much attention to developing new products and product uses for metals (Richardson, 1984; Bumstead, 1984; Hendrick, 1984b). For example, total outlays on both product- and market-research development for copper by industry associations equals less than 0.1 percent of the current sales value of output (Bumstead, 1984). Although world markets for zinc have held up better than those for copper, the product-research emphasis in this industry is just as dismal as that for copper. As for the nickel producers, it was not until 1984 that they even formed an International Nickel Development Institute. It was only in 1984, as well, that governments of nickel-producing countries took initiatives to form an intergovernmental association to gather statistical and other information on developments affecting nickel (Canada, Department of Energy, Mines and Resources, 1984b). In contrast, R&D as a proportion of sales was 4.6 percent for the automotive industry, 3.8 percent for the electronics industry, 2.9 percent for the chemical industry (Hendrick, 1984b, citing *Business Week*), and between 2 and 3 percent for the plastics industry (Bumstead, 1984). It is little wonder that a number of metals have been losing ground to other materials.

The one R&D exception for the metals sector is the aluminum industry. It spends between 1 and 2 percent of sales on R&D, a proportion still below the plastics industry and some other large industrial sectors, but better than other minerals. Generally, the aluminum industry has devoted much more attention to developing new product uses for its material than have the other metal industries for theirs. Even the Canadian aluminum industry, however, has until recently paid little attention to technological advance at the smelting end.

Consequences for Competition
Many of Canada's metal mining, smelting and refining industries are under considerable competitive pressure. This is particularly so for copper, which has lost a number of its traditional product uses. As for nickel, even though Canada is the lowest-cost producer in the world, subsidized production from the less-developed countries and COMECON countries will produce excess capacity and depressed prices in industry for years to come. Production costs have been reduced substantially in Canada in the last two years, but even with the Canadian

dollar at US$0.73, Canadian costs are still somewhat above prevailing world prices.

A significant chunk of the traditional market for lead was lost when the use of that metal was discontinued in paints and cut back in gasoline. To date, no substitute appears imminent for lead's most important market, the lead-acid battery, which accounts for about 50 percent of sales, although the downsizing of cars has reduced demands even here. Moreover, if Alcan's experimental air battery, which uses aluminum, becomes sufficiently successful to reach commercial production, more electric-powered cars are a possibility; this development would further reduce the demand for lead.

Zinc depends greatly on its symbiotic relationship with steel to support sales. Thus the successful development of ever-improved qualities of steel and other materials that encroach on the traditional markets for steels will affect not only the iron and steel industry, but zinc as well. Metallic glasses, which are strong and highly resistant to corrosion may, as their manufacturing technology is improved, change the market situation for a variety of metals (Jewett, 1983). Similarly, developments in new metal composites such as metal-plastics and metal-ceramics, although not likely to alter greatly the total market for metals, may alter the composition of demand (ibid., 1983).

Of the major metals that Canada produces, aluminum and gold are in a somewhat different category from the rest. Although for about a quarter of a century after the mid-1950s, no more aluminum smelters were constructed in Canada, even though much expansion of capacity occurred throughout the world, this situation is now changing. Because of Canada's cheap electric power, much of it owned by the smelting companies themselves, the Canadian share of world aluminum production has risen modestly over the last decade, from 9.4 percent in 1973, to 10.3 percent in 1983. Unlike in the rest of the world, where plant closures are occurring, energy-efficient plants are being opened in Canada. The old Canadian plants were not energy efficient by today's standards (Maule, 1985). The future of aluminum production in Canada consequently looks quite promising, provided that hydro-electric rates are kept relatively low, that federal or provincial governments do not impose taxes that cancel the effects of the low electricity rates, and that consuming nations such as the United States do not attempt to impose countervailing duties on shipments from Canada, on the ground that Canadian production is being subsidized by energy inputs priced below market levels.

Gold is the major focus of exploration and development activity in the Canadian mining industry at this time. Between January 1979 and December 1983, 48 (60 percent) of the 85 new deposits either commencing production or scheduled for production were gold mines. In 1983, 70 percent of the more than one billion dollars of new capital for mines, and 20 out of 28 new mine- and concentrator-development projects announced, were for gold production (Canada, Department of Energy, Mines and Resources, 1984d, 1984e). In contrast, mine-production capability for base metals and silver is expected to continue to decline for some time to come, and employment will continue to decline as producers strive for greater efficiency (Canada, Department of Energy, Mines and Resources, 1984d).

Concerning the future production and exports of the three major nonmetallic minerals, asbestos, potash and sulphur, the situation is mixed. The industry likely to face the most difficult future is asbestos because substitution of this product takes place wherever human health is at stake. World demand for potash will grow substantially in the years ahead, since this product is essential for plant growth; potash, however is found in many countries throughout the world and Canadian supplies will face a competitive market. Saskatchewan has the largest and lowest-cost reserves and will therefore undoubtedly play a major role in world markets in the years ahead. The most likely markets for Saskatchewan's potash are expected to be in the United States, Latin America, Asia and possibly Africa (Ekedahl, 1984; Parsons, 1984). A major issue is whether Canada should be content to remain a marginal supplier in many markets and thus suffer the major ups and downs of any marginal supplier, or should attempt to take over more markets under long-term contracts (Parsons, 1984).

The third non-metallic mineral, sulphur, is produced in Canada, in contrast to some countries, largely as a required by-product of the natural gas industry, which removes it to "sweeten" the gas. While world-wide demand for sulphur is large and diverse, it is also quite price inelastic. The issue, treated more fully below, thus becomes one of pricing that will maximize the long-run returns to the industry.

In summary, the Canadian minerals sector faces a host of challenges. Consider briefly some options for the future in response to these challenges.

Policies for the Future

The Industries' Policies

At the Thirteenth Policy Discussion Seminar at the Centre for Resource Studies, held in Kingston in 1984, the focus was on productivity improvement in mining. Enhanced management attitudes and skills were pinpointed as of first importance if this improvement were to take place (Wojciechowski, 1984). The severe straits that many metal-mining companies have found themselves in during the last few years have put the process of management self-assessment and change already well under way in many companies. Accordingly, profits have been rising or losses have been falling. Still, self-initiated change will have to be a continuous process in the future, rather than a series of *ad hoc* projects initiated as crises arise. Greater attention to improved employee relations and human resource development will have to be part of this process. Improved relations with governments are necessary, too, so that a spirit of cooperation rather than an adversarial atmosphere may prevail.

Companies and industry associations will have to give much greater attention to research and development that might lead to new products and uses for the traditional metals, both by themselves and in combination with other materials. R&D on new technology for smelting, refining and processing will be essential, too, in order to lower costs to users. This means that a much larger portion of each sales dollar will have to be spent on R&D. To this end, corporations might well strive to cooperate much more with universities, to sponsor university research of interest to themselves, and to draw on university researchers' knowledge of new developments throughout the world. This undertaking would, of course, be a "two-way street," for university personnel could benefit greatly from what corporations have to tell them.

In financing matters, the companies will have to switch back to a greater reliance on equity capital. New share issues may have to be priced very attractively to encourage sales (Sultan, 1984). Companies should not be rescued by government bail-outs; it was largely by the companies' own choices that they are in their current debt-equity positions.

Mining companies might also consider more forward integration into industries using their products, both domestically and in foreign markets. By this means they could become better informed about the needs of the final consumers of metal-based products and about competitive products that are likely to be substituted for metals. Through such integration, research into new uses could be carried out, as well.

Above all, the companies must avoid the danger of ever again being satisfied with an inward-looking approach and with failing to keep abreast of what is going on in the world outside their own small domains. From now on, an outward-looking perspective must be the order of the day.

Government Policies

Governments, too, will have to maintain an outward-looking approach. They must make a concerted effort to keep themselves informed of advances throughout the world in mine expansions, mining technology, new uses for the minerals that Canada produces, and new substitutes that will compete with Canadian materials. This can be done in cooperation with industry and universities.

Only with this background information can government properly support the mineral companies in the other types of policies that have been outlined in the previous section. The indications are that both provincial and federal governments must develop and maintain open honest relationships with industry so that government-industry cooperation becomes the norm. In addition, provincial and federal governments should provide a stable and fairly predictable environment relating to taxes, pollution control and other regulations. When changes are deemed necessary, wide consultation with industry would be much preferable to an adversarial approach.

It is also important to avoid federal-provincial contests over taxation, particularly when economic rents are at issue. Such situations as occurred in the mid-1970s, when marginal tax rates in British Columbia were reputed to be greater than 100 percent, must be avoided if a spirit of trust and cooperation is to be preserved. Moreover, taxes have to be levied with an eye to what other producing nations are requiring from their companies. For Canadian governments to get too far out of line, particularly with other developed producing nations where political stability is high, can only discourage further investment in this country.[24]

The Canadian government, too, must be constantly aware of the importance of the current U.S. value of the Canadian dollar to the life of many Canadian mining companies, particularly those in metals production. Given that the high value of the U.S. dollar relative to most other currencies in the world today, the Canadian dollar should remain no higher than it is now. Advice that argues for a higher dollar to reduce inflation should be ignored. If anything, the Canadian dollar could well be even lower than it is at present.

At the same time, wages and salaries in this country will have to be kept under control, even if this means that the current level of inflation erodes real incomes to some degree. To the extent that in the past any portion of real incomes in this country, both within and outside the minerals sector, contained an element of economic rent, it is worth recognizing that that part no longer exists. Real wages and salaries may well have to be adjusted downwards, particularly in the metals sector, to reflect this change. Management, who must bear much of the responsibility for the condition that industry is now in, should share in real income reductions. The need for a downward trend in real wages and salaries is not likely to change in the foreseeable future.

Beyond these broad macroeconomic issues, a number of other policies are likely to be important in the years ahead.[25] First, Canada needs to capitalize as much as possible both on its position as a politically stable supplier of resources with a well-adjusted labour force and well-developed transportation systems and infrastructure, and on its membership in NORAD and NATO. Canada also cooperates with the United States in the Canada-U.S. Defence Production Sharing Agreement. Under this last agreement, Canada is deemed to be a secure source of supply. Yet periodically, proposals are put forward in the United States to bar imports of foreign (including Canadian) minerals so as to preserve U.S. domestic industries producing uranium, potash, zinc, lead and copper. The basis for such proposals is that foreign sources are insecure and unreliable in times of crisis such as war. These are nothing but protectionist measures. Canada might therefore attempt to have minerals covered by the Canada-U.S. Defence Production Sharing Agreement and to be included as a supplier as and when the United States wishes to stockpile certain minerals. If minerals were covered by NATO, Canada might also gain better access to Western European markets.

Canada can also work for a liberalized world trading system whereby there would be tariff- and quota-free access to foreign markets, particularly those of the developed nations and newly industrialized countries (NICs), not only for Canadian raw materials but also for materials at higher stages of processing. An attempt might be made to persuade the U.S.S.R. to join GATT and to adhere to GATT rules. If the U.S.S.R. declines, as is likely, Canada might take the initiative to have the OECD nations unite to thwart Soviet dumping of minerals by imposing countervailing duties (Caragata, 1984).

There may also be merit in encouraging companies from the European Community or Japan to enter joint ventures with Canadian firms in developing new deposits of minerals. In slack times these nations might then be more inclined to buy from Canada (Caragata, 1984). But this policy could backfire. It could be used to the advantage of foreign countries, as Japan seems to have used it with regard to coal. That is, foreigners might take a minority interest in encouraging production to be developed here, and do the same in a variety of other places in the world, thereby bringing about world overcapacity. At that point they might be able to negotiate for lower prices on the minerals they import from supplier countries such as Canada. The net result might be long-run gains to the foreign nations involved at Canada's expense.

This suggests another strategy that Canada could profitably follow. As much as possible, it should discourage its domestic financial institutions and international institutions, as well as its own foreign-aid programs, from making loans and grants that increase the world supply of minerals for which adequate supplies already exist.

At the same time, Canada might well, either through federal-provincial cooperation or through private enterprise, develop trading companies to handle countertrade negotiations that are becoming more and more necessary in trade with less-developed countries (LDCs) and communist countries (Caragata, 1984).

Canada might also direct its foreign aid to help LDCs to diversify so that they are less dependent on a few minerals for their foreign exchange and therefore have less need to keep producing and selling raw materials at depressed prices in order to acquire foreign exchange. If Canada took this approach, it would also have to be prepared to reduce its tariffs and quotas on these new products from these developing countries.

Finally, Canada may have to consider possible periodic participation in commodity cartels if the circumstances warrant, as they might, in the future, for asbestos or even nickel. As Caragata mentions, to avoid the expensive business of U.S. antitrust laws, where the United States objects to cartels, there could be two different arrangements: a cartel on sales to the world, excluding the United States, and a separate marketing agency for sales to U.S. markets plus an export tax on such sales.

In products such as potash, Saskatchewan might take the lead in developing strong cooperation among the various places in Canada that produce potash. That province might work, through aggressive marketing pricing to discourage new entrants, and research on agronomic matters, to become the first-choice supplier of potash to more countries in the world, rather than remaining the marginal supplier to many nations that it is now (Parsons, 1984).

For sulphur, where Canada is largely an involuntary producer, acquiring new supplies as a by-product of the natural gas industry, the best strategy is probably to price approximately at the average cost of voluntary producers (Canada, Department of Energy, Mines and Resources, 1983c). Here greater cooperation among Canadian suppliers in meeting foreign demands might help to preserve the long-run price. If prices were "competed down" by individual Canadian suppliers attempting to expand their markets, and if voluntary producers matched these prices, market shares would remain unchanged, and total revenues would drop. There would be no gain from such a strategy, and it would be better to leave prices higher. Another possibility might be barter trade in sulphur (ibid.).

All these possible policy moves might be summed up as follows: much more effort must be devoted to finding out as clearly as possible what is happening in world markets; to ensuring that this information is shared with all interested parties in government, industry and universities; and to developing new research, production and marketing strategies as necessary, while working for cooperation among all the Canadian actors in each industry for the benefit of the country as a whole.

Canadians should not be upset by any forecasts of declining Canadian reserves of its traditional minerals. It is highly improbable, given the recent trends in world-resource developments, that Canadian mineral deposits are anywhere near the exhaustion point (Wilkinson, 1980). They are only awaiting the appropriate incentives for development.

Water Resources

The West is not running out of water. It is running out of low-cost water. . . .
Kenneth Frederick and James Hanson (1982a)

The World Situation

Although the hydrosphere contains massive quantities of fresh water, and annual global precipitation is 525,100 km³,[26] the actual amount of this water that is easily accessible for human use each year amounts to about 9,000 km³. The difference between these two figures results from the 78 percent of the precipitation that falls into the oceans, the flood runoff that flows into the oceans, and the amount that falls in relatively uninhabited areas of the globe (L'vovich, 1979).

Although particular regions of the world currently are experiencing a scarcity of water, no overall world scarcity exists. Around 1970, the total withdrawal of water for human use equalled about 40 percent of the 9,000 km³ of annual precipitation available, and the portion of the total available not ultimately being discharged as some form of sewage (i.e., irrecoverable consumption) was about 27 percent. L'vovich (1979) estimates that to the year 2000, assuming that pollution has been brought under control, but without allowance for the more economical use of water that would be stimulated by price increases and other such policies, water withdrawals will nearly double, growing at an annual rate of 2.1 percent, while irrecoverable consumption will expand by more than two and one-half times, increasing at an annual rate of 3.3 percent, to 6,335 km³. Water shortages would then become extremely serious in some portions of the globe if nothing were done to increase storage facilities, thereby reducing runoff, and to develop much more efficient water use. However, with reasonable investments in expanded storage facilities, the same margin of safety could exist then as exists at present. Moreover, if water prices are permitted to rise and other policy moves are made, there need be no difficulty in providing ample water supplies (Rogers, 1984, p. 71).

Irrigation represents 87 percent of the world's water consumption (L'vovich, 1979, p. 56). The four most populous nations, which are also the four largest international users of water, China, India, the U.S.S.R. and the United States, account for 60 to 70 percent of the world's irrigated lands.

The U.S. Situation

From a Canadian trading perspective, the water supply-demand situation in the United States is of the upmost importance. A question frequently asked in Canada is: Will the United States wish to import water from Canada in the future? To answer this question a brief review of U.S. circumstances is appropriate.

Although agricultural output accounts for only 3 percent of U.S. gross national product, it absorbs 83 percent of the nation's yearly water consumption. In 1977, irrigated acreage comprised 11 percent of total cropland and pasture, or 61 million acres. In the 17 rather more arid western states, where the most rapid expansion of irrigation has occurred, 22 percent of the cultivated land was under irrigation (Rogers, 1984, p. 56). Most of the water has come from underground sources. Since 1950, the enlargement of groundwater usage has been growing by 3.8 percent per year on average, about double the growth rate of surface water utilization (ibid., p. 58). This pace cannot continue, for in many areas anything from 4 to 95 percent *more* water is being withdrawn annually from the aquifers than is being replaced by the usual processes of nature. For the entire United States, about one-quarter of the groundwater extracted each year is not being replenished. On 15 million acres under irrigation, the water table is dropping, on average, about 2 metres a year.

The overwhelming reason that the rapid — and in most instances, wasteful — consumption of water has occurred is that governments have so heavily subsidized its provision. Water has not been and is not being priced anywhere near its marginal cost of production. Average cost or even below-average cost is the normal standard. In California, for instance, a proposed new supply of irrigation water costing about US$63 per acre-foot is scheduled to be pooled with existing water supplies selling for anywhere from $2.50 to $15 per acre-foot, and the average cost of all this water will be increased by $3.25 per acre-foot. Thus, at most, some consumers of such water would be paying $18.25 per acre-foot. This figure is still a long way from the cost of the planned new water addition, for which the users should be paying $63 per acre-foot (Rogers, 1984, p. 25). More generally, Frederick and Hanson (1982b, p. 244) report the following:

Analysis of eighteen irrigation districts by the U.S. Department of Interior shows an average subsidy of $792 per acre in 1978 dollars. The range in the subsidy varies widely among projects, varying from $58 per acre . . . to $1,787 per acre. The subsidy ranges from 57 percent of the total project costs to 97 percent. . . . An alternative estimate of irrigation subsidies suggests that at current collection rates and costs, farmers will repay only 3.3 percent of the $3.62 billion the Bureau has spent for irrigation construction. In some cases the effects of inflation on long-term fixed charges have reduced the rates paid by irrigators below the point where they even cover the project's operating and maintenance costs.

As the nation moves toward recognizing that the days of low-cost water are over and begins to price water closer to its economic value, the incentives for inefficient use of water will gradually be removed, and water will be transferred to higher-value uses. A variety of results will follow. Reductions in irrigation will likely occur in the high plains of Kansas, Nebraska, Texas and Oklahoma, as well as in the southern and western mountain regions, while some expansion will take place in the Nebraska sandhills and the Dakotas.

Overall, even with significant real crop-price increases of about 25 percent, total irrigated acreage, in about 2005, is expected to expand by no more that 15.5 percent, for an annual average growth rate of about 0.5 percent. Simultaneously, however, other inputs such as capital and labour will substitute for additional water. These will include reduction of water losses through either or both of piping and lining of canals and field distribution systems; better water-control systems on farms; tail-water recovery systems; land levelling; and reduction of water evaporation from cropped areas. Other changes will include shifts to crops requiring less water or having higher commercial value and to superior seed varieties (Frederick and Hanson, 1982b, pp. 226–29). It is unlikely that farmers will continue to receive subsidies to grow crops that use huge quantities of water and that have a small market, such as rice grown in California (Rogers, 1984, p. 77).

Although irrigation is the main user of water, at least two research studies suggest that if no supply controls existed growth areas of crops in the United States could be redistributed according to interregional comparative advantages. This change would enable the U.S.A. to meet its domestic and export needs for agricultural products in the year 2000, using only about one-half its presently irrigated acreage (33.4 million acres) (cited in Frederick, 1980, pp. 186–87).

The transmission of water from surplus to deficit areas within the United States is not an economic solution to water shortages in the western states. One study, conducted in the early 1970s, of moving water to the high plains of Texas and New Mexico from the Mississippi River indicated that costs exceeded benefits on a four-to-one ratio. This study assumed that the water itself had no cost, and it also greatly underestimated energy costs, which at 1980 electricity prices would, by themselves, have caused the delivered cost of the water to exceed $400 per acre-foot.[27] The cost would have been even greater had the water itself been assigned a value equivalent to what it would be worth in other uses. Another more recent study assessed water costs to the same area from four alternate sources. The delivered costs varied between $352 and $880 per acre-foot.[28] Compared to the costs that farmers are now accustomed to paying of just a few dollars per acre-foot of water, these costs are extremely high. As Frederick and Hanson (1982a, p. 103) say, "Although economic feasibility has not been a necessary requirement for authorization and funding of western water projects, the economics of such a water transfer project appear poor even by the standards of other water projects."

The two other main uses of water, for industry and households, are clearly much higher-valued uses in the sense that at present much higher prices can be charged for the water used. Hence if institutions in the United States are altered so that farmers and other holders of water rights are permitted to sell their water to the highest bidder, much wasteful use of water in agricultural irrigation will cease. These uses are more price-sensitive than is sometimes believed. In industry, which uses about 6 percent of U.S. water, 90 percent of it for cooling, water is used an average of 2.2 times before being discharged. One study found that an increase in price by a multiple of five reduces industrial use of water by 50 times.[29] Where marginal cost pricing is employed in charging for domestic consumption, large reductions in water use occur.[30] Accordingly, if the price mechanism is allowed to operate, there will also be water conservation for these uses.

Thus for the United States as a whole, as Table 1-39 shows, total withdrawals of fresh water to the year 2000 are expected to diminish by 7.3 percent between 1985 and 2000. Actual consumption of water, that is, the use of water that is not returned to the surface-flow systems, will rise modestly, however, by 12 percent, or about 3/4 percent per year on average. Generally speaking, however, this is not a scenario suggesting dramatic shortages of water in the United States in the coming years.

Relevance for Canada

What does this situation mean for Canada? Our nation is certainly one with an overall surplus of water. Within our boundaries, covering 7.6 percent of its surface, lies 25 percent of the world's fresh water. Demand for water is relatively small because Canada has developed relatively little irrigation compared with many nations; only about 2 million acres are irrigated in Canada, or approximately one-thirtieth as much land as in the United States. Over one-half of this acreage is in southern Alberta. Much of Canada's water flows into the Arctic Ocean and Hudson Bay. For example, 83 percent of Alberta water flows to the Arctic Ocean. Hence it is not being used at all, other than for minimal transportation and recreational purposes. There would therefore seem to be an abundance to export. We could go into the ecological arguments for and against this possibility, but these arguments probably are not and will not be the determining considerations. More important in the final analysis is the water situation in the United States outlined above.

What has our review of the U.S. circumstances told us? Briefly this: that that nation as a whole is not short of water. Because of generous government subsidies, water has been used inefficiently in irrigation programs. As the realization dawns upon Americans that water can no longer be considered a free good or even a cheap one, many new measures will be taken to economize on the use of water. Moreover, within the United States, even without considering the value of water for the other uses to which it might be put, it is not economically feasible to transport water from surplus areas, such as the Mississippi River, to deficit areas on the western plains.

The implication of these findings for Canada is that the grandiose schemes that periodically appear for the transportation of northern Canadian waters to the southwestern U.S. states are not likely to come

TABLE 1-39 Total Withdrawals and Consumption, by Functional Use, for the United States, 1975, 1985, 2000

Functional Use	Total Withdrawals			Total Consumption		
	1975	1985	2000	1975	1985	2000
	(millions of gallons per day)					
Fresh water						
Domestic						
Central (municipal)	21,164	13,983	27,918	4,976	5,665	6,638
Noncentral (rural)	2,092	2,320	2,400	1,292	1,408	1,436
Commercial	5,530	6,048	6,732	1,109	1,216	1,369
Manufacturing	51,222	23,687	19,669	6,059	8,903	14,699
Agriculture						
Irrigation	158,743	166,252	153,846	86,391	92,820	92,506
Livestock	1,912	2,233	2,551	1,912	2,233	2,551
Steam electric generation	88,916	94,858	79,492	1,419	4,062	10,541
Minerals industry	7,055	8,832	11,328	2,196	2,777	3,609
Public lands and others[a]	1,866	2,162	2,461	1,236	1,461	1,731
Total fresh water	338,500	330,375	306,397	106,590	120,545	135,080
Saline water,[b] total	59,737	91,236	118,815			
Total withdrawals	398,237	421,611	425,212			

Source: U.S. Water Resources Council, *Second National Water Assessment* vol. 1 (Washington, D.C.), p. 29.
a. Includes water for fish hatcheries and miscellaneous uses.
b. Saline water is used mainly in manufacturing and steam electric generation.

to pass in the foreseeable future. The economics simply do not warrant such transmission. A scheme of that sort would not be an economic use of either Canadian or American capital, public or private.

Thus, those citizens who have thought of the sale of Canadian water to the United States as a tragedy equivalent to the selling of the family homestead can put their minds at rest. They are not unlikely to see such an undertaking in their lifetimes. Those, however, who might dream of the sale of Canadian water as a means of strengthening the future Canadian balance of payments, should our competitive position in sophisticated manufactures, labour-intensive and mass-produced manufactures, and even some other natural resources be eroded, had best cease their daydreaming and exert more of their energy toward improving Canada's competitive position in these other sectors.[31]

Conclusions

> Development is not just getting rich; it is getting wise. If we simply see development as getting rich, we will frustrate it.
>
> Kenneth Boulding (1983)

This study was commenced with a deep foreboding about the future of Canada's natural resource sectors in an international context. It concludes on a note of cautious optimism that apart from a world financial or economic collapse, nuclear war or some other catastrophe of these proportions, Canadian resource sectors are far from finished.

There remains much scope for growth, development and profitability in the resources sectors. Some of these sectors are in a more favoured position than others. Some will require more innovation through research and development or in managerial techniques than others. But in each of them, if executives and workers face realistically the particular competitive positions and problems of their own industry, are willing to make changes, and do not let their industry be destroyed by their own personal acquisitiveness, the future in international trade can be reasonably bright, even if new employment prospects are minimal. There is an important role for supportive governments in this future, too.

In this section we shall first summarize the main findings from the previous sections. Then we shall make some qualitative comparisons among the various resource sectors. Finally, we shall draw several broad conclusions.

Summary of Main Findings

Agriculture
1. There will continue to be increasing demands for agricultural imports, particularly of cereals and, to a lesser extent, of oilseeds,

by the developing world, as well as by many centrally planned economies.

2. Nevertheless, this does not mean that real agricultural prices will increase in the long term. Instability of prices is likely to continue, but persistent world food shortages are not now generally anticipated, so that real prices may well remain at current levels or once again return to their long-run pattern of decline.

3. There is considerable scope for expansion in Canadian cereal grain, feedgrain, and oilseed exports, although such exports will likely face severe competition from subsidized European Community exports, some instability in purchases by our main buyers, such as the U.S.S.R. and China, and the possibility that developing lands may occasionally have difficulty in paying for their imports.

4. For enlarged exports to occur, increases in cultivated acreage, decreases in the proportion of summerfallow, and growth in yields will be necessary. Moreover, much research will be required concerning the development of improved techniques of managing land, water and snow resources; the countering of soil salinity and other soil-quality deterioration problems; the appropriate use of fertilizers; optimal crop rotations and other farming techniques; and development of higher-yielding, drought-resistant and sprouting-resistant crops, including improved varieties of white, winter and 3-M wheats. Results of such work must be communicated effectively to farmers.

5. Major changes leading to greater flexibility in Canada's grain grading, handling and transportation systems will be necessary so that farmers can shift more readily to the white, winter and 3-M grades of wheat, where the most growth in future exports will be.

6. Because agriculture is by far the most capital intensive of the resource industries, financing can be a major problem for farmers, particularly those with smaller holdings and those attempting to modernize. The research leading to greater productivity will be an important long-run aspect of facing this difficulty, as will the upgrading of managerial skills of farmers with respect to financing, time management, record keeping, risk spreading, and all the technical aspects of producing farm products.

7. Canada will continue to export red meats to the United States and Japan, but the value will likely remain substantially less than the value of grain exports. To maintain or improve competitiveness attention will have to be given to enhancing farmers' managerial skills, permitting comparative advantage to operate within Canada, and becoming more flexible in production, grading, processing and pricing of meat products so as to satisfy foreign tastes. More vertical integration of the industry may be necessary to increase efficiency. Supply-management systems should be avoided, and wage levels in

processing plants will have to be kept competitive with those in the United States.

8. Canadian poultry, eggs and milk-products production is not competitive by world standards. Supply-management systems by producer-controlled boards, often with a narrow provincial focus, have restricted competition domestically and raised prices to consumers. These systems must be amended or even dismantled so that greater efficiency can be achieved, prices to consumers can be lowered, and the economic rents that go to holders of quotas can be removed.

9. Canada is a net importer of large quantities of fresh fruits and vegetables. Although the southern United States may have some cost advantages in this respect, Canadian producers could become more competitive through achieving greater scale economies, adopting the most up-to-date technology, and giving much more attention than they have so far given to matters of reliability and quality of supply. Similar types of improvements are necessary in the greenhouse industry in Canada, and greater use could be made of waste heat from industrial processes. As with other agricultural products, marketing boards, which only protect inefficiency, should be terminated.

10. In general, more research, upgrading of agriculturalists' skills, continued modernization and adjustment to changing technology and competitive conditions are essential for improved viability of the agricultural sector. Care should be taken to ensure that rigidities which prevent adjustment to changing conditions are reduced, and that new ones are not built into the agricultural supply system. If adjustment to change in this industry had been prevented in the past, the agricultural community and all of Canada would be much worse off today.

Energy

1. Barring an all-encompassing war in the Middle East, real oil prices, and with them all energy prices, are not expected to rise much, if at all, between now and the end of the century; they could even continue their recent decline. Even with greater conflict in the Middle East, the decreasing reliance on oil, and the general energy-saving measures now in place and in process, will mean that real energy prices probably will not rise beyond about 2.5 percent yearly.

2. Canada's dependence on oil as a source of energy will continue to diminish, so that by the year 2005 it will be about 25 to 30 percent. Whether self-sufficiency in light crude oil can be sustained will depend on how quickly the non-conventional sources of supply, particularly the oilsands and heavy oil reserves of Alberta and, to a lesser extent, Saskatchewan, are developed. Significant frontier supplies will be necessary, too. The projects going forward today

suggest that the pace of exploitation may well be increased, provided that a stable, cooperative, federal-provincial environment is maintained, and that government taxation arrangements are sufficiently flexible and predictable and are not confiscatory. This implies that modifications are necessary in National Energy Policy taxes and in the federal-provincial equalization scheme, which is due to expire in 1987.

3. Exports of western natural gas to the United States will increase quite rapidly after the current gas surplus is worked off by about 1986. The lower export prices permitted to start in the autumn of 1984 may well be sustained. If they are, it will be important to gas producers for the Canadian dollar to remain at current levels if netbacks on exports are not to be seriously eroded. Exports are expected to be maintainable from conventional sources of supply until at least the year 2000 or beyond. By that time, Arctic gas may be on stream, with exports going both to the United States and to Japan. Arctic exports to Japan could even commence within the current decade as Japan strives to diversify its sources of energy supply. East Coast gas may eventually be exported to the U.S. Northeast, as well, but anticipated delivery costs leave this possibility in doubt.

4. Excess coal-production capacity exists in the world. Coal is of more environmental concern than oil and gas, so that world real coal prices are not expected to rise much from their 1981 level till about the turn of the century. Canada's coal exports could expand — at most, double — by the 1990s and then level out, but this is far from certain.

5. Increased Canadian coal sales abroad may have to depend on nations such as Japan diversifying their sources of supply, for on a delivered-cost basis, Canadian coal is often not as low-priced as coal from other sources. This stems from the long distances that coal must be transported to reach the sea coast.

6. It may be advantageous for Canadian federal and provincial governments to work cooperatively with the coal industry in negotiating with Japan to maximize the present discounted value from the nation's coal resources. Japan has a tendency to play supplying firms and countries off against one another to minimize its costs of resources.

7. Domestic demand for coal is expected to increase by about 50 percent over the next two decades. Ontario, currently the province with the greatest consumption, will be shifting to nuclear power and away from coal, while other areas, such as Alberta, Saskatchewan and Atlantic Canada, will become increasingly dependent on coal.

8. If Canadian governments were to agree to move more rapidly toward requiring lower sulphur emissions than the 50 percent reduction scheduled to occur by 1994, there might be greater scope for immedi-

ate increased use of low-sulphur (although higher-priced) Alberta coal in Ontario until such time as Ontario has appropriately expanded its nuclear capacity.

9. The greatest potential for sustained long-term exports of energy may well be electricity to the United States, based on hydro- and possibly nuclear generation facilities. But if the full potential is to be realized, Canada as a whole should consider, as well as export negotiations, the interprovincial coordination of electricity usage so that potential economic rents are not given away unnecessarily in the competition for U.S. sales. In addition, as for oil and gas, taxation of the economic rents is required for efficiency as well as equity among sources of energy.

10. Uranium exports and prices tend to be volatile. Canada's reserves are more than adequate until well into the 21st century, and new finds in Saskatchewan make Canada the most economical uranium producer in the world. In volume of output, Canada now is about equal to the United States, and indications are that it will be the leading uranium producer in the world outside centrally planned economies. The host of factors influencing uranium exports, in addition to those affecting demand and supply for energy products in general, make predictions of exports quite unreliable. The foremost market remains the United States, although western Europe will be important, too. Exports can be expected to expand, but compared with the value of coal, gas and electricity exports, the value of such shipments abroad is likely to be fairly small.

Fisheries

1. Because world natural fish stocks are limited, greater emphasis is being placed, and will continue to be placed, on reducing fish wastage during processing, increasing the proportion of fish used for human food, and enhancing aquaculture and mariculture production.

2. Canada's resources should allow her to expand very substantially her output of fish and fish products. Before the end of the 1980s, the cod catch off the East Coast could be 75 percent greater than it is today. With proper management, the catch of salmon, herring and other species could be expanded greatly over the coming decades.

3. The Canadian fishing industry faces three major problems. The first is enormous overcapacity in the fishing fleet and, particularly on the Atlantic Coast in processing facilities as a consequence of government-assisted overexpansion of the industry following the extension of Canada's control on fishing to the 200-mile limit. The second is the need to be able to market abroad the extra supplies of fish that are becoming available, for the nation consumes no more than 15 percent of its production. The third, perhaps less is that aquacultural skills and applications are much behind those of other major countries.

4. Measures are already under way to reduce capacity of the fishing

fleets through a buy-back program, and to institute a transferable licensing system whereby each fishing operation has the right either to take a certain proportion of the total allowable catch itself or to sell its rights to other fishermen wishing to utilize their fishing boats' capacity more fully. In this way, overfishing can be eliminated and unit costs lowered.

5. Rationalization of the fish-processing sector is necessary, too, if efficiency is to be improved, costs reduced, and quality improved. This policy will require that attention be given to other job-creation possibilities, such as in aquaculture, tourism or perhaps the incipient oil and gas industry.

6. Sales expansion, both domestically and abroad, will require more attention to quality of product, new product development, generic advertising and other aggressive marketing techniques, including, perhaps, exchange of fishing rights to less-wanted species by European nations, in return for commitments to purchase Canadian fish.

7. As industry efficiency is enhanced and unit-production costs are lowered, these reduced costs will have to be reflected, to a considerable extent, in lower prices to consumers if sales are to be increased, rather than in higher incomes to workers, greater profits to owners, or expanded economic rents to society.

8. Aquacultural research and development needs attention in Canada. This project will require not only more dollars and people committed to such research, but also mobilization of existing aquaculture-related research programs in the universities. The research will have to include work on such topics as the types of facilities to employ, stock selection and improvement, fish health and nutrition, handling and harvesting techniques, and organizational administrative and marketing technology.

9. Throughout all segments of the fishing sector, federal and provincial governments as well as both management and the workforce employed in fishing and fish processing, a greater spirit of cooperation and trust will enable the necessary adjustments to be made more readily and less painfully for all concerned.

Forest Products

1. World demand for pulp and paper products and for lumber is expected to grow over the next two decades, but at about only one-half the rate of its growth in the 1960s. The weakest part of the market is expected to be in lumber.

2. Major new suppliers of pulp and paper are coming onto the world markets, and they are placing increased emphasis on silviculture. In many tropical and subtropical countries where silviculture is being practised, growth rates of new wood are much more rapid than they have traditionally been for Canadian softwoods. As more of the

world's wood supply is managed in this way, less land area will have to be devoted to timber production.

3. Canada's traditional softwood forests are being depleted rapidly, both by harvesting for lumber and pulp and paper production, and by disease, pestilence and forest fires. Thus, for Canada to continue its large export trade and to expand it, emphasis will have to be placed on reforestation, much-improved forest-management techniques, and the development of faster-growing species.

4. Much new investment will also be required to modernize and rationalize Canada's processing industry, a large proportion of which was established earlier than in many other parts of the world and is accordingly less efficient. Simultaneous research is needed into the improved use of forests and the wood therefrom, and into exploiting for pulp and paper uses, especially for large-volume newsprint production, Canada's hardwood resources, such as poplar, which grow much faster than softwood coniferous trees.

5. Since about 94 percent of Canada's forests are owned by the government, the tenure system on leases has not been conducive to the undertaking of reforestation and forest management by private forestry companies. The auctioning-off of prime forest lands to private interests may be one means of increasing the incentives to companies to do this work. The recent federal-provincial agreements, along with provisions for financing of silviculture, should also help resolve this problem.

6. Canada may well have to increase the proportion of its forest harvest that is exported as raw logs from the present level of about 4 percent of the total cut. This step would cause employment to rise in the forestry harvesting sector and to fall somewhat in sawmilling. Attention to greater efficiency and to new-product developments to match market needs should help the wood-processing sectors to compete internationally.

7. Canada has an advantage in one way over major competitors such as the U.S. South, in that hydro-electric costs for the energy-intensive pulp and paper industry are much lower here, provided that the United States does not view Canada's cheap hydro-electric power as an export subsidy subject to countervailing duties.

8. On the negative side, Canadian labour costs are substantially above those in the United States, and labour strife has not infrequently aggravated Canada's marketing problems. Restraint needs to be exercised in wage and salary demands, particularly in British Columbia.

9. Employment prospects for the traditional parts of the industry, even with the massive new investments in modernized equipment, are mixed. For many jobs, the skill levels required will be considerably higher. For expanded reforestation and intensive forest management, however, which include weed control, fertilization, thinning, and

control of disease, pestilence and forest fires, much of the labour requirement may involve relatively low-skill levels. These jobs could employ many young people during the summer months.

Minerals, Excluding Energy

1. Future real price increases of the minerals that Canada produces are generally expected to be quite modest or even negative up to 1990. The large price increases of the 1970s were an irregularity compared with their world-wide decline for many decades previously. No long-run shortage is expected in mineral resources.
2. Some continued growth in demand for minerals is anticipated, but this growth, too, will be at a much more modest pace than in the decades since World War II. It will depend not only on a renewal of expansion in the world economy, but also on much research on new product uses for many metals and on trends toward making products smaller and lighter, substituting plastics, ceramics or glass for metals, and increased recycling.
3. Canada will be challenged to prevent its export shares diminishing because of subsidized production from developing or COMECON nations, markets closed by regional trading agreements, and foreign governmental controls on trade.
4. These challenges should not be overwhelming given the following conditions.
   - Canadian firms, especially those in the non-precious metals sector, must undertake more research on exploration, mining, smelting and refining techniques to lower their mining and processing costs. They must undertake, individually and within their respective industry associations at home and abroad, research on new product uses for metals. They must also improve their management techniques relating to longer-range planning, market development, human resource development and employee relations, and relations with governments and the public.
   - Canadian governments must maintain a stable and predictable tax regime that is flexible with respect to industry-profitability conditions and that does not discourage development of new mineral resources. Maintenance of an exchange value for the Canadian dollar that permits the industry to compete abroad is also essential. This line of action requires that the advantage from a lower dollar not be lost through wage and salary increases. In other words, the industry, especially the metals sector, may have to be content with lower real wages and salaries. Management will have to share this experience.
   - Canada must attempt to capitalize on its position as a politically stable source of resources and a member of NORAD and NATO so as to have as free access as possible to the markets of the

United States and the European Community for its raw materials and processed minerals. Continued advocacy of a more liberalized world trading system can be important too.

- While supporting a freer world trading environment, Canada cannot ignore the fact that countertrade is now a significant part of world trade. Thus, trading companies that can participate effectively in this process may have to be established. Other aggressive marketing techniques may be necessary on occasion, too, as with potash, where Canada is still a marginal world supplier to many markets in spite of its vast resources in Saskatchewan.
- And finally, the Canadian government might also work to discourage loans or grants by government agencies, or loans by national or international institutions, that are for development of additional mineral resource production abroad.

5. A problem that will affect many firms in the industry for some time to come is the financial one that they placed themselves in: that is, an extremely high debt-to-equity ratio, which is particularly troublesome for this industry, given the natural variability in annual returns. They will have to shift more to equity, even if it means a dilution of existing shareholders' positions.

Water Resources
1. Although much is heard on the subject of water shortages in particular areas of the United States, the major problem has been that the predominant use of water for agricultural purposes has been heavily subsidized from public funds. As water is allowed to approach its market value, uneconomic uses of water in agriculture will be discouraged.
2. If prices are allowed to reflect the value of water, imports from Canada will not be necessary. Moreover, it would not be an economic proposition from the viewpoint of either Canada or the United States to undertake the massive investments necessary to transport water from Canada to the U.S.A.

An Intersectoral Comparison

To summarize the previous section and to provide a cross-industry comparison of the relative situations of the resource industries, Table 1-40 has been prepared. Most of the table is self-explanatory. The ranking of current competitive strength may need some comment, however. It was derived by weighing, in a qualitative way, the extent to which the various industries are now competitive in world markets, the extent to which they depend for their survival on particular situations, which might change, and the amount of internal adjustment, in the form of new investment, new research and development, and so forth, that is neces-

TABLE 1-40 An Intersectoral Comparison

Industry	Rank by Current International Competitive Strength	Expected Real Price Changes to 2000	Potential for Expanded Exports or Reduced Imports	Direct Employment Prospects
Energy	1	Same as now or modest increase if Middle-East situation worsens	• Good to excellent depending on the energy product	• Gradual expansion from 1982 lows as conventional oil and gas activity picks up and more conventional and nonconventional development occurs • Weakness in coal • Little new construction in electricity generation until surpluses reduced
Agriculture	2 (Except dairying and poultry)	Same as now or modest decline	• Good for cereals and feedgrains; small increases in beef and pork	• Little change from present

Industry	Rank by Current International Competitive Strength	Main Industry Requirements for Improved Competitive Performance	Government Roles
Energy	1	• Continuing research on efficiently exploiting surface oilsands and on in situ technology • Control wage and salary increases, especially in coal mining, but also in mega- and mini-oil and other construction projects	• Provide taxation regimes that encourage new investments and share the revenue risks on new ventures; tax systems should be predictable • Keep open communication with industry • Coordinate and assist in negotiations on new coal developments and exports to Japan and on gas and uranium exports generally
Agriculture	2 (Except dairying and poultry)	• Reduction in summer-fallowing • Greater flexibility in crops grown • Improvements in farm management skills • Avoidance or reduction of supply-management or other programs reducing the flexibility and competitiveness of the industry; • Rationalization and upgrading of technology in the horticultural sector	• Improve grain gathering, grading, and transportation methods so greater flexibility is possible in handling soft grades of wheat and other varieties of grains to meet world demands • Reduce use of supply-management of other systems that raise prices to consumers or prevent flexibility in supply systems to market forces • More research on soil-quality preservation, new seed varieties, and improved farming techniques, with adequate communication of results to farmers

TABLE 1-40 (cont'd)

Industry	Rank by Current International Competitive Strength	Expected Real Price Changes to 2000	Potential for Expanded Exports or Reduced Imports	Direct Employment Prospects
Forestry	3	Modest increases	• Good for woodpulp • Poorest for lumber • Newsprint and other paper products are in between • Log exports could be increased if desired	• Skill levels required in many sectors will increase • Some increases in forestry section as intensive forest management is expanded
Fishing	4	Same as now or modest increase; could be decrease if efficiency improvements passed to consumer in lower prices	• Modest	• Decline in traditional areas as excess capacity reduced • Some increases in aquaculture

Industry	Rank by Current International Competitive Strength	Main Industry Requirements for Improved Competitive Performance	Government Roles
Forestry	3	• More reforestation, forest management, and protection programs • More research on improved, faster-growing tree varieties and use of hardwood trees for such as newsprint • Investment in modernization and rationalization of plants • Limit wage and salary increases	• Assist with research on new tree varieties, forest management techniques and reduction of forest losses from disease, pestilence, etc. • Set the example in keeping wages and salaries under control so advantage of lower Canadian dollar is not eroded • Possibly some sale of forest lands to private corporations to increase their interest and participation in silviculture
Fishing	4	• Reduce excess capacity in fishing fleet and fish-processing sector • Attention to improved quality of product, new products, generic advertising • More aquaculture • Improve management-worker relations	• Continued work on reducing excess capacity and increasing the use of transferable property rights to fish stocks • Improve labour-management, industry-government, and intergovernmental relations • Assist in negotiations for expanded markets in other countries • Much more research in and encouragement of aquaculture

TABLE 1-40 (cont'd)

Industry	Rank by Current International Competitive Strength	Expected Real Price Changes to 2000	Potential for Expanded Exports or Reduced Imports	Direct Employment Prospects
Minerals	5	Same as now or return to a secular decline, providing technological change outweighs increased anti-pollution costs	• Least favourable of the five sectors, but potash, sulphur, gold, aluminum, and possibly zinc look quite good	• Some improvement from 1982 lows as exploration picks up • But new technology will reduce need for rehiring as output is expanded again

Industry	Rank by Current International Competitive Strength	Main Industry Requirements for Improved Competitive Performance	Government Roles
Minerals	5	• Shift back from debt to equity financing • More research to enhance productivity in all mining, smelting, and refining processes • More research on new product uses for minerals, especially metals • Improved management techniques in planning, employee relations, and human resource development generally • Limit wage and salary increases of workers and management	• Provide stable, predictable taxation regimes which encourage new investment on exploration, and research on processes and new product uses • Policies to keep Canadian dollar well below U.S. currency and to discourage wage-salary increases that would erode this benefit to industry • Work for expanded role of Canada as a stable, long-term supplier to NORAD and NATO • Discourage loans and grants that subsidize additional mineral resource production in other lands

sary to ensure their future. It was not difficult to choose the top two sectors, energy and agriculture, for their positions are clearly superior to the other three. There might be some debate as to which of these two should have been ranked first. But apart from some present excess capacity in gas, electricity generation, and coal, much of which will be worked off over the next few years, the future of the energy industry, at least for gas and electricity, looks bright. It would appear that governments, especially the federal government, have learned an expensive lesson about taxing too heavily the leading resource sector of the economy so that tax arrangements to encourage the development of the oil industry in Western Canada, particularly heavy oil and oil sands, will likely be more accommodating and supportive in the future. Current world excess capacity in coal will not as easily be worked off so that expanded exports of that product are less certain, but in terms of quality and low sulphur content, its position is favourable.

In the agriculture industry, exports of cereals, feedgrains and canola promise to remain strong. Nevertheless, some important steps must be taken to prevent deterioration of soil quality to improve seed varieties, and to enhance the western grain-handling and transportation systems, so that production can be adapted to world tastes. In addition, a sizeable segment of the industry, consisting of poultry and dairying, is nowhere near competitive with foreign production and has so protected itself that barring some courageous acts by governments that might rectify the situation, it never will be competitive. Another disturbing factor is that this protective mentality seems to be growing within the total agricultural sector, and it could only harm the world-wide competitiveness of the entire sector. Horticultural work is inefficient by U.S. standards and should be rationalized and upgraded in its use of technology. For these reasons, it seemed wise to place agriculture in second place.

The fifth or last spot in the ranking was not hard to select. The minerals sector in aggregate, apart from promising segments such as potash, or possibly gold, sulphur or aluminum, is in difficulties. Only major restructuring and a low value for the Canadian dollar have kept this industry afloat. Continued efforts will have to be made along the lines indicated for this industry to grow again in the future.

Positions 3 and 4 were not as easily identified. Although much new investment and research is necessary in the forestry and the pulp and paper industries, the sector does have tremendous strength. The magnitude of the task before it in adjusting to increasingly competitive world circumstances does not seem overwhelming. Moreover, world markets will continue to expand for the major product groups. Hence forestry was given third position. Fishing has been ranked fourth because it has few options. Reducing the overcapacity in the industry will certainly make it more efficient and possibly enable it to lower prices of its exports. Yet world competition for markets will be intense, particularly as other nations improve and develop their aquaculture and mariculture techniques. Hence, although there is substantial potential capacity for supply increases, there will probably continue to be a problem at the marketing end.

Final Conclusions

The first major conclusion of this review is that the day of Canada's resource industries is not over. Their expansion is not likely to match again the heady days of the 1950s or 1960s, but they still have much to contribute to the Canadian economy in the years ahead, and there is considerable potential for growth in output and exports or, in some commodities, such as oil, in import replacement.

This statement must be qualified, however. Although the industries will be able to survive and prosper, there is little scope in most of them for increased direct employment. The best prospects for higher-than-present employment levels in the longer term are in the energy industries, particularly oil and gas exploration and development, hydro-electricity projects and, possibly, nuclear projects. There will also be some potential in the forestry sector as intensive management practices are increasingly used. Many jobs will be upgraded in terms of skill levels, but there should be opportunity for many labour-intensive techniques in this sector to use the large body of unemployed youth during the months that they are not in schools and universities. Apart from these two sectors, the scope for greater direct employment in the resource sectors is minimal. Nevertheless, this is not the whole story. The substantial increases in investment required, in industries other than fishing, to modernize the resource sector will generate considerable employment. The impact multipliers for some of the resource sectors are certainly as good as, and frequently better than those for a variety of other products in the economy. Table 1-41 supplies evidence. The contribution of the resource sectors to the total economy can be substantial.

The second general conclusion of this study is that it is not a question of choosing between "high-tech" industries and the continued development of our resource industries. Every nation seems to be choosing to support much the same high-tech industries so that there are bound to be some significant losers. Canada has immense resources of almost every type. It is thus a matter of taking the best of high technology, wherever it is developed, and applying it to the enhancement of the productivity, competitiveness, and environmental and conservation needs of our resource sectors. It is also necessary to undertake much more research and development in the resource industries. If anything, Ottawa could be accused of having too much of a Niagara Peninsula-Ottawa Valley focus when it comes to encouraging R&D. This focus needs to be rectified. High technology can be of immense benefit to Canadian resource

TABLE 1-41 Impact Multipliers for Selected Canadian Commodities

Commodity	Multiplier
Grains	1.76
Live animals	1.76
Other agricultural products	1.76
Forestry products	1.97
Fish landings	1.40
Iron ores and concentrates	1.63
Other metal ores and concentrates	1.66
Coal	1.66
Crude mineral oils	1.66
Natural gas	1.66
Nonmetallic minerals	1.68
Services incidental to mining	1.66
Meat products	2.21
Dairy products	2.27
Fish products	2.26
Fruits and vegetable preparations	2.26
Feeds	2.25
Flour, wheat, meal and other cereals	2.27
Fabrics	1.80
Clothing and accessories	1.70
Lumber and timber	2.13
Veneer and plywood	2.13
Pulp	2.03
Newsprint and other paper stock	2.03
Paper products	2.00
Iron and steel products	1.91
Aluminum products	1.92
Copper and copper alloy products	1.92
Nickel products	1.92
Other nonferrous metal products	1.91
Fabricated structural metal products	1.91
Agricultural machinery	1.68
Motor vehicles	1.60
Motor vehicle parts	1.64
Gasoline and fuel oil	2.05
Other petroleum and coal products	1.93
Fertilizers	1.74
Pharmaceuticals	2.02
Other manufactured products	1.85
Electric power	1.30
Other finance, insurance, real estate	1.46
Health services	1.39
Accommodation and food services	1.78
Travel, advertising and promotions	2.42

Source: Statistics Canada, *The Input-Output Structure of the Canadian Economy 1971–1979* (Ottawa; Statistics Canada, 1983), Table 80, Impact (Inverse) Matrix (Aggregation-M), 1979.

industries. To dismiss the resource sectors as mere sunset industries would be to do our nation and each person in it a sore disservice. We would be ignoring what will continue to be a major source of production and income for Canadians for generations to come.

These comments lead to a third general conclusion of this study. Benefits to Canada from its abundant endowments of natural resources will not come without effort. It will not be simply a matter of lying back and collecting the economic rents while someone removes and sells our replenishable and non-replenishable resources. Rather, it will require much more attention by the industries themselves to research and development, to the latest technology, to improved management-planning and scheduling techniques, better labour-management relations, more cooperation with governments, and so on. It will also require that governments undertake much more R&D, particularly in sectors such as agriculture and aquaculture, where individual firms are often too small to do this themselves, and that they provide a climate in which business is consulted, not dictated to; where the taxation rules are accommodating and predictable, not punitive; where there is cooperation, not competition, among provinces and between them and the federal government so that industries, where necessary, are assisted to negotiate with foreign industries or governments, which themselves are attempting to assert their individual or collective market power, and where provincial and federal governments do not dissipate their collective intellects and energies in narrowly protecting their own locales or rights, at the expense of the nation as a whole.

The economic rents that Canada has unquestionably enjoyed from a number of its resource sectors in the past will not likely be as large in the future if they exist at all. Some of these rents have gone to consumers, for example, when oil prices were less than world market levels. Some have gone to workers in the form of higher wages than those collected by their colleagues in other sectors (Copithorne, 1979),[32] and some have gone to the owners of capital and the owners of the resources themselves. The fact that the world is a much more competitive place than it was 10, 15 or 20 years ago implies that these rents are greatly reduced or eliminated. In turn, this suggests that workers in the resource industries, both wage-earners and executives, as well as in other industries where incomes are largely determined by the pace of development in the resource sectors, such as construction, will have to come to grips with the idea that their real incomes, which have in the past contained a segment of economic rent, will have to be lower. This lowering may come about in several ways: through a depreciated Canadian dollar such as we are now experiencing, without compensating increases in wages and salaries; by actual reductions in nominal wages, which some industries are now attempting to bring about; or simply by the failure of nominal wages to keep up with the general rate of inflation.

Whatever way their future develops, this review of the resource sectors suggests that in several of the sectors, such as forestry products and minerals, including coal, industries which are to survive, must be able to generate funds for investment without always requiring government assistance and to move forward. Even in the energy sector, apart from coal, where economic rents are more likely to persist, it would be desirable because of the favourable demonstration effect it could have upon construction and other industries to limit real wage increases. The high unemployment rates in the economy enlarge this possibility. As for fishing, any rents that may have existed have largely been dissipated through overcapacity and the resulting inefficiency. As rationalization in the industry occurs, rents may be instituted. But if increased sales abroad are to be made, by such means as encouraging greater consumption of fish in the huge U.S. market, these rents may also have to disappear in the competition for markets. The major observation about agriculture is that artificial rents have been created in the poultry and dairy industries by means of the supply-management and quota systems. The owners of quotas enjoy rents at the expense of the consuming public. If governments dismantled the system, consumers would gain, and productivity would increase.

Governments have another role to play in this context. Moves to lower real incomes in industry will be more acceptable if governments, with all their direct and indirect employees, set the example through practising wage and salary restraints. Without such an example it will be difficult to hold the line in the private sector. Governments need to be realistic and courageous in publicizing the message that most of our abundant natural resources, although still capable of helping us to earn a living, will no longer support an easy living for anyone.

Closely related to the previous point is the fact that Canadians need not bemoan the current low value of the Canadian dollar in comparison to the U.S. dollar. Although our dollar is at an historic low, it is still relatively high compared with the currencies of other nations. Its value as compared to the U.S. dollar means that Canadian products sold in the United States, be they metals or other minerals, forestry products, fish products, or red meats, are better able to compete effectively than they would be if our dollar rose to a level approaching the parity to which Canadians in the past were more accustomed. Given the current — and probably continuing low rate of employment in this country, the existing or even a lower exchange value of the Canadian dollar is all to Canada's benefit.

Finally, if we Canadians fail to adjust to changing circumstances, as our resource sectors must continue to do, our only path must be downward. If each group in society attempts to build protective systems to prevent itself from being touched by the vicissitudes of the international economy, it will only hasten its own decline and the decline of the entire economy.

Notes

I appreciate the willing and enthusiastic assistance of Rampersaud Rameshwar and Ardeshir Sephri-Borojeni on the sections relating respectively to minerals and agriculture. Moreover, the completion of this study would have been impossible without the cheerful, accurate, and efficient typing and duplicating assistance of Maryon Buffel, Leslie Haugan and Charlene Hill, who together enabled me to meet the various deadlines involved in preparing this manuscript. I am also grateful to my colleagues, Mike Percy and Terry Veeman, for valuable discussions concerning forestry and agriculture respectively, and to Ken Norrie and John Whalley who provided advice and encouragement. The comments of two anonymous referees were helpful, too. The responsibility for the final product, however, remains mine alone.

This study was completed in February 1985.

1. In this study it is assumed that it will take six years to reclaim the entire land. If crops or yields decline by 10 to 20 percent, the project will be marginally feasible at best. However, if the reclamation occurred in only three years, as in the Montana experiments, the economies would be improved accordingly.

2. The recent innovation by United Grain Growers to load directly from farmers' trucks to hopper cars is a first step toward greater efficiency in the reorganization of the grain-handling system (*Alberta Report*, October 1984).

3. See Economic Council of Canada, 1984, pp. 89–90.

4. With regard to *soil acidity*, more research is required on monitoring soil acidity, on changes therein in response to fertilizers and industrial emissions, on developing fertilizers that minimize acidity, on determining lime requirements and the effects of lime amounts on crop yields, and on the development of plants tolerant to soil acidity. The reasons why poor growth occurs in *solonetzic soils* need investigation, as do the effects of deep plowing, crop rotation, and chemical applications (Racz, 1984). More details on the extent and rate of expansion of *soil salinity* are required, along with hydrological studies of affected and susceptible areas, models of salt and water movements, micro- and macroclimatic effects, techniques for identifying recharge areas, improved land-management practices for recharge and discharge areas, and plant breeding and selection for salt tolerance. The *loss of soil organic matter* requires more study in relation to soil type, tillage and cropping methods, and of methods of reducing this loss. Research is needed with respect to *farming* itself and to *plant varieties*, to determine optimum tilling practices, to illuminate fertilizer and herbicidal usage, disease, drought, and winter-kill resistance, and yield enhancement for new varieties of grains and oilseeds. Frontier research is needed on increasing nitrogen fixation by legumes, on developing nitrogen-fixing cereal grains and grains able to use deeper moisture reserves, on adapting presently unused food-plant species to human use, on using bioregulators to augment plant productivity, and on removing ice-nucleating bacteria from plants to lengthen growing seasons (Anderson and Associates, 1982).

5. The italics are mine.

6. See possibilities in Jensen, 1980, p. 69.

7. The simple average of eight different forecasts of world prices to 1990, made over a series of years up to 1981, by a variety of forecasters representing many different perspectives, was about US $43 (in 1979 constant dollars) (Reddy, 1984). In mid-1982, the World Bank consensus was that by 1990, the oil price would be only US $37 in 1981 constant dollars, and US $41 by 1995. By September 1984, the World Bank estimates for 1990 and 1995 were reduced to US $30.1 and US $36.8 respectively (in 1983 dollars). From the 1984 price of US $27.5 per barrel (in 1983 dollars), the growth rate to 1995 represented by these latter estimates would be about 2.7 percent per year. Lower again are the April 1984 reference Informetrica assumptions (see Nelles, 1984) of annual oil-price increases in real terms of 2 percent in 1985 and 1 percent thereafter.

8. Petro-Canada has negotiated a sale of 2.5 million cubic metres a day with a consortium of three major U.S. pipeline companies (*Globe and Mail*, December 11, 1984).

9. At present Hydro-Québec can simultaneously deliver 3,100 megawatts (MW) to points outside the province. New projects now under construction will greatly increase this

capacity, by an additional 1,000 MW to Ontario and New York, 500 MW to New Brunswick, and 690 MW to New England (Bérubé, 1984).

10. Quebec now has over 32,000 MW of capacity. Another 14,000 MW can be developed more cheaply than by nuclear or coal-fired plants, and an additional 16,000 MW can be developed if markets and costs warrant (Bérubé, 1984).

11. Ontario Hydro is currently paying about $79 per pound, although the world price is now only about $25 per pound.

12. In 1983, four large firms were identified: Fishery Products Ltd., the Lake Group Ltd., National Sea Products Ltd., and H.B. Nickerson and Sons Ltd. (Weeks and Mazany, 1983). The last firm is a subsidiary of National Sea Products, and in 1984, Fishery Products Ltd. merged with the Lake Group and another firm, John Penny and Sons Ltd.

13. It is ironic that Canada's extension of fishing rights to the 200-mile limit, and thus the removal of most foreign ships from this sphere, has only meant two things for most Canadians: massive increase in government subsidies to the fishing industry, and simultaneously, fish-product price rises more rapid than for other foods.

14. For example, during the autumn of 1984, Congressional representatives from New England wanted a delay in instituting the World Court judgment on how the Georges Banks should be divided between Canadian and U.S. fishermen. A part of their strategy included making charges that Canadian fish going to the United States are subsidized by government financing to the industry and attempting to have counter-vailing duties applied against Canadian fish.

15. U.S. tariffs are 1.875 cents per pound on cod and similar fish, 3 percent on salmon, and 6.5 percent on a wide range of canned fish.

16. Total aquaculture (both finfish and shellfish) output in Canada in 1984 was about 6,000 tonnes. A recent entrant is mussel culture which amounted to about 2,000 tonnes in 1984, compared with 40 tonnes in 1982 (Pritchard, 1984b).

17. Apparently it is only recently that Canada's federal Department of Fisheries and Oceans has committed itself to ensuring that eggs passed to farmers are taken from disease-free fish (*Globe and Mail*, October 15, 1984).

18. The document *A Review of Canadian Trade Policy: A Background Document to Canadian Trade Policy for the 1980s* (Canada, Department of External Affairs, 1983, p. 73) suggests that world demand for pulp and paper over the next 10 years will be about 3 percent per year. For the reasons given in the text, I suggest that this figure is too high.

19. The resurgence in the American economy during 1983 and 1984 produced actual and anticipated growth rates of shipments for the pulp and paper industry of 8 percent, a figure much above these estimates. But it is not expected that these rates will be sustained in the longer term.

20. The Canadian Pulp and Paper Association suggests that intensive forest management can produce growth in Canada of about 63 cubic feet per acre per year to 128 cubic feet per acre per year. These amounts are still much less than tropical plantations can produce, but far better than the average AAC in all Canadian forests of 13 cubic feet per acre per year.

21. The one exception is that if the forests have to be utilized for pulpwood rather than lumber, increases in costs of processing wood pulp could negate the advantage of the southern hemisphere's plantations (Sedjo 1983a, chap. 6).

22. Refer to the first column of Table 1-37.

23. Buck (1984) reports some estimates by David Williamson of Shearson/American Express on the share of the world production under state control. These range from 63 percent for copper to 44, 39, 36, and 34 percent for nickel, lead, zinc, and aluminum, respectively.

24. It is sometimes argued that Canadian taxes are less than those in developing countries with mineral endowments. But a recent study by the Centre for Resource Studies, Kingston, suggests that developing nations frequently expect their mining industries to contribute much to the welfare needs of their society. When the costs of these are

counted, including the inefficiency and low productivity that can result from over-employment, companies sometimes may be less well off than they are in Canada. Canada, in fact, along with the Philippines, apparently expects less from its mining sector relative to the benefits the sector received than do the governments of the other nations in the study: Chile, Indonesia, Peru, Zaire, and Zambia (*CRS Perspectives*, June 1984).

25. See Caragata, 1984.
26. 1 km^3 = 264.2 × 10^9 U.S. gallons.
27. Cited in Frederick and Hanson, 1982a, p. 103.
28. Reported ibid.
29. Reported in Rogers, 1984, p. 28.
30. Reported ibid., p. 22.
31. A thorough analysis of Canadian water resources, their implications for economic growth, and issues such as interbasin transfers and possible export of these resources is found in Veeman (1984). The author reaches the same negative conclusion about water-export possibilities.
32. Casual empiricism supports this statement. Average 1980–81 hourly wages in the mineral, fuel and forestry resource sectors and related primary manufacturing averaged about $11.00 to $11.50, whereas for manufacturing outside of these sectors, the hourly wage rate was about $8.10. In construction, hourly wages for the same two years were $12.75.

Bibliography

Introduction

Reynolds, Lloyd. 1983. "The Spread of Economic Growth to the Third World." *Journal of Economic Literature* 21 (3) September: 941–80.

Statistics Canada. 1983. *System of National Accounts, National Income and Expenditure Accounts*. Ottawa: Statistics Canada.

_____. 1984. *Summary of External Trade: December 1983*. Ottawa: Statistics Canada.

Agriculture

Alberta. Alberta Agriculture. 1980. *Proceedings of Alberta Horticulture Conference*. Edmonton: The Department.

_____. 1981. *Agricultural Land: Our Disappearing Heritage — A Symposium*. Proceedings of the 18th Annual Alberta Soil Science Workshop. Edmonton: The Department.

_____. 1983. *Proceedings of the First Annual Western Provincial Conference Rationalization of Water and Soil Research Management: Soil Salinity*. Edmonton: The Department.

_____. 1984a. "Agricultural Land Base Study Economic Analysis: Direct Benefits and Costs." Edmonton: The Department, Production and Resource Economics Branch, Economic Services Division.

_____. 1984b. "Agricultural Land Base Study Economic Component: Phase-I." Edmonton: The Department, Production and Resource Economics Branch, Economic Services Division.

_____. 1984c. *Executive Summary: Alberta Vegetable Processing Industry Sector Profile*. Edmonton: The Department, Plant Industry Division.

_____. 1984d. *Response to Environment Council of Alberta Questions Arising from Public Hearings into Maintaining and Expanding the Agricultural Land Base in Alberta*. Edmonton: The Department.

_____. Greenhouse Industry Task Force. 1983. *The Economics Viability and Future Expansion of Alberta's Greenhouse Industry*. Edmonton.

———. Horticulture Research Centre. 1983. *1980 Alberta Horticulture Conference Follow-up Proceedings*. Edmonton: The Centre.

Anderson, Marv. and Associates Ltd. 1981. *Factors Affecting Summerfallow Acreage in Alberta*. ECA81-17/IB1. Edmonton: Environment Council of Alberta.

———. 1982. *Research and Agricultural Productivity in Alberta*. ECA82-17/IB23. Produced in cooperaton with Alberta Agriculture. Edmonton: Environment Council of Alberta.

———. 1983. *An Analysis of Agricultural Research and Productivity in Alberta*. ECA83-17/IB30. Edmonton: Environment Council of Alberta.

Anderson, Robert. 1981. "Government Regulation of the Canadian Dairy Processing, Distributing and Retailing Sector." Working Paper 25. Ottawa: Economic Council of Canada.

Barichello, Richard. 1981. *The Economics of Canadian Dairy Industry Regulations*. Technical Report E/12. Study prepared for the Economic Council of Canada and the Institute for Research on Public Policy. Ottawa: Economic Council of Canada.

Barney, G.O., P.A. Freeman, and C.A. Ulinski. 1981. *Global 2000: Implications for Canada*. Toronto: Pergamon Press.

Bigland, C.H. 1984. *Potential for the Application of Biotechnology in the Development and Production of Animal Vaccines and Monoclonal Antibodies in Canada*. Ottawa: Science Council of Canada.

Birch, Alfred. 1983. "The Economics of Agricultural Drainage: Irrigated Saline Soils in Southern Alberta." Edmonton: Alberta Agriculture, Resource Economics Branch.

Bjarnason, Harold. 1984. "Marketing High-Yielding Wheats." An Address to the Annual Meeting of Palliser Wheat Growers. Winnipeg: Canadian Wheat Board.

Borland, S., and G. Robertson. 1985. "A Sectoral View of the Longer-term: Agriculture." In *Long-Term Economic Prospects for Canada: A Symposium*, vol. 23 of the research studies prepared for the Royal Commission on the Economic Union and Development Prospects for Canada. Toronto: University of Toronto Press.

Bushak, W. 1984. "New South Wales System of Variety Identification for the Prime Hard and Hard No. 1 Grades of Wheat." Winnipeg: University of Manitoba, Department of Plant Science.

Canada. Department of Agriculture. 1981. "Challenge for Growth: An Agri-Food Strategy for Canada." Discussion Paper AGR-6-81DP. Ottawa: The Department.

———. 1983. *Annual Unload Report: Fresh Fruit and Vegetables on 12 Canadian Markets*. Ottawa: The Department, Marketing and Economics Branch.

Canada Grains Council. 1982a. "Grain Handling for Efficiency and Profit." A Report Submitted by the Grain Grading Committee. Winnipeg: The Council.

———. 1982b. *Prospects for the Prairie Grain Industry, 1990*. Winnipeg: The Council.

Canadian Agricultural Research Council. *Biotechnology: Research and Development for Canada's Agricultural and Food System*. Ottawa: The Council.

Canadian Federation of Agriculture. 1983. Paper submitted to the Royal Commission on the Economic Union and Development Prospects for Canada, September.

Canadian Wheat Board. 1984. *Grain Matters* (December–January).

Cargill Bulletin: Current Domestic and International Market Conditions and Public Policy Questions Involving Agriculture and World Trade. Various Issues. Minneapolis: Cargill.

Chaudhary, G.N. 1981. *The Economics of Production and Marketing of Greenhouse Crops in Alberta, 1970–80*. Edmonton: Alberta Agriculture, Production Economics Branch, Economic Services Division.

———. 1984. *The Economics of Production and Marketing of Greenhouse Crops in Alberta, 1982–83*. Edmonton: Alberta Agriculture, Production Economics Branch, Economic Services Division.

Chaudhary, G.N., and Lloyd J. Andruchow. 1980. *The Economics of Production and Marketing of Greenhouse Crops in Alberta*. Edmonton: Alberta Agriculture, Production Economics Branch, Economic Services Division.

Clarke, John M., John V. Christensen, and Ronald M. DePauw. n.d. "The Effect of

Weathering on Falling Numbers of Standing and Winnowed Wheat." *Canadian Journal of Plant Science* (forthcoming).

Cole, David, and S. Horton. 1983. "World Grain Trade and Its Financing: Past Patterns and Future Prospects." Montreal: Institute for Research on Public Policy.

Coote, D.R. 1984. "The Extent of Soil Erosion in Western Canada." In *Proceedings of the Second Annual Western Provincial Conference Rationalization of Water and Soil Research and Management: Soil Erosion and Land Degradation*. Saskatoon: University of Saskatchewan.

DePauw, R.M. n.d.(a) "Registration of a Sprouting Resistant White-Seeded Spring Wheat Germplasm Line." *Crop Science* (forthcoming).

———. n.d.(b) "3M Wheat Crop Development Status Report for Canada Grains Council." Mimeographed.

———. 1982c. "Recombining Dormancy and White Seed Color in a Spring Wheat Grass." *Canadian Journal of Plant Science* 63 (July): 581–89.

———. 1984. "Development of Wheat Varieties in Canada (C) Triple-M and Utility." Paper presented to the International Flour Technology Course, sponsored by the Canadian International Grains Institute, August 29.

DePauw, R.M., and T.N. Craig. 1983a. "Evidence for a Genetic Mechanism Controlling Seed Dormancy Independent of Seed Color." In *Proceedings of the 6th International Wheat Genetics Symposium*, Kyoto, Japan, November 28–December 3.

———. 1983b. "Falling Numbers and Alpha-Amylase in Sawfly-Resistant Wheats." In *Third International Symposium on Pre-Harvest Sprouting in Cereals*, edited by James E. Kruger and Donald E. LaBerge. Boulder: Westview Press.

Desjardins, R., K. Macdonald, and D. Wutzke. 1984. "The Economics of Drainage in Alberta." Edmonton: Alberta Agriculture, Production and Resource Economics Branch.

Economic Council of Canada. 1984. *Western Transition*. Ottawa: Minister of Supply and Services Canada.

Environment Council of Alberta. 1982. *Irrigation Agriculture in Alberta*. ECA81-17/IB8. Edmonton: Environment Council of Alberta.

Farrell, Kenneth R., Fred Sanderson, Trang T. Vo, and Michael F. Brewer. 1984. "Meeting Future Needs for United States Food, Fiber and Forest Products." Washington, D.C.: Resources for the Future.

Food and Agriculture Organization of the United Nations (FAO). 1981. *Agriculture: Toward 2000*. Rome: FAO.

Forbes, J.D., R.D. Hughes, and T.K. Warley. 1982. *Economic Intervention and Regulations in Canadian Agriculture*. Study prepared for the Economic Council of Canada, and the Institute for Research on Public Policy. Ottawa: Economic Council of Canada.

Fowler, D.B. 1984. "The Potential for Winter Wheat." In *Proceedings of the Second Annual Western Provincial Conference Rationalization of Water and Soil Research and Management: Soil Erosion and Land Degradation*. Saskatoon: University of Saskatchewan.

Funk, Thomas F. 1984. *An Examination of Policy Issues Related to the Adoption of Biotechnology Research by the Canadian Seed Industry*. Ottawa: Science Council of Canada.

Gillen, David W., and Tae H. Oum. 1984. *Railways in Western Canada: Bottlenecks, Capacity Expansion and Financing*. Study prepared for the Economic Council of Canada. Ottawa: Minister of Supply and Services Canada.

Gilson, J.C. 1982. "Evolution of the Hog Marketing System in Canada."Working Paper E/12. Study prepared for the Economic Council of Canada and the Institute for Research on Public Policy. Ottawa: Economic Council of Canada.

Gordon, M.E. 1981. *Agricultural Land and Land Use Planning in Alberta*: *Summary and Issues*. ECA81-17/IB6. Edmonton: Environment Council of Alberta.

———. 1982. *Options for Protecting Agricultural Land*. ECA82-17/IB15. Edmonton: Environment Council of Alberta.

Govindasamy, Nithi. 1984. "The Economics of On-firm Salinity Control and Reclamation." Paper presented at the Canadian Society of Soil Science Annual Meeting, Banff, Alberta. Edmonton: Alberta Agriculture, Statistics Branch.

Groenewegen, J. 1982. "Feed Grain Policy Objectives in Canada." Discussion Paper. Ottawa: Department of Agriculture.

Harborszky, Janos. 1984. "Agriculture: The Land Base." Background paper prepared for the Conference: "The Global Possible: Resources, Development and the New Century." Washington, D.C.: World Resources Institute.

Harvey, R.D. 1981. *Government Intervention and Regulation in the Canadian Grain Industry*. Technical Report E/16. Study prepared for the Economic Coundil of Canada and the Institute for Research on Public Policy. Ottawa: Economic Council of Canada.

Hedlin, R.A. 1980. "The Place of Summerfallow in Agriculture on the Canadian Prairies." Winnipeg: University of Manitoba, Department of Soil Science.

Hole, Ted. 1980. "Production and Marketing of Fresh." In *Proceedings of Alberta Horticulture Conference*. Edmonton: Alberta Agriculture.

Hoos, Sidney, ed. 1979. *Agricultural Marketing Boards — An International Perspective*. Cambridge, Mass.: Ballinger.

Hoyt, P.B., M. Nyborg, and H. Ukrainetz. 1981. "Degradation by Acidification." In *Agricultural Land: Our Disappearing Heritage — A Symposium*. Proceedings of the 18th Annual Alberta Soil Science Workshop. Edmonton: Alberta Agriculture.

Huff, B., and J. Graham. 1981. "Resource and Infrastructure Constraints Affecting the Growth of Canadian Agriculture." In *Food for All in a Sustainable World*, edited by Kirit Parikh and Ference Kabar. Laxenberg, Austria: International Institute for Applied Systems Analysis, Food and Agriculture Program.

Jensen, Merle H. 1980. "Energy Alternatives for Horticulture." In *Proceedings of Alberta Horticulture Conference*. Edmonton: Alberta Agriculture.

Josling, Tim. 1981. *Intervention and Regulation in Canadian Agriculture: A Comparison of Costs and Benefits Among Sectors*. Technical Report E/14. Study prepared for the Economic Council of Canada and the Institute for Research on Public Policy. Ottawa: Economic Council of Canada.

Kelly, Michael L. 1981. *Factors Affecting Summerfallow Acreage in Alberta: Summary*. ECA81-17/IB2. Edmonton: Environment Council of Alberta.

_____. 1982. *A Summary of the Economics of Agriculture in Alberta: Selected Issues*. ECA82-17/IB20. Edmonton: Environment Council of Alberta.

Kelly, Michael L., and E. Moreau. 1982. *The Economics of Agriculture in Alberta: Selected Issues*. ECA82-17/IB19. Edmonton: Environment Council of Alberta.

Kerr, William, and S. Ulmer. 1984. "The Importance of Livestock and Meat Processing Industries to Western Growth." Discussion Paper 255. Ottawa: Economic Council of Canada.

Kirsch, Ken. 1983. "Market Status — Vegetable Crops." In *1980 Alberta Horticulture Conference Follow-up Proceedings*. Edmonton: Alberta Horticulture Research Centre.

Koester, U. 1982. *Policy Options for the Grain Economy of the European Community: Implications for Developing Countries*. Washington, D.C.: International Food Policy Research Institute.

Konandreas, P., and H. Hurtado. 1978. "Analysis of Trade Flows in the International Wheat Market." *Canadian Journal of Agricultural Economics* 26 (November).

Krahn, Thomas R. 1980. *Alberta Horticultural Crops Storage Task Force Report*. Edmonton: Alberta Horticulture Research Centre.

Lattimore, Ralph. 1983. "Government Expenditure in Agriculture: A Database for Decision Making." Paper prepared for the federal Department of Agriculture.

Lilley, J. 1982. *An Analysis of Legislation Affecting Agricultural Land in Alberta*. ECA82-A/IB21. Edmonton: Environment Council of Alberta.

_____. 1983. *Dryland Salinity in Alberta*. ECA82-17/IB13. Edmonton: Environment Council of Alberta.

Lindwall, C.W., and S. Dubetz. 1984. "Conservation Tillage." In *Proceedings of the*

Second Annual Western Provincial Conference Rationalization of Water and Soil Research and Management: Soil Erosion and Land Degradation. Saskatoon: University of Saskatchewan.

Loyns, R.M.A., and Colin A. Carter. 1984. *Grains in Western Canadian Economic Development to 1990*. Study prepared for the Economic Council of Canada. Ottawa: Minister of Supply and Services Canada.

Macdonald, Kathleen. 1984. "Rangeland Improvement: Procedures, Costs, and Benefits." Paper presented at the Canadian Society of Soil Science Annual Meeting, Banff, Alberta. Edmonton: Alberta Agriculture, Economic Services Division.

Manning, E.W. 1983. *Agricultural Land Protection Mechanisms in Canada*. ECA83-17/IB31. Edmonton: Environment Council of Alberta.

McGill, W.B. 1982. *Soil Fertility and Land Productivity in Alberta*. ECA82-17/IB16. Edmonton: Environment Council of Alberta.

McMullin, Ronald W. 1984. "Irrigation Management on a Saline Soil." Paper presented at the Canadian Society of Soil Science Annual Meeting, Banff, Alberta. Edmonton: Alberta Agriculture, Conservation and Development Branch.

Meat Industry Research Service Ltd. 1979. *The Economic Viability of Increased Beef Feeding in Alberta*. ECA79-OP/2. Edmonton: Environment Council of Alberta.

Nicholaichuk, W. 1983. "Snow Management." In *Proceedings of the First Annual Western Provincial Conference Rationalization of Water and Soil Research and Management: Soil Salinity*. Edmonton: Alberta Agriculture.

Nicholaichuk, W., and D.W.L. Read. 1980. "Snow Management by Swathing at Alternate Lengths." In *Proceedings of the Soil and Crops Workshop*. Saskatoon: University of Saskatchewan.

Nonnecke, I.L., and D.P. Ormrod. 1977. "Horticultural Crops for Food." In *Canada's Role in the Feeding of the World*. Conference Report. Guelph: University of Guelph.

Nowland, J., J. Dumanski, R. Steward, and W. Saidak. 1982. "Production Base and Production Potential of the Eastern Grain Industry." Paper prepared for the Eastern Grain Conference, Montreal, October.

Prairie Sun Greenhouse. n.d. *An Energy Conservation Project*. Edmonton: Noval Technologies Ltd., a wholly-owned subsidiary of Nova — an Alberta Corporation.

Racz, G.J. 1984. "Research Needs." In *Preparing of the Second Annual Western Provincial Conference Rationalization of Water and Soil Research and Management: Soil Erosion and Land Degradation*. Saskatoon: University of Saskatchewan, 1984.

Rennie, D.A. 1980. "Components of the Agricultural Production System: A Summary Statement." Saskatoon: University of Saskatchewan, Saskatchewan Institute of Pedology.

Rigaus, R. 1971. "Market Shares Analysis Applied to Canadian Wheat Exports." *Canadian Journal of Agricultural Economics* 19.

Robertson, G. 1983. "The Medium-Term Outlook for Canadian Agriculture." Ottawa: Department of Agriculture.

Sanderson, K. 1981. *Agriculture and the Environment*. ECA81-17/IB5. Edmonton: Environment Council of Alberta.

_____. 1982a. *Agriculture and Environment: Summary*. ECA82-17/IB14. Edmonton: Environment Council of Alberta.

_____. 1982b. *Greenhouse Production in Alberta*. ECA82-17/IB24. Edmonton: Environment Council of Alberta.

_____. 1982c. *Irrigation Agriculture in Alberta: Summary*. ECA81-17/IB9. Edmonton: Environment Council of Alberta.

_____. 1982d. *Recreation on Agricultural Land in Alberta: Summary*. ECA82-17/IB9. Edmonton: Environment Council of Alberta.

_____. 1982e. *Soil Fertility, Land Productivity, and Dryland Salinity in Alberta: Summary*. ECA82-17/IB22. Edmonton: Environment Council of Alberta.

Saskatchewan Federation of Agriculture. 1983. "A Greater Commitment to Agriculture." Brief presented to the Royal Commission on the Economic Union and Development Prospects for Canada, November.

Saskatchewan Institute of Pedology. 1984. *Proceedings of the Second Annual Western Provincial Conference Rationalization of Water and Soil Research and Management: Soil Erosion and Land Degradation*. Saskatoon: University of Saskatchewan.

Schaupmeyer, C. 1977. "Production and Marketing Potentials for Vegetables and Special Crops." Paper presented to the Alberta Irrigation Projects Association Annual Meeting, November 30.

Shapiro, Robert G., D.R. Hughes, Broadwith Hughes and Associates Ltd. 1980. "An Analysis of the Effect of Government Regulations on the Canadian Fruit and Vegetable Processing Industry." Working Paper 11. Ottawa: Economic Council of Canada.

Slinkard, A.E. 1984. "The Role of Forages and Legumes in Conservation — Tillage Systems." In *Proceedings of the Second Annual Western Provincial Conference Rationalization of Water and Soil Research and Management: Soil Erosion and Land Degradation*. Saskatoon: University of Saskatchewan.

Smith, Stewart. 1983. "Research Direction in Resource Industries in the 1980's." Address to the Canadian Agriculture Outlook Conference, Ottawa, December.

Soper, R.J. 1980. "The Agricultural Soil and Climatic Resources of the Prairie Provinces." Winnipeg: University of Manitoba, Department of Soil Science.

Statistics Canada. 1972. *Census of Canada 1971: Agriculture*. Ottawa: Statistics Canada.

———. 1982. *Census of Canada 1981: Agriculture*. Ottawa: Statistics Canada.

———. 1983. *Farm Cash Receipts, 1982*. Ottawa: Statistics Canada.

———. 1984. *Cereals and Oilseeds Review, 1983*. Ottawa: Statistics Canada.

Tanner, J. 1983. "Vegetable Industry Review — Production." In *1980 Alberta Horticulture Conference Follow-up Proceedings*. Edmonton: Alberta Horticulture Research Centre.

Taylor, M.C., and K.R. Leggat. 1982. *Agriculture and Public Land Management in Alberta*. ECA82-17/IB23. Edmonton: Environment Council of Alberta.

Thomas, J.B., and R.M. DePauw. n.d. "A Proposed Structure for Western Canadian Varieties of Common Wheat." Mimeographed.

Thompson, P.S. 1981a. *The Agricultural Land Base in Alberta*. ECA81-17/IB3. Edmonton: Environment Council of Alberta.

———. 1981b. *The Agricultural Land Base: Summary*. ECA81-17/IB7. Edmonton: Environment Council of Alberta.

———. 1981c. *Urbanization of Agricultural Land*. ECA81-17/IB10. Edmonton: Environment Council of Alberta.

———. 1981d. *Urbanization of Agricultural Land: Summary*. ECA81-17/IB11. Edmonton: Environment Council of Alberta.

United States. Council on Environmental Quality and the Department of State. 1980. *The Global 2000 Report to the President: Entering the Twenty-First Century*. Washington, D.C.: U.S. Government Printing Office.

Vander Pluym, H.S.A. 1983. "Salinity in Western Canada." In *Proceedings of the First Annual Western Provincial Conference Rationalization of Water and Soil Research and Management: Soil Salinity*. Edmonton: Alberta Agriculture.

Vander Pluym, H.S.A, B. Paterson, and H.M. Holm. 1981. "Degradation by Salination." In *Agricultural Land: Our Disappearing Heritage — A Symposium*. Proceedings of the 18th Annual Alberta Soil Science Workshop. Edmonton: Alberta Agriculture.

Veeman, T., and Michele Veeman. 1984a. *The Future of Grain: Canada's Prospects for Grain, Oilseeds, and Related Industries*. Ottawa: Canadian Institute for Economic Policy.

———. 1984b. "Western Canadian Agriculture: Prospects, Problems and Policy." Paper presented at the Conference on the Economic Transition of Western Canada. Edmonton: University of Alberta.

Vogely, William A. 1984. "Nonfuel Minerals and Materials." Background paper prepared for the Conference: "The Global Possible: Resources, Development and the New Century." Washington, D.C.: World Resources Institute.

Weble, C. 1981a. *The Impacts of Linear Developments, Resource Extraction, and Industry on the Agricultural Land Base*. ECA82-17/IB25. Edmonton: Environment Council of Alberta.

_____. 1982b. *The Impacts of Linear Developments, Resource Extraction, and Industry on the Agricultural Land Base: Summary*. ECA82-17/IB26. Edmonton: Environment Council of Alberta.

Whalley, G. 1980. *The Western Canadian Hog Industry in the Eighties*. Calgary: Canada West Foundation.

Whelan, Eugene. 1983. "Issues for the Agri-Sector to 2000." Brief submitted to the Royal Commission on the Economic Union and Development Prospects for Canada, November 24.

_____. 1984. Speech to the Royal Commission on the Economic Union and Development Prospects for Canada.

Wiebe, John. 1980. "The Alberta Industry." In *Proceedings of Alberta Horticulture Conference*. Edmonton: Alberta Agriculture.

Woloshyn, Peter A. 1984. "An Economic Comparison of Summerfallow Reduction in the Major Soil Zones of Alberta." Edmonton: Alberta Agriculture, Production and Resource Economics Branch.

World Bank. 1982. *Price Prospects for Major Primary Commodities*. Volume III. *Agricultural Raw Materials*. Report No. P14/82. Washington, D.C.: The Bank.

Zentner R.P. 1984. "Economics of Soil Conservation in Western Canada." In *Proceedings of the Second Annual Western Provincial Conference Rationalization of Water and Soil Research and Management: Soil Erosion and Land Degradation*. Saskatoon: University of Saskatchewan.

Energy

Adelman, M.A. 1984. "The International Context." In *Canada's Energy Policy, 1985 and Beyond*, edited by E.A. Carmichael and C.M. Herrera. Toronto: C.D. Howe Institute.

Alberta Report. 1984. *Alberta Coal: Looking Forward*. Edmonton: Government of Alberta.

Alkema, H.J. 1983. "Short Notes: Present and Future Coal Trade Patterns (with particular reference to developing countries)." *Natural Resources Forum* 4, (October).

Anderer, Jeanne. 1983. "A Word on Energy Forecasting." *Options* (International Institute for Applied Systems Analysis).

Aylsworth, Jim. 1983. "Coal, Coal, Coal, Coal." *Canadian Mining Journal* (February).

Bain, W.A. 1984. "Prospects for Energy in Western Canada and Implications for Economic Growth." Notes for a Presentation to the Western Economic Transition Conference. Edmonton, November 1984.

Battle, Ellen F., Gordon S. Gislason, and Gordon W. Douglas. 1983. *Potential Benefits and Costs of Canadian Electricity Exports. Client Research Report No. 83-1*. Calgary: Canadian Energy Research Institute.

Bérubé, Yves. 1984. "Notes for Speech [by the Minister of Education of Quebec] to New York State Legislators." Quebec, August 21.

Blix, Hans. 1983. "Energy Supplies in the Long Term." *Skandinaviska Enskilda Banken Quarterly Review* 4: 100–104.

Bourque, Michèle. 1984. *Évolution du prix international de pétrole, de 1870 à nos jours*. Study prepared for the Economic Council of Canada. Ottawa: Minister of Supply and Services Canada.

Bradley, Paul G. 1984. *Costs and Supply of Natural Gas from Alberta: An Empirical Analysis*. Study prepared for the Economic Council of Canada. Ottawa: Minister of Supply and Services Canada.

Campbell, Paul G. 1984. *Exhaustible Resources and Economic Growth: The Case of Uranium Mining in Saskatchewan*. Study prepared for the Economic Council of Canada. Ottawa: Minister of Supply and Services Canada.

Canada. Department of Energy, Mines and Resources. 1983. *Long-Term Energy Demand Outlook: Summer '83 Forecast*. Ottawa: The Department, Energy Strategy Branch, Energy Market Analysis and Statistics Division.

Canadian Electrical Association. 1982. *Nuclear Energy in Canada: A National Policy*. Montreal: The Association.

———. 1983a. *A National Policy Regarding Electricity Export and Interchanges with the United States of America*. Montreal: The Association.

———. 1983b. *Outline of Submission by the Canadian Electrical Association to the Royal Commission on the Economic Union and Development Prospects for Canada*. Montreal: The Association.

———. 1983c. *Submission by the Canadian Electrical Association to the Royal Commission on the Economic Union and Development Prospects for Canada*. Montreal: The Association.

Canadian Energy Research Institute. 1983. *Workshop on Benefit-Cost Analysis in Energy Economics*. Ottawa: Minister of Supply and Services Canada.

———. 1984. "A Review of Oil and Gas Drilling Activity Forecasting Techniques." Working Paper 84-1. Calgary: The Institute.

Canadian Petroleum Association and Independent Petroleum Association of Canada. 1983. *Submission to the Royal Commission on the Economic Union and Development Prospects for Canada*. Calgary.

Carmichael, Edward A., and Corina M. Herrera, eds. 1984. *Canada's Energy Policy, 1985 and Beyond*. Toronto: C.D. Howe Institute.

Daly, Michael J., and Someshwar Rao. *Productivity Growth, Economies of Scale, and Capacity Utilization in the Canadian Electric Power Industry. The Case of Ontario Hydro*. Study prepared for the Economic Council of Canada. Ottawa: Minister of Supply and Services Canada.

Dawson, John A. 1983. "Development Options for Maritime Coal." Working Paper 83-1. Calgary: Canadian Energy Research Institute.

Duhaime, Yves L. 1984. "Notes for Remarks [by the Minister of Energy and Resources] to the Conference on Canada/U.S.A. Business Perspectives." Montreal, October 1.

Dyack, Brenda. 1983. "Western Canada's Minerals — Coals." Ottawa: Economic Council of Canada 1983. Mimeographed.

Eck, Ted R. 1983. "The U.S. Natural Gas Market 'Perspective of a Producer'." In *Proceedings of the International Gas Markets Conference*, edited by S.S. Streifel. Calgary: Canadian Energy Research Institute.

Economic Council of Canada. 1978. *Energy Production from Oil Sands and Heavy Oils*. Edmonton: Environment Council of Alberta.

———. 1984a. *Au Courant* 4 (3).

———. 1984b. *Au Courant* 5 (1).

———. 1984c. *Oil and Gas Price Changes Would Develop Economy. News Release*. Ottawa: The Council.

———. 1984d. *Submission by the Chairman of the Economic Council of Canada to the Standing Senate Committee on Energy and Natural Resources*. Ottawa: May 24.

———. 1984e. *Western Transition*. Ottawa: Minister of Supply and Services Canada.

Eglington, Peter, and Maris Uffelman. 1984a. *An Economic Analysis of Hydrocarbon Developments in the Beaufort Sea*. Study prepared for the Economic Council of Canada. Ottawa: Minister of Supply and Services Canada.

———. 1984b. *An Economic Analysis of the Oilsands Policy in Canada — The Case of Alsands and Wolf Lake*. Study prepared for the Economic Council of Canada. Ottawa: Minister of Supply and Services Canada.

———. 1984c. *An Economic Analysis of the Venture Development Project and Hibernia*. Study prepared for the Economic Council of Canada. Ottawa: Minister of Supply and Services Canada.

———. 1984d. *Observed Costs of Oil and Gas Reserves in Alberta, 1957–79*. Study prepared for the Economic Council of Canada. Ottawa: Minister of Supply and Services Canada.

Eglington, Peter, and James A. Nugent. 1984. *An Economic Analysis of Enhanced Oil Recovery in Conventional Light Oil Pools in Alberta*. Study prepared for the Economic Council of Canada. Ottawa: Minister of Supply and Services Canada.

Foster, J.S. 1983. "The World Energy Conference and International Energy Suppliers." *Skandinaviska Enskilda Banken Quarterly Review* 4: 84–89.

Gas Energy Review. 1984. "Status of Canadian/U.S. Natural Gas Arrangements." *Gas Energy Review* (January).

Grignon, Michael M. 1984. "Seminar on Long-Term Prospects for Canadian Economy: Issues and Estimates." Sponsored by the Royal Commission on the Economic Union and Development Prospects for Canada, January 10.

Haessel, W. 1983. "Issues in Canadian-U.S. Energy Trade." Paper prepared for the Research Symposium on Canada-U.S. Free Trade Issues, sponsored by the Royal Commission on the Economic Union and Development Prospects for Canada, October 6.

Haughey, Douglas J. 1981. *Crude Oil Supply and Demand: Major Issues and Alternate Scenarios*. Calgary: Canadian Energy Research Institute.

Haughey, Douglas, and Donald A. Bruton. 1983. *The Impacts of Crude Oil Supply Changes and Supply Allocation*. Calgary: Canadian Energy Research Institute.

Haughey, Douglas, and Leonard Coad. 1984. *Exportable Natural Gas Surplus: Sensitivity to Oil Prices and Economic Growth*. Calgary: Canadian Energy Research Institute.

Hazledine, Tim, Steve Guiton, Lorraine Froehlich, and Pierre Mercier. *OPEC and the Value of Canada's Energy Resources: A Long-Range Simulation Model*. Study prepared for the Economic Council of Canada. Ottawa: Minister of Supply and Services Canada.

Helliwell, J.F., M.E. MacGregor, and A. Plourde. 1983. "The National Energy Program Meets Falling World Oil Prices." *Canadian Public Policy* 9 (September): 284–96.

International Institute for Applied Systems Analysis. 1983. *Options* (March).

Leader, H.H. Roger. 1983. *IIASA '83 Scenario of Energy Development: Summary*. Laxenberg, Austria: International Institute for Applied Systems Analysis.

MacMillan, J.A. 1984. "Draft Comments on Western Transition." Edmonton: University of Alberta Seminar, November 8.

Marshall, R.T. 1984. "Coal's Role in the Future Economic Development of the West." The Conference on Western Economic Transition. Edmonton, November 8.

McCormack, T.W. 1984. "Long-Term Forecast Comparison: Long-Term Prospects for the Canadian Economy: Issues and Estimates." Ottawa: Data Resources of Canada, January 10.

McDonald, Alan. 1981. *Energy in a Finite World. Executive Report 4*. Laxenberg, Austria: International Institute for Applied Systems Analysis.

Miles, Peter. 1983. "Charts Accompanying a Talk on Energy Issues to a Seminar on Long-Term Projections — Issues and Estimates — a Preliminary Report. Ottawa: Research Staff of the Royal Commission on the Economic Union and Development Prospects for Canada.

Mossavar-Rahmani, Bijan. 1983. "The OPEC Natural Gas Dilemma." In *Proceedings of the International Gas Markets Conference*, edited by S.S. Streifel. Calgary: Canadian Energy Research Institute.

National Energy Board. 1982. *Reasons for Decision: In the Matter of Phase I — The Review Phase of the Gas Export Omnibus Hearing, 1982*. Ottawa: The Board.

———. 1983a. *Request for Submissions*. Ottawa: The Board.

———. 1983b. *NEB Update of Energy Supply and Demand, 1983–2005*. Ottawa: The Board.

———. 1984a. *Canadian Energy Supply and Demand 1983–2005: Summary Report*. Ottawa: The Board.

———. 1984b. *Canadian Energy Supply and Demand 1983–2005: Technical Report*. Ottawa: The Board.

Nelles, D., ed. 1984. *The Canadian Economy to 2005: Assumptions and Summary Workshop* 1-84. Ottawa: Informetrica.

Niering, Frank E. 1983. "Brighter Outlook for Oil Industry." *Petroleum Economist* (October).

Nixon, A.J. 1981. "Natural Gas Pricing in Canada: An Economic Analysis." Working Paper 81-2. Calgary: Canadian Energy Research Institute.

Norrie, K.H., and M.B. Percy. 1984a. "Energy Price Increases, Economic Rents, and Industrial Structure in a Small Regional Economy." Discussion Paper 220. Ottawa: Economic Council of Canada.

Oil and Gas Journal. 1983. *Oil and Gas Journal.* 81(52)(December 26).

Ontario Hydro. Systems Planning Division. 1982. *Cost Comparison of Candu Nuclear and Coal-Fuelled Generating Stations.* Toronto: Ontario Hydro.

_____. 1984. *Cost Comparison of Candu Nuclear and Coal-Fuelled Generating Stations Report 620SP.* Toronto: Ontario Hydro.

Osten, J.A. 1983/84. "Changes in the Energy Forecast, Executive Summary." *Canadian Energy Review* 3 (2) (Winter).

Owen, A.D. 1983. "The Economics of Uranium Demand." *Resources Policy* (June).

Portney, Paul R., and Ruth B. Haas, eds. 1982. *Current Issues in Natural Resources Policy.* Washington, D.C.: Resources for the Future.

Quarterly Energy Review. 1983. "Regional Review: Summary and Outlook." *Quarterly Energy Review* 1 (3).

Reddy, Amulya K.N. 1984. "Energy: Issues and Opportunities." Background paper for the Conference: "The Global Possible: Resources, Development and the New Century." Washington, D.C.: World Resources Institute.

Scarfe, Brian L. 1983. "The New Oil Price Scenario and the Chrétien-Zaozirny Agreement: A Comment." Edmonton: University of Alberta. Mimeographed.

_____. 1984. "New Technologies: Oil Sands." Edmonton: University of Alberta. Mimeographed.

_____. 1985. "Energy Policy and Industry Activity: A Rejoinder." Edmonton: University of Alberta. Mimeographed.

Sharp, Mitchell. 1983. "Canada's Role in the Expanding International Gas Markets." In *Proceedings of the International Gas Markets Conference,* edited by S.S. Streifel. Calgary: Canadian Energy Research Institute.

Shimizu, Shun-Ichi. 1983. "Characteristics of the Japanese LNG Market and Keys to Success in LNG Projects." In *Proceedings of the International Gas Markets Conference,* edited by S.S. Streifel. Calgary: Canadian Energy Research Institute.

Skandinaviska Enskilda Banken. 1983. *Quarterly Review* 4.

Slagorsky, Charles. 1982. *Alternative Transportation Fuels in Canada.* Calgary: Canadian Energy Research Institute.

Statistics Canada. 1984. *Trade of Canada, Exports.* Ottawa: Statistics Canada.

_____. 1985. *The Labour Force: March 1985.* Ottawa: Statistics Canada.

Streifel, Shane, ed. 1982. *World Oil Market Conference Proceedings.* Calgary: Canadian Energy Research Institute.

_____. 1983. *Proceedings of the International Gas Markets Conference.* Calgary: Canadian Energy Research Institute.

Sumner, Brian D. 1983. "The Potential for Energy Substitution in Canada." Working Paper 83-6. Calgary: Canadian Energy Research Institute.

Varangu, Kristi E. 1983. *Development Options for British Columbia Coal.* Working Paper 83-3. Calgary: Canadian Energy Resource Institute.

Waverman, Leonard. 1984. "Canadian Energy Policy After 1985: Lessons from The Present." In *Canada's Energy Policy: 1955 and Beyond,* edited by E.A. Carmichael and C.M. Herrera. Toronto: C.D. Howe Institute.

Wilkie, Gary. 1983. *Canadian Energy Policy and Canada's Balance of Payments.* Downsview: York University, Faculty of Administrative Studies.

Wilkinson, B.W. 1984. "Energy Revenue Sharing." In *Canada's Energy Policy: 1985 and Beyond,* edited by E.A. Carmichael and C.M. Herrera. Toronto: C.D. Howe Institute.

Whillans, R. 1983. "Uranium Uranium Uranium Uranium." *Canadian Mining Journal* (February).

World Bank. 1984. *Price Prospects for Major Primary Commodities.* Vol. 5. *Energy.* Washington, D.C.: The Bank.

Youston, D.J. 1980. *Summary Report on Environmental Effects and Social Costs of Air Pollution*. Toronto: Ontario Hydro.

Zuker, Richard C., and Glenn P. Jenkins. 1983. *Blue Gold: Hydro Electric Rent In Canada*. Study prepared for the Economic Council of Canada. Ottawa: Minister of Supply and Services Canada.

Fisheries

Aiken, D.E. 1983. "Aquaculture in Atlantic Canada." Study prepared for the Department of Fisheries and Oceans, Fisheries and Environment Sciences Branch. Ottawa: Department of Fisheries and Oceans.

Anderson and Associates. 1980. *A Development Plan for Atlantic Salmon Aquaculture in the Maritimes Region*. Report to Department of Fisheries and Oceans. Ottawa.

Boulanger, Y., and Lars E. Hansen. 1982. "Survey of Aquaculture Practices in Quebec." Draft paper.

Bourne, N., and J.R. Brett. 1983. "Aquaculture in British Columbia." Vancouver: Department of Fisheries and Oceans, Fisheries Research Branch, Pacific Biological Station.

Campbell, Harry F. 1981. "The Bay of Fundy Herring Fishery." *The Public Regulation of Commercial Fisheries in Canada*. Case Study No. 5. Technical Report 20. Ottawa: Economic Council of Canada.

Canada. Commission on Pacific Fisheries Policy. 1982. *Turning the Tide: A New Policy for Canada's Pacific Fisheries*. (Peter H. Pearse.) Ottawa: Minister of Supply and Services Canada.

_____. Department of Fisheries and the Environment. 1978. *Food from Water: Fisheries and Aquaculture*. Fisheries and Marine Service Special Publication.

_____. Department of Fisheries and Oceans. 1980. *Annual Statistical Review of Fisheries, 1978*. Ottawa: The Department.

_____. 1983. *Annual Statistical Review of Fisheries, 1981*. Ottawa: The Department.

_____. 1984a. *Fish Health Protection Regulations: Manual of Compliance*. Fisheries Marine Service. Special Publication 31 (Revised).

_____. 1984b. "The Buy-Back Program." *Information* (June).

_____. 1984c. "Community Adjustment and Economic Development Measures." *Information* (June).

_____. 1984d. "Developing the Sport Fishing Sector." *Information* (June).

_____. 1984e. "The Financial Condition of the Pacific Salmon Fleet." *Information* (June).

_____. 1984f. "Legislation to Restructure the Pacific Fisheries: An Overview." *Information* (June).

_____. 1984g. "Native Participation in the Fisheries." *Information* (June).

_____. 1984h. "New Regulatory Measures for the Commercial Pacific Salmon Fisheries: Rationale and Highlights." *Information* (June).

_____. 1984i. "Status of Pacific Salmon Stocks." *Information* (June).

_____. Department of Fisheries and Oceans and Science Council of Canada. 1983. *Report of the Proceedings of the National Aquaculture Conference*, St. Andrews, N.B., July 10–14, 1983. Ottawa: The Department.

_____. Task Force on Atlantic Fisheries. 1982. *Navigating Troubled Waters: A New Policy for the Atlantic Fisheries; Highlights and Recommendations*. (Michael J.L. Kirby, Chairman.) Ottawa: Minister of Supply and Services Canada.

Castledine, Allan J. 1982. "An Evaluation of Fish Feed Supply in Canada." Policy Discussion Paper. Ottawa: Department of Fisheries and Oceans, Fisheries Research Directorate.

Crutchfield, James A. 1981. "The Pacific Halibut Fishery." *The Public Regulation of Commercial Fisheries in Canada*. Case Study No. 2. Technical Report 17. Ottawa: Economic Council of Canada.

Daneau, Marcel. 1984. "Quebec-Canada Relations with Respect to Ocean Fisheries." Quebec: Laval University, Faculty of Social Sciences, Department of Economics.

Farrell, Kenneth R., Fred H. Sanderson, Trang T. Vo, and Michael F. Brewer. 1984. "Meeting Future Needs for United States Food, Fiber and Forest Products." Washington, D.C.: Resources for the Future.

Fisheries Research Board of Canada. 1977. *Fisheries and Aquatic Sciences in Canada: An Overview*. Ottawa: Minister of Supply and Services Canada.

Dawson, John A. 1983. "Development Options for Maritime Coal." Working Paper 83-1. Calgary: Canadian Energy Research Institute.

Duhaime, Yves L. 1984. "Notes for Remarks [by the Minister of Energy and Resources] to the Conference on Canada/U.S.A. Business Perspectives." Montreal, October 1.

Dyack, Brenda. 1983. "Western Canada's Minerals — Coals." Ottawa: Economic Council of Canada 1983. Mimeographed.
Streifel. Calgary: Canadian Energy Research Institute.

Economic Council of Canada. 1978. *Energy Production from Oil Sands and Heavy Oils*. Edmonton: Environment Council of Alberta.

———. 1984a. *Au Courant* 4 (3).

———. 1984b. *Au Courant* 5 (1).

———. 1984c. *Oil and Gas Price Changes Would Develop Economy. News Release*. Ottawa: The Council.

———. 1984d. *Submission by the Chairman of the Economic Council of Canada to the Standing Senate Committee on Energy and Natural Resources*. Ottawa: May 24.

———. 1984e. *Western Transition*. Ottawa: Minister of Supply and Services Canada.

Eglington, Peter, and Maris Uffelman. 1984a. *An Economic Analysis of Hydrocarbon Developments in the Beaufort Sea*. Study prepared for the Economic Council of Canada. Ottawa: Minister of Supply and Services Canada.

———. 1984b. *An Economic Analysis of the Oilsands Policy in Canada — The Case of Alsands and Wolf Lake*. Study prepared for the Economic Council of Canada. Ottawa: Minister of Supply and Services Canada.

———. 1984c. *An Economic Analysis of the Venture Development Project and Hibernia*. Study prepared for the Economic Council of Canada. Ottawa: Minister of Supply and Services Canada.

———. 1984d. *Observed Costs of Oil and Gas Reserves in Alberta, 1957–79*. Study prepared for the Economic Council of Canada. Ottawa: Minister of Supply and Services Canada.

Eglington, Peter, and James A. Nugent. 1984. *An Economic Analysis of Enhanced Oil Recovery in Conventional Light Oil Pools in Alberta*. Study prepared for the Economic Council of Canada. Ottawa: Minister of Supply and Services Canada.

Foster, J.S. 1983. "The World Energy Conference and International Energy Suppliers." *Skandinaviska Enskilda Banken Quarterly Review* 4: 84–89.

Gas Energy Review. 1984. "Status of Canadian/U.S. Natural Gas Arrangements." *Gas Energy Review* (January).

Grignon, Michael M. 1984. "Seminar on Long-Term Prospects for Canadian Economy: Issues and Estimates." Sponsored by the Royal Commission on the Economic Union and Development Prospects for Canada, January 10.

Haessel, W. 1983. "Issues in Canadian-U.S. Energy Trade." Paper prepared for the Research Symposium on Canada-U.S. Free Trade Issues, sponsored by the Royal Commission on the Economic Union and Development Prospects for Canada, October 6.

Haughey, Douglas J. 1981. *Crude Oil Supply and Demand: Major Issues and Alternate Scenarios*. Calgary: Canadian Energy Research Institute.

Haughey, Douglas, and Donald A. Bruton. 1983. *The Impacts of Crude Oil Supply Changes and Supply Allocation*. Calgary: Canadian Energy Research Institute.

Haughey, Douglas, and Leonard Coad. 1984. *Exportable Natural Gas Surplus: Sensitivity to Oil Prices and Economic Growth*. Calgary: Canadian Energy Research Institute.

Hazledine, Tim, Steve Guiton, Lorraine Froehlich, and Pierre Mercier. *OPEC and the Value of Canada's Energy Resources: A Long-Range Simulation Model*. Study prepared for the Economic Council of Canada. Ottawa: Minister of Supply and Services Canada.

Helliwell, J.F., M.E. MacGregor, and A. Plourde. 1983. "The National Energy Program Meets Falling World Oil Prices." *Canadian Public Policy* 9 (September): 284–96.

International Institute for Applied Systems Analysis. 1983. *Options* (March).

Schrank, W.E., E. Tsoa, and N. Roy. 1984. *An Econometric Model of the Newfoundland Groundfishery: Estimation and Simulation*. Ottawa: Department of Fisheries and Oceans.

Science Council of Canada. 1983. *In Touch* 1 (October–November).

———. 1984. *Aquaculture: A Development Plan for Canada*. Ottawa: The Council.

Scott, Anthony. "The Maritime Lobster Fishery" *The Public Regulation of Commercial Fisheries in Canada. Case Study No. 1*. Technical Report 16. Ottawa: Economic Council of Canada.

Scott, Anthony, and Phillip Neher. 1981. *The Public Regulation of Commercial Fisheries in Canada*. Ottawa: Economic Council of Canada.

Statistics Canada. 1977. *Summary of External Trade, 1976*. Ottawa: Statistics Canada.

———. 1984. *Summary of External Trade, 1983*. Ottawa: Statistics Canada.

Technology, Growth and Employment: Report to the Seven Heads of State and Government and to the Representatives of the European Communities. 1983. Versailles Summit, June 4, 5 and 6, 1982. Paris.

Weeks, E.P., and L. Mazany. 1983. *The Future of the Atlantic Fisheries*. Montreal: Institute for Research on Public Policy.

Wildsmith, Bruce H.. 1984. *Federal Aquaculture Regulation. No. 1252*. Ottawa: Department of Fisheries and Oceans, Fisheries Research Directorate, Aquaculture and Resource Development Branch.

———. 1985. "Fisheries, Harmonization and the Economic Union." In *Case Studies in the Division of Powers*, volume 62 of the research studies prepared for the Royal Commission on the Economic Union and Development Prospects for Canada. Toronto: University of Toronto Press.

Wilen, James E. 1981. "The British Columbia Roe Herring Industry." *The Public Regulation of Commercial Fisheries in Canada. Case Study No. 6*. Technical Report 21. Ottawa: Economic Council of Canada.

Forest Products

Adams, Darius M., Richard W. Haynes, George F. Dutrow, Richard L. Barber, and Joseph M. Vasievich, 1982. "Private Investment in Forest Management and the Long-Term Supply of Timber." *American Agricultural Economics Association*. Iowa: Iowa State University, Department of Economics.

Armson, K.A. 1983. *Canadian Forestry Association Brief to the Royal Commission on the Economic Union and Development Prospects for Canada*. Ottawa: Canadian Forestry Association, September.

Bank of Canada. *Bank of Canada Review*.

Boyd, George. 1982. "Pulp Production Costs Compared." *Pulp and Paper International* (June 1982): 65–68.

Bowonder, B. 1983. "Forest Depletion: Some Policy Options." *Resources Policy* (September).

Canada. 1984a. *Federal Government Response to the Recommendations of the Forest Industries Advisory Committee*. Ottawa: Minister of Supply and Services Canada.

———. 1984b. *Canada/Manitoba Forest Renewal Agreement*. Ottawa: Minister of Supply and Services Canada.

———. Department of the Environment. 1981a. *A Forest Sector Strategy for Canada Human Resources Component*. Ottawa: Minister of Supply and Services.

———. 1981b. *A Forest Sector Strategy for Canada Discussion Paper*. Ottawa: Minister of Supply and Services, September 1981.

———. 1983. *Departmental Strategic Plan 1984–1989*. Ottawa: Minister of Supply and Services Canada.

———. 1982. *Canada's Forests, 1981*. Ottawa: Minister of Supply and Services Canada.

———. Department of the Environment. 1982. *Policy Statement: A Framework for Forest Renewal*. Ottawa: Minister of Supply and Services Canada.

———. Department of External Affairs. 1983. *A Review of Canadian Trade Policy: A Background Document to Canadian Trade Policy for the 1980s*. Ottawa: Minister of Supply and Services Canada.

Canadian Council of Resources and Environment Ministers. 1979. *Forestry Imperatives for Canada: A Proposal for Forest Policy in Canada*. Prepared for the Annual meeting of the Canadian Council of Resource and Environment Ministers, June 6–7.

Canadian Forest Congress. 1980. *Proceedings: The Forest Imperative*. Montreal: Canadian Pulp and Paper Association.

Canadian Pulp and Paper Association. 1983. *Submission to the Royal Commission on the Economic Union and Development Prospects for Canada*. Montreal: Canadian Pulp and Paper Association.

———. 1984a. "Outlook for the Canadian Pulp and Paper Industry in 1984." Montreal: Canadian Pulp and Paper Association.

———. 1984b. "The Outlook for the Canadian Pulp and Paper Industry in 1984." Press Release. Montreal: Canadian Pulp and Paper Association.

———. 1984c. *Response to Challenges and Choices — the Interim Report of the Royal Commission on the Economic Union and Development Prospects for Canada*. Montreal: Canadian Pulp and Paper Association.

Copithorne, Lawrence. 1979. *Natural Resources and Regional Disparities*. Study prepared for the Economic Council of Canada. Ottawa: Minister of Supply and Services Canada.

Denny, M., M. Fuss, and J.D. May. 1981. "Intertemporal Changes in Regional Productivity in Canadian Manufacturing." *Canadian Journal of Economics* 14 (3) (August): 390–408.

Diesen, Magnus. 1983. "Prospects for Publication Papers." *Pulp and Paper International* (March): 44–48.

Domtar, Inc. 1984a. *Domtar Forest Products Hybrid Poplar Program 1984*. Cornwall: Domtar Forest Products.

———. 1984b. *Rapport Annuel 1983*. Montreal: Domtar Inc.

Economic Council of Canada. 1984. *Western Transition*. Ottawa: Minister of Supply and Services Canada.

The Economist. 1984. "Economic and Financial Indicators 1, 2." *The Economist* 291 (April 7), pp. 101–102.

Ehrntooth, Eric. 1981. "Chequered Future for Market Pulp Supply." Second PPI Symposium. *Pulp and Paper International* (September): 76–78.

Environment Conservation Authority. 1977a. *The Environmental Effects of Timber Production in Alberta*. Alberta: The Authority.

———. 1977b. *Perspectives II: The Forest Industry in Alberta*. Alberta: The Authority.

———. 1977c. *Terms of Reference and Background Information on the Environmental Effects of Forestry Operations in Alberta*. Alberta: The Authority.

Environment Council of Alberta. 1979. *The Environmental Effects of Forestry Operations in Alberta*. Edmonton: The Council.

Farrell, Kenneth R., Fred H. Sanderson, Trang T. Vo, and Michael F. Brewer. 1984. "Meeting Future Needs for United States Food, Fibre and Forest Products." Washington, D.C.: Resources for the Future.

Food and Agriculture Organization of the United Nations (FAO). 1977. "Forestry Paper: World Pulp and Paper Demand, Supply and Trade." Rome: FAO.

———. 1982a. *World Forest Products, Demand and Supply, 1990–2000*. Rome: FAO.

_____. 1982b. "World Paper and Paperboard Consumption Outlook." Report of an Industry Working Party. Rome: FAO.

_____. 1983. *1981 Year Book of Forest Products*. Rome: FAO, 1983.

Forest Industries Advisory Committee. 1983. *Interim Report, August 1983*. Ottawa: Minister of Supply and Services Canada.

Graff, Peter. 1983. "Paper Consumption — A Global Forecast." *Pulp and Paper International* (May): 52–58.

Haas, Leonard. 1982. "Finncell Pulp Symposium — Short Supply by '85?" *Pulp and Paper International* (July).

Hagler, Robert. 1983. "Supply Side Forestry in the U.S. South." *Pulp and Paper International* (July).

Haley, David. 1984. "The Forest Tenure System as a Constraint on Efficient Timber Management — Problems and Solutions." Edmonton: Conference on the Economic Transition of Western Canada held at the University of Alberta, November 8–9.

Hall, Claes G. 1984. "Brazil and Its Economy — A Few Highlights." Mimeographed.

Heaps, Terry. 1984. "The Sensitivity of the Present Value of Stumpage Under Alternative Criteria for Harvesting." Ottawa: Economic Council of Canada.

Hohol, Roman. 1984. "Export: The Canadian Pulp and Paper Industry." *Pulp and Paper Journal* (March).

Industrial Forestry Ltd. 1982. "Provincial Changes for Timber in Canada." Prince George: Industrial Forestry Services Ltd.

MacDonald, Cecil. 1983. "Tropics Could be Major Fiber Source." *Pulp and Paper International* (July): 26–28.

McClay, Brian. 1984. "Remarks to the Wood Pulp Section Annual Meeting of February 1, 1984." Montreal: Canadian Pulp and Paper Association.

O'Donoghue, David. 1982. "Confidence in the Print Media." *Pulp and Paper International* (December): 36–40.

Ottens, Hans, and Keith L. Aird. 1980. "An Outlook for Timber Utilization in Canada." A conference paper. Ottawa: Canadian Forestry Service.

Peat Marwick and Partners. 1977. *Analysis of Wood Costs in the North American Forest Products Industries*. Ottawa: Department of Industry, Trade and Commerce.

Percy, M.B. 1984. "The Forestry Industry of the West." Ottawa: Economic Council of Canada.

Phelps, Robert B. 1979. "Projected Timber Use by Product and Market Sector." Washington, D.C.: U.S. Dept. of Agriculture, Forest Service.

Pinard, Raymond R. 1984. "The Forest Industry: Main Driving Force of Quebec's Industry." 1983–84 Hautes Études Commerciales Lectures. Montreal: DOMTAR Inc.

Quebec. 1984a. "La politique forestière du Québec: Problématique d'ensemble." Quebec: Ministry of Energy and Natural Resources.

_____. 1984b. *Quebec's Forests and Forest Industry: Statistical Information*. 1984 edition. Quebec: Ministry of Energy and Natural Resources.

Reed, F.L.C. and Associates Ltd. 1978. *Forest Management in Canada*. Volumes I and II. Ottawa: Forest Management Institute of Canada.

_____. 1980. "Recent Reductions in the Canadian Timber Base." Appendix IV. In *Proceedings of the Canadian Forest Congress: The Forest Imperative*. Toronto.

Sandwell Management Consultants Ltd. 1977. *Analysis of the Manufacturing Costs in the North American Forest Products Industries*. Ottawa: Department of Industry, Trade and Commerce.

_____. 1981. *Forest Products Industry, B.C. Regions: Manufacturing Cost Update*. Victoria, B.C.: Ministry of Small Business Development.

Science Council of Canada. 1983. *Canada's Threatened Forests*. Ottawa: The Council.

Sedjo, Robert A. 1983a. *The Comparative Economics of Plantation Forestry: A Global Assessment*. Washington, D.C.: Resources for the Future.

_____. 1983b. ed. *Governmental Interventions, Social Needs, and the Management of U.S. Forests*. Washington, D.C.: Resources for the Future.

Smyth, J.H., K.L. Ramsay, and D.E. Barron. 1984. *Forest Management Expenditures in Canada, 1977–81*. Ottawa: Department of the Environment, Canadian Forestry Service.

Spears, John, and Edward S. Ayensu. 1984. "Sectoral Paper on Forestry." Background paper for the Conference: "The Global Possible: Resources, Development and the New Century." Washington, D.C.: World Resources Institute.

Statistics Canada. 1984. *Summary of External Trade: December 1983*. Ottawa: Statistics Canada.

———. 1985. *Historical Labour Force Statistics*. Ottawa: Statistics Canada.

Udell, Jan G. 1983. *The Outlook for the Economy and Newsprint Consumption in the U.S.A.* Montreal: ANPA Newsprint Committee of Canadian Pulp and Paper Association, Newsprint Section.

United States. Department of Agriculture. Forest Service. 1983. *America's Renewable Resources: A Supplement to the 1979 Assessment of the Forest and Rangeland Situation in the United States*. Washington, D.C.: The Department.

Wansbrough, John. 1985. "Sectoral View of the Longer Term: Forest Products." In *Long-term Economic Prospects for Canada: A Symposium*, volume 23 of the research studies prepared for the Royal Commission on the Economic Union and Development Prospects for Canada. Toronto: University of Toronto Press.

Minerals

Albrecht, Oscar W., Ernest H. Manuel Jr., and Fritz W. Efaw. 1981. "Recycling in the U.S.A." *Resources Policy* (September).

Anderson, David L. 1983. *The Saskatchewan Potash Industry: Alternative Strategies for Future Development*. Study prepared for the Economic Council of Canada. Ottawa: Minister of Supply and Services Canada.

———. 1984. *Foreign Investment Control in the Canadian Mineral Sector: Lessons from the Australian Experience*. Kingston: Queen's University, Centre for Resource Studies.

Barclays Bank. 1984. *Countertrade — What Is It and Is It Here to Stay?* London: The Bank.

Barnett, H., and J. Myers. 1984. "Minerals and Economic Growth." In *Economics of the Mineral Industry*, 4th ed., edited by W.A. Vogely. New York: American Institute of Mining, Metallurgical and Petroleum Engineers.

Beigie, Carl, and Alfred O. Hero Jr.. 1980. *Natural Resources in US-Canadian Relations*. Vols. I and II. Boulder, Col.: Westview Press.

Bohi, Douglas R., and Michael A. Toman. 1983. *Understanding Nonrenewable Resource Supply Behavior*. Washington, D.C.: Resources for the Future.

Boyd, B.W. 1982. *Sulphur Market Profile*. Ottawa: Department of Energy, Mines and Resources.

Buck, W. Keith. 1984. "Minerals Canada — Looking Outward." *CRS Special Paper*.

Bumstead, David L. 1984. "The Competition for Canadian Producers of Copper, Lead, Zinc, Gold and Silver." St. Jovite, Quebec: Metal Mining Association, June 18–19.

Business Week. 1984. "The Death of Mining." December 17.

Butt, N.A., and T. Atkinson. 1982. "Shortfalls in Minerals Investments." *Resources Policy* (December).

Cairns, Robert D. 1981. "An Application of Depletion Theory to a Base Metal: Canadian Nickel." *Canadian Journal of Economics* 14 (November).

Calaway, Lee, and W.C.J. Rensburg. 1982. "U.S. Strategic Minerals, Policy Options." *Resources Policy* (June).

Callot, Francis, G. 1981. "World Mineral Production and Consumption in 1978." *Resources Policy* (March).

Canada. Department of Energy, Mines and Resources. 1982a. *Mineral Policy. A Discussion Paper*. Ottawa: Minister of Supply and Services Canada.

———. 1982b. *Statistical Summary of the Canadian Mineral Industry*. Ottawa: Minister of Supply and Services Canada.

_____. 1983a. *Annual Review of the Canadian Mineral Industry in 1982*. Ottawa: Minister of Supply and Services Canada.

_____. 1983b. *Canadian Mineral Survey*. Ottawa: Minister of Supply and Services Canada.

_____. 1983c. *Sulphur Market Profile*. Ottawa: Minister of Supply and Services Canada.

_____. 1984a. *Canada's NonFerrous Metals Industry: Nickel and Copper. A Special Report*. Ottawa: Minister of Supply and Services Canada.

_____. 1984b. *The Canadian Mineral Industry Monthly Report* (October). Ottawa: Minister of Supply and Services Canada.

_____. 1984c. *Canadian Minerals Yearbook, 1981*. Ottawa: Minister of Supply and Services Canada.

_____. 1984d. *Canadian Mines: Perspective from 1983*. Ottawa: Minister of Supply and Services Canada.

_____. 1984e. *Canadian Reserves as of January 1, 1983*. Ottawa: Minister of Supply and Services Canada.

_____. 1984f. *The Medium Term Outlook for Minerals* (a preliminary view). Ottawa: Minister of Supply and Services Canada.

Caragata, Partick James. 1984. *National Resources and International Bargaining Power: Canada's Mineral Options*. Kingston: Queen's University, Centre for Resource Studies.

Clark, Joel P., and Martin R. Neutra. 1983. "Mining Manganese Nodules." *Resources Policy* (June).

Cooney, Jim. 1984. "Issues Management and Mining." *CRS Perspectives* 19 (October).

Crowson, P.C.F. 1982. "Mineral Development, Financing and Cooperation." *Resources Policy* (June).

Ekedahl, Erik. 1984. "Canpotex and the World Potash Market." Notes for a speech to the Canadian Fertilizer Institute, August, 29. St. John's, Newfoundland.

Goeller, H.E., and Alvin M. Weinberg. 1978. "The Age of Substitutability." *American Economic Review* 68 (6) (December): 1–11.

Govett, M.H., and G.S. Govett. 1982. "Gold Demand and Supply." *Resources Policy* (June).

Groten, Eric, and W.C.J. Rensburg. 1983. "Barriers to Investment in Third World Mineral Industries." *Resources Policy* (March).

Hendrick, Keith C. 1984a. "The Long Road Back." Notes for Capitals Metals Forum, Washington, February 16.

_____. 1984b. "The Right Price for Zinc." Brussels Metal Bulletin International Conference, June 12.

Jewett, G.A. 1983. *The Impact of Materials Technology on the Markets for Metals: A Multi-Client Report*. Toronto.

Kirthisingha, P.N. 1982. "Viability of Processing in Copper-Mining Areas." *Resources Policy* (December).

_____. 1983. "International Policies on the Economic Resources of the Deep-Seabed." *Resources Policy* (June).

Landsberg, Hans H. 1983. "Key Elements Common to Critical Issues on Engineering Materials and Minerals." Washington, D.C.: Resources for the Future.

Leontief, Wassily, James Koo, Sylvia Nasar, and I.R.A. Sohn. 1982. *The Production and Consumption of Non-fuel Minerals to the Year 2030 Analyzed Within an Input-Output Framework of the U.S. and World Economy*. New York: New York University.

Mackenzie, Brian W. 1984. "Economic Mineral Targets." Working Paper 28. Kingston: Queen's University, Centre for Resource Studies.

Mackenzie, Brian W., and Charles H. Pye. 1982. "Effects of Public Policy on Investment Demand: The Case of Taxation in Canadian Base Metal Mining." Working Paper 26. Kingston: Queen's University, Centre for Resource Studies.

Mackenzie, Brian W., and Michel L. Bilodeau. 1979. *Effects of Taxation on Base Metal Mining in Canada*. Kingston: Queen's University, Centre for Resource Studies.

Maule, C.J. 1985. "Industrial Adjustment." The Case of the Aluminum Industry." In *Canada Among Nations: 1984 — A Time of Transition*, edited by M. Molot and B. Tomlin. Toronto: James Lorimer.

Miksell, Raymond F. 1979a. *New Patterns of Mineral Development*. Washington, D.C.: British-North America Committee.

———. 1979b. *The World Copper Industry*. Baltimore: Johns Hopkins University Press for Resources for the Future.

Mining Association of British Columbia. 1983. *Submission by the Mining Association of B.C. to the Royal Commission on the Economic Union and Development Prospects for Canada*, Ottawa.

———. 1984. "Taxation and Economic Development in British Columbia: The Mining Industry." A brief submitted by the Mining Association of British Columbia to the Honourable Hugh Curtis, Minister of Finance, Province of British Columbia, October.

Olewiler, Nancy. 1981. *The Regulation of Natural Resources in Canada: Theory and Practice*. Technical Report 4. Ottawa: Economic Council of Canada.

———. 1981. "Inco and the World Nickel Markets." Part of a Report to the Harvard Institute for International Development. Kingston: Queen's University, Centre for Resource Studies.

Parsons, G.F. 1984. "Issues in the Development of the Potash Industry of Saskatchewan." Paper prepared for the Conference on the Economic Transition of Western Canada, University of Alberta, November 8–9.

Pye, Charles H. 1981. *Profitability in the Canadian Mineral Industry*. Kingston: Queen's University, Centre for Resource Studies.

Richardson, Peter. 1984. "Evaluating Mining Management." *CRS Perspectives* 18 (June).

Ridker, R.G., and William D. Watson. 1980. *To Choose a Future*. Baltimore: Johns Hopkins University Press for Resources for the Future.

Ryba, André. 1983. Economic Council of Canada, Financial Group, personal communication.

Smith, Kerry V., and John V. Krutilla, eds. 1982. *Explorations in Natural Resource Economics*. Baltimore: Johns Hopkins University Press.

Statistics Canada. 1984a. *Exports by Commodities: December 1983*. Ottawa: Statistics Canada.

———. 1984b. *Summary of External Trade: December 1983*. Ottawa: Statistics Canada

Stollery, Kenneth R. 1983. *Productivity Trends and Their Causes in the Canadian Mining Industry 1957–79*. Study prepared for the Economic Council of Canada. Ottawa: Minister of Supply and Services Canada.

Sultan, Ralph. 1984. "Financing the Future." In *Financing Canadian Mining in the 1980s: Strategies for Action*, edited by David Yudelman. Kingston: Queen's University, Centre for Resource Studies.

Tilton, John E. 1977. *The Future of Nonfuel Minerals*. Washington, D.C.: Brookings Institution.

United Nations. 1968. *Growth of World Industry*. 1967 Edition. Vol. 2. New York: United Nations.

———. 1969. *Growth of World Industry*. 1967 Edition. Vol. 1. New York: United Nations.

———. 1971. *Growth of World Industry*. 1969 Edition. Vols. 1 and 2. New York: United Nations.

———. 1974. *Growth of World Industry*. 1972 Edition. Vol. 2. New York: United Nations.

———. 1976. *Yearbook of Industrial Statistics*. 1974 Edition. Vol I. New York: United Nations.

———. 1983. *Yearbook of Industrial Statistics*. 1981 Edition. Vol. 2. *Commodity Production Data, 1972–81*. New York: United Nations.

United States Bureau of Mines. 1980. *Mineral Facts and Problems 1980*. Washington, D.C.: U.S. Government Printing Office.

———. Council on Environmental Quality and the Department of State. 1980. *The Global*

2000 Report to the President: Entering the Twenty-First Century. Washington, D.C.: U.S. Government Printing Office.

Urquhart, Elizabeth. 1978. *The Canadian Nonferrous Metals Industry: An Organizational Study.* Kingston: Queen's University, Centre for Resource Studies.

Vogely, William. 1984. "Nonfuel Minerals and Materials." Background paper prepared for the Conference: "The Global Possible: Resources, Development and the New Century." Washington, D.C.: World Resources Institute.

Walsh, James I. 1982. "The Growth of Develop-For-Import Projects." *Resources Policy* (December).

Webb, Michael C., and Mark W. Zacher. 1983. "Canada and International Regulation of Primary Commodity Markets: The Case of Minerals." Vancouver: University of British Columbia, Institute of International Relations.

Wilkinson, Bruce W. 1980. *Canada in the Changing World Economy.* Montreal: C.D. Howe Research Institute.

Wojciechowski, Margot. 1984. "Mining Productivity." *CRS Perspectives* (October).

World Bank. 1984. *Price Prospects for Major Primary Commodities, Vols. I, II and IV.* Washington, D.C.: World Bank, Economic and Research Staff.

Yudelman, David, ed. 1984a. Canadian Mineral Policy Formulation: A Case Study of the Adversarial Process." *New CRS Announcement.* Kingston: Queen's University, Centre for Resource Studies.

_____. 1984b. *Financing Canadian Mining in the 1980s: Strategies for Action.* Kingston: Queen's University, Centre for Resource Studies.

Water

Crabbe, Philippe J. 1984. "The Columbia River Treaty: Twenty Years After." Paper delivered at the Canadian Economics Association Annual Meetings, Guelph.

Frederick, Kenneth D., and James C. Hanson. 1982a. *Water for Western Agriculture.* Research paper prepared for Resources for the Future, Washington, D.C.

_____. 1982b. "Water Supplies." In *Current Issues in Natural Resource Policy,* edited by Paul R. Portney. Washington, D.C.: Resources for the Future.

Frederick, Kenneth D. 1980. "Irrigation and the Future of American Agriculture." In *The Future of American Agriculture as a Strategic Resource,* edited by Sandra S. Batie and Robert G. Healy. Washington, D.C.: The Conservation Foundation.

Kovacs, Jerry D. 1982. "Managing Alberta's Water: The Decision-Making Process." *Resources Policy* (December).

L'vovich, M.I. 1979. *World Water Resources and Their Future.* Translation by the American Geophysical Society, edited by Raymond L. Nace. Washington, D.C.: American Geophysical Society.

Rogers, Peta. 1984. "Fresh Water." Background paper prepared for the Conference: "The Global Possible: Resources, Development and the New Century." Washington, D.C.: World Resources Institute.

Veeman, Terrance S. 1984. "Water and Economic Growth in Western Canada." Discussion Paper. Ottawa: Economic Council of Canada.

Conclusions

Boulding, Kenneth. 1983. "National Defense Through Stable Peace." *Options* 3 (International Institute for Applied Systems Analysis).

Copithorne, Lawrence. 1979. *Natural Resources and Regional Disparities.* Study prepared for the Economic Council of Canada. Ottawa: Minister of Supply and Services Canada.

Statistics Canada. 1983. *The Input-Output Structure of the Canadian Economy: 1971–79.* Ottawa: Statistics Canada.

People Contacted For This Study

Angevin, G. Canadian Energy Research Institute, Calgary.

Baribeau, R. Executive Assistant to Executive Vice President and Chief Executive Officer of Domtar, Montreal.

Birch, Alf. Resource Economics Branch, Alberta: Agriculture.

Bjarneson, Harold. Executive Director – Planning, The Canadian Wheat Board, Winnipeg.

Brewer, Keith. Director General, Economic and Financial Policy Analysis Branch, Department of Energy, Mines and Resources, Ottawa.

Briggs, Keith. Department of Plant Science, University of Alberta, Edmonton.

Burke, Paul J. Supervisor, Economic Studies, Economics and Forecasts Division, Ontario Hydro, Toronto.

Burgess, Bernard. President. Pulp and Paper Research Institute.

Bushak, W. Department of Plant Science, University of Manitoba, Winnipeg.

Chaudhary, G.N. Production Economics Branch, Economic Services Division, Alberta Agriculture, Edmonton.

Colgan, Brian. Land Use Branch, Alberta Agriculture, Edmonton.

Cornell, Peter. Director, Economic Council of Canada, Ottawa.

Cramm, Bill. Director General, Resource Processing Industries Branch, Department of Regional Industrial Expansion, Ottawa.

Cummer, H.C. Director, Market Development, Canpotex Limited, Saskatoon.

Cupp, Calvin. Science Council of Canada, Ottawa.

Curtis, John. Research Director, Institute for Research on Public Policy, Ottawa.

Davis, John. Assistant Deputy Minister, Pacific and Freshwater Fisheries, Department of Fisheries and Oceans, Ottawa.

Deeks, W. Vice-President of Sales, Noranda Mines, Toronto.

Desjardins, Ronald. Production and Economics Branch, Alberta Agriculture, Government of Alberta, Edmonton.

De Pauw, R.M. Research Station, Research Branch, Agriculture Canada, Swift Current, Saskatchewan.

Enemark, Tex. President, Mining Association of British Columbia, Vancouver.

Fox, R. Strategic Planning. Department of Economic Development, Government of Edmonton, Alberta.

Frederick, Kenneth. Director, Renewable Resources, Resources for the Future, Washington, D.C., U.S.A.

Haessel, W. Canadian Energy Research Institute, Calgary.

Harwood, J. V.P. Research, Metropolitan Center for High Technology, Detroit.

Heath, Rod. Canpotex Limited, Toronto.

Hedley, D.D. Director, Strategic Planning Division Agriculture Canada, Ottawa.

Helleiner, G. Department of Economics, University of Toronto.

Herring, Richard J. Assistant Deputy Minister, Canadian Forestry Service, Environment Canada, Ottawa.

Ho Lem, Stephanie. Division Vice-President, Noval Enterprises, a Division of Nova, an Alberta Corporation, Calgary.

Holling, C.S. International Institute for Applied Systems Analysis, Vienna, Austria.

Huff, H.B. Director, Commodity Markets Analysis Division, Marketing and Economics Branch, Agriculture Canada, Ottawa.

Hughes-Anthony, Nancy. Department of Energy, Mines and Resources, Ottawa.

Jarvis, W. Department of Economics, Energy, Mines and Resources, Ottawa.

Jewett, George A. P. Engineer, Toronto.

John, Joshua. Director General, Marketing Directorate, Department of Fisheries and Oceans, Ottawa.

Kiel, Dave. Regional Director, Canadian Forestry Service, Edmonton.

Kondra, Zenon. Department of Plant Science, University of Alberta, Edmonton.

Mark, David. Consultant, Aluminum Company of America.

Miles, Peter. Chief Economist, National Energy Board, Ottawa.

Miller, Mel. Land Use Branch, Alberta Agriculture, Edmonton.

Nonnecke, I.L. Chairman, Department of Horticultural Science, Ontario Agricultural College, University of Guelph, Guelph, Ontario.

Olewiler, Nancy. Centre for Resource Studies, Queen's University, Kingston.

Parsons, Scott L. Assistant Deputy Minister, Atlantic Fisheries Service, Department of Fisheries and Oceans, Ottawa.

Percy, Mike. Department of Economics, University of Alberta, Edmonton.

Pierce, Max. Corporate Finance Division, Department of Finance, Ottawa.

Pound, Del. Chief Commissioner, Canadian Grains Commission, Winnipeg.

Pritchard, G. Ian. Director, Aquaculture and Resource Development Branch, Department of Fisheries and Oceans, Government of Canada, Ottawa.

Proulx, Pierre-Paul. Department of Regional and Industrial Expansion, Ottawa.

Rabinovitch, V. Assistant Deputy Minister, Fisheries Economic Development and Marketing, Department of Fisheries and Oceans, Ottawa.

Repetto, Robert. World Resource Institute, Washington, D.C. U.S.A.

Richardson, Peter. School of Business, Queen's University, Kingston.

Robertson, Gerald. Marketing and Economics Branch, Agriculture Canada, Ottawa.

Roehle, Robert. Director of Market Analysis, Canadian Wheat Board, Winnipeg.

Rothman, M.P. Chief Economist, Ontario Hydro, Toronto.

Schaupmeyer, C. Research Station, Alberta Agriculture, Brooks, Alberta.

Schindler, Dave. Secretary, Continuing Advisory Committee on Biotechnology, Science and Technology, Ottawa.

Slater, David. Chairman, Economic Council of Canada, Ottawa.

Smith, Eric. Canmet.

Smith, Mike. Ministry of State for Science and Technology, Ottawa.

Steed, Guy. Science Council of Canada, Ottawa.

Stern, Robert, Department of Economics, University of Michigan, Ann Arbor, Michigan.

Veeman, Michele. Department of Rural Economy, University of Alberta, Edmonton.

Veeman, Terry. Departments of Economics and Rural Economy, University of Alberta, Edmonton.

Wonsbrough, John. Director, Forest Products Directorate. Resource Processing Industries Branch, Department of Regional Industrial Expansion, Ottawa.

Wiebe, John. Director, Plant Industry Division, Alberta Agriculture, Government of Alberta, Edmonton.

Wilde, Keith. Agriculture Canada, Ottawa.

Wilson, Art. Research Director, Canada Grains Council, Winnipeg.

Wilson, Dave. Chief Economist, Canadian Pulp and Paper Association, Montreal, Quebec.

Wise, Tom. Manager, Economic Research Division, Economic Development Directorate, Fisheries Economic Development and Marketing, Department of Fisheries and Oceans, Ottawa.

Zuker, R. Economic Council of Canada, Ottawa.

2

The Design of Water-Export Policy

ANTHONY SCOTT
JOHN OLYNYK
STEVEN RENZETTI

Introduction

The Terms of Reference

Economic modes of thought have much to contribute to the drafting of
Canadian policy on water exports. This report expands on this theme
and makes suggestions about what the message of such a policy should
be. If governments do not prepare themselves now, proposals to transfer
water from Canadian rivers and lakes to the United States will find us
with our facts unmarshalled and our points of view unclarified. We will
then likely give our usual response: federal-provincial confusion providing a background for diverse trumpetings about the national interest,
provincial rights, the sanctity of water, and government interference. If
governments begin to formulate a policy now, they can avoid this rhet-
orical stage and instead use tested principles and procedures to look
analytically at any export proposal that may suddenly be waved before
them.

How should governments prepare themselves? An economic
approach to policy formulation, apart from its intrinsic merits, has the
additional merit of indicating what bodies should be formed, what
information collected and what procedures set out. The problem here is
to avoid mistaking action for preparation. In our work on this study we
have heard from well-informed experts almost too quick to warn of a
crisis in our water affairs, but less helpful where concrete advice is
required. For example, after a recent Canadian-American conference
convened by the U.S. Council on Foreign Relations, the author of the
proceedings wrote:

Fresh water, long considered inexhaustible and hence a "free good", now begins to appear as a — perhaps *the* — major long-range resource issue on the continent. Although the quality of both surface water and ground water is already of concern in some places, the issue of water quantity is further down the road in terms of impact and, for that reason, suggests a different kind of bilateral attention than acid rain now receives. If unaddressed, rising demand over the next decades, especially by Americans, can cause problems of unprecedented seriousness since water is clearly the most precious of all continental resources. Complex and expensive schemes for water diversion have been and will be proposed. Long-term planning is essential, taking into account such diverse factors as climate change, world population pressures, and food needs. It would be desirable for the two governments to initiate now a systematic and coordinated review of impending or future changes and problems so as to have early warning and the capacity for whatever joint or separate action may be appropriate or possible. (Council on Foreign Relations, 1984, p. 8)

The warning is timely, but is the specific advice correct? Should Canada start by a "coordinated review" of impending problems even before it has examined its own needs and resources, even before it has seized the opportunity to analyse for itself what actions would harm and what would help the contribution that water can make to Canadian well-being? This report is intended to take us a few steps in the direction of forming a water export policy by exploring the advantages and difficulties inherent in an economic approach, and their implications in terms of governments, agencies and institutions. As our objectives were set out in our terms of reference, the study was to:

• identify the varieties of meanings of water export (e.g., tanker export, diversion from international watercourses, hydro-electric export) and their significance;
• explore the alternative policy positions that Canada might adopt, ranging from prohibition through regulation to free trade, and the economic and political implications of each;
• develop broad benefit/cost calculations that assess various economic, environmental and political factors, and include considerations of flexibility, reversibility, timing and scale;
• develop a framework in which governmental machinery at different levels might be brought to bear on the subject of water export; and
• recommend appropriate measures (e.g., research, data collection, planning) for the federal government to address the water-export issue more effectively in future.

Contents

The next two sections of this study present some important background information on water exports, to provide a context for the subsequent discussions of economic analysis of and policies for export proposals. The first section examines physical factors that affect water-export costs, environmental impacts of water exports, and important aspects of international law and Canadian constitutional law that could affect management of water exports. The section also discusses potential American demand for Canada's water and briefly discusses Canadian water supply.

The second background section presents some historical information relevant to Canadian water exports. Two existing "exports" are described, and a number of water-export proposals, including three active proposals, are outlined. Current federal policies for exports of a number of other Canadian natural resources are then briefly surveyed, and a discussion of current Canadian water-export policies concludes the section.

The report then describes the range of possible export policies. The benefits of a flexible, adaptable — but rigorous — approach to dealing with export proposals are argued. We then propose a new approach to water-export policy based upon economic analysis of the benefits and costs that each export project would involve for Canada.

The section on the benefits and costs of exports discusses the issues of valuation, uncertainty and commensurability as they relate to economic analyses of water-export projects. An illustrative calculation is presented to suggest how the proposed economic approach might be applied in practice.

The section on organization and machinery focuses on possible administrative arrangements for water exports. A number of existing examples of intergovernmental arrangements — federal-provincial, interprovincial and international — are described, and a number of criteria for establishing an administrative arrangement are presented. Finally, we propose one possible arrangement of this nature.

Some key findings and recommendations conclude the study.

Some Basic Considerations

A large number of factors determine whether Canada can or should export water. This section provides background information on types of water exports, physical factors affecting costs of water exports, legislative jurisdiction over water exports, demand for water in the United States, and the availability of Canadian water for export.

Water Export and its Physical Costs

The term "water export" can be applied to a wide range of activities. Perhaps the most common image evoked by the term is the diversion of water from rivers within Canada through canals or pipelines to the

United States. This type of water-export project typically involves moving large volumes of water over long distances, with correspondingly large expenditures. A second type of export is the movement of water by large tankers from Canada to another country. This type would involve much smaller volumes of water and, likely, lower costs as well.

While the above clearly constitute water exports, there are a number of other activities that border on being exports, but are not obviously so. For example, some rivers flowing between Canada and the United States are subject to water-apportionment understandings between the two nations. A change in the apportionment that allocated more water to the United States and less to Canada would amount to a water export. As with any physical diversion, Canada would have less water to use; the United States would have more.

Other activities that bear mention are what may be termed "water-based exports." Several hydro-electric developments in Canada rely on American markets for the sale of the power they generate. By importing hydro-electricity from Canada, the United States is placed in the same position as it would be if it paid for the use of a Canadian river and its generating site (Lucas and Saunders, 1983). A second kind of water-based export is of goods that are produced with Canadian water. An example could be agricultural produce from irrigated lands. Indeed, Rogers (1984, p. 56) goes so far as to suggest that international trade in foodgrains constitutes a form of water transfer; this line of reasoning could be applied to other agricultural crops as well. Increased exports of industrial products, from beer to aluminum, that require water or water power in their manufacture could also be included in this exportation category. However, while such water-based activities may scientifically be argued to lead to water exports, they will not be so considered here. It would appear to be more productive to view them as domestic economic activities that significantly affect the supply of, and the demand for, water. These domestic activities represent alternatives to water exports, albeit only to a limited extent, and should therefore be included in an analysis as among the forgone opportunities or economic costs of a water-export proposal.

In this study, the term "water exports" is taken to mean physical transfers of water from Canadian drainages to a foreign country. For purposes of illustration, we refer at length to a hypothetical large-volume transfer from a Canadian river, through canals, across the border to an American river or basin. However, our analysis is intended to be sufficiently flexible to apply equally to smaller-scale water exports.

What physical factors are most important in any consideration of the success or costliness of any proposal to export water? The most obvious factor is the distance between the point of water withdrawal and the foreign receiving basin or point of use. The greater the distance of the diversion, the higher the infrastructure cost will be, other things being equal. Closely related is the pattern of topography and water drainages along the route of the diversion. In some cases it may be possible to divert water along existing basins with only short canals in between, which may prove less costly than having to construct a canal to cover the whole distance.

Related to the distance of the diversion is water loss along the transfer route. Water may be lost through evaporation or through seepage from canals. This rate of loss will be affected by climatic conditions as well as soil conditions along the route. Water loss can be mitigated by diverting more water to allow for losses or by using construction techniques (such as lining) that minimize losses, each of which would increase costs.

Watershed storage capacity is also a very important physical factor. Because of the seasonal variability of natural waterflow, a number of dams and impoundments would be necessary for any large-scale water transfer, to ensure that the flow of exported water was reliably available when needed.

Elevation is similarly important. If water were to be exported to a basin at a higher elevation, or between two low basins across an area of higher elevation, additional costs would be faced in lifting the water to the higher level. These pumping costs would be affected not only by the total difference in elevation, but also by the topography along the route. Transferring water across hilly or mountainous terrain would likely incur greater pumping costs than moving water a comparable distance across a plain. It is worth noting here that some of the proposals made for water exports from Canada suggested that the energy required to lift the water be provided by hydro-electric generators in the diversions' own dams. (This is discussed in more detail below, under the heading "Proposals for Water Exports.")

A final physical factor that will affect the cost of exports is the quantity of water to be exported. The choice or design of infrastructure will be dictated largely by this factor. The extent to which economies of scale can be obtained is uncertain. While there are real economies when the scale of very small projects is increased, it must be recognized that there is a definite upper limit. One study cited by Howe and Easter "indicates that scale economies in canal construction are virtually exhausted at a capacity of 7,000 cfs [cubic feet per second, or about 200 cubic metres per second] . . ." (1971, p. 61).[1] While this threshold may be higher or lower today, it is nonetheless clear that the principle of diminishing returns to increases in scale must be watched for in economic analyses of water-export proposals.

Environmental Impacts of Water Exports

Large-scale transfers of water out of Canadian streams would create large-scale environmental impacts. These can be categorized into two types: the effects of project construction, and the effects of the actual water diversion.

Impact of Project Construction

The construction of water-export projects would have effects on both aquatic and terrestrial ecosystems. Some of these effects arise from the impoundment, temporary diversion and disturbance of rivers and lakes. These could damage or destroy fish habitats by increasing erosion and turbidity. Construction of a dam could create a barrier preventing fish migration. The construction activity could also affect wildlife and flora around the sites, as quarries, roads and dumps scar the landscape, especially in those valleys that provide the key winter habitats for big game and smaller animals.

Building canals would cause the physical destruction of a certain amount of wildlife habitat, mainly in the area of the right-of-way for the canals and their associated infrastructure. This would be a long-term impact. In some regions, the canals could also present a physical or psychological barrier to movement for large mammal species. For example, migrations of mountain caribou in the eastern slopes region of Alberta conceivably could be blocked by a canal from the Peace River to the Athabasca River. Where the canals cross small streams and rivers, there could be adverse effects on local fish populations due to increased stream situation, habitat losses and stream blockages.

Nor would such effects be limited to fish and wildlife and their habitats. Construction work on canals could interfere with farmers' access to their lands, raising their costs or demanding more time. (The permanent loss of agricultural land, discussed in the section below on the "Benefits and Costs of Water Exports," is additional to this more temporary effect.) There are other social costs of construction — mainly those associated with the temporary influx of construction workers to "boom" communities along the canal route. These social costs would be similar in nature to those Canada has already experienced during construction of railways, pipelines and other linear facilities.[2]

Impact of Water Diversion

Once construction has been completed and water diversions initiated, the benefits begin. But permanent environmental impacts also begin. Four main categories of impacts have been identified: levels (flooding); streamflow reduction; drying of marshes and lakes; and risks of transferring harmful exotic species into Canadian drainages.

The most important effect would occur when the reservoirs were filled after the dams were built. As previously mentioned, valley bottoms typically are important wildlife habitats: filling a reservoir would flood some of this key habitat. Flooding also precludes future use of an area for forestry and agriculture; the proposed B.C. Hydro development at Site C on the Peace River is an example. However, it is to be noted that stream diversion will reduce some levels and so mitigate flood damage there.

The increased amplitude of water-level changes would be most noticeable in the systems' newly created lakes. Although artificial reservoirs are often touted as having recreational benefits, these depend on water levels remaining relatively constant. Taylor (1967, p. 24) points out that reservoirs "are constructed to move water from one time period to another." Most reservoirs, especially those associated with large-scale water diversions, have large fluctuations in their water levels, as the reservoir or lake is drawn down during dry periods of low natural flows and recharged during high-flow periods. For example, according to Bocking (1972, p. 62), the level of the Mica Reservoir can fluctuate up to 45 metres. These fluctuations may cause shoreline erosion, and in any case they obviously reduce the utility of the reservoir for recreation and as a habitat for fisheries and wildlife.

Streamflows would be affected in both quality and quantity. Flows downstream would be reduced when impoundments were being filled, not only initially when a dam was first built, but later, as well, each time the impoundment was replenished after a period of drawdown. Reduced streamflows may have a number of effects. Oxygen levels usually drop if turbulence is reduced, probably with harmful consequences for aquatic species; streambank erosion may increase near the impoundment; spawning beds for fish could be damaged by increased scouring; and estuarine salinity may increase (Bryan, 1973). Other possible impacts listed by Ortolano (1979) include changed rate of groundwater recharge, altered water temperature and quality, and modified sediment-transport characteristics. Two final important effects of reduced streamflow are reduced pollution-assimilation capacity and reduced power-generation capability (Howe, 1979).

An effect described by Bryan (1973) is the drying up of marshes and lakes below the dams and diversions. This occurs due to reduced average streamflow or reduced peak streamflow (during the spring freshet, for example) or both. Perhaps the best-known example of this effect is found in the Peace-Athabasca delta, where elimination of spring floods by the Bennett Dam on the Peace River resulted in large areas of the delta drying up, with consequent effects on populations of fish and fur-bearing species such as muskrats and beaver (Bryan, 1973). These effects in turn harmed the Indian and Métis populations in the region (Bocking, 1972). The problem has been mitigated by artificially controlling water levels in the delta (Canada West Foundation, 1982, p. 271).

One other environmental effect associated with water transfers is the increased risk of the introduction of a non-native, or exotic, species into northern drainages. A canal between Canada and the U.S.A. would provide a conduit through which some undesirable plants or animals could move or be transported. This was demonstrated in the early 20th century, when lampreys invaded the upper Great Lakes, following the opening of the Welland Canal, and decimated the commercial fisheries. Changing the drainage patterns around the Garrison Dam will, it is argued, have similarly undesired side effects.

Environmental Impacts: A Concluding Note

These brief listings suggest that water exports can cause a wide variety of effects. It is almost impossible to say anything definite about their general tendency, for some may be regarded as beneficial and some as harmful. Indeed there is great doubt about how much of any particular impact will occur. As Holling (1978) has said, it is impossible to predict in advance all the environmental effects of a large development project. This impossibility must be kept in view in economic appraisals to offset the deceptive definitiveness of numerical estimates.

For example, mid-century dam construction affected fish migrations and populations in many rivers. Uncertainty took a number of forms: uncertainty about the actual severity of the impacts on fish; uncertainty in placing a value on those impacts; uncertainty as to whether the impacts should be treated as unavoidable or as susceptible to mitigative measures; uncertain success of any mitigative measures; and so on. The fishery example suggests the difficulties of identifying and quantifying environmental costs of water exports, involving putting values both on alternative ecological states and on alternative attempts to preserve them. Both problems, uncertainty and valuation, are discussed later in the section on the "Benefits and Costs of Water Exports."

Control and Jurisdiction over Water Exports

There is probably less uncertainty surrounding citizens' and governments' ability to exercise control over water exports. Since no studies addressed specifically to water-export aspects of this subject have been found, the following examination of the subject relies on literature on related themes — for example, on studies of how the constitutional division of powers affects water management, environmental management or natural resources management in general. There has been no judicial decision dealing with water exports in particular, and so this "analysis" must be limited to suggesting possible or likely arguments for establishing jurisdiction over water exports. The discussion is divided into two parts: private ownership of water and jurisdiction over exports.

Private Ownership of Water

Under our traditional or common law, property interests in water are a consequence of ownership of land. While it is common to refer to "ownership of water," the phrase is technically inaccurate, because

. . . the law has never recognized the ownership of such ["fugitive"] commodities while they remain in their natural state. . . . This is not to say that there can be no legal *rights* over water . . . in the natural state. Various rights of exploitation of water and its contents accrue to those who own the land underlying or adjacent to the water. (Gibson, 1969, p. 73)

These "riparian" rights of water use and exploitation are incidental to or run with the riparian land (that land bordering or underlying the watercourse). A person who owns such land can use the adjoining water freely so long as that use does not harm other riparian owners along the stream. This condition tends to limit the amount of water owners can withdraw completely to prevent their transferring water away from their riparian property.

In Canada, the simple system of private landowners having riparian rights to adjoining water is rarely in effect today.[3] Instead the provincial governments exercise, more or less, all rights over water within their boundaries. This provincial control is typically based on one of three foundations. In some cases the main basis for government control is simply that the provincial Crown is itself the largest holder of "private" riparian rights; in some provinces the government has used its regulatory powers to restrict private landowners' use of their riparian rights; and the third foundation is that some of the governments have essentially abolished the system of riparian rights and have replaced it with a system of water licences similar to the "appropriative" private water rights in the southwestern United States.

The second approach, based on permits to use water, is found in Ontario and the eastern provinces. The third approach, in which a government vests in the provincial Crown all property in and all rights to use water, is predominant in the western provinces.

While it is not certain that these three bases are clear enough to deprive every landowner in Canada of all riparian rights to water in all adjoining streams, they do go far enough to justify an assertion that in most situations where it might be proposed to re-apportion or divert water to exports, the "owner" to be dealt with would not be local citizens but the provincial government.

Jurisdiction over Water Exports

So much for "ownership" of exportable water. This section deals with power to legislate under our federal constitution. The federal and provincial governments would each have roles.

The *Constitution Act* (1982) contains a number of sections that could establish federal jurisdiction over water exports. First, the combined operation of sections 91(29) and 92(10)(a) grants Parliament jurisdiction over certain classes of works and undertakings that stretch beyond the boundaries of one province, especially shipping lines, railways, canals, telegraphs "and other Works and Undertakings connecting the Province with any other or others of the Provinces, or extending beyond the Limits of the Province . . ." (section 92(10)(a)).[4] This term "undertaking" has been given a broad legal definition. La Forest describes an undertaking as "not being a physical thing, but an arrangement under which physical things are used" (1973, p. 49). In the provinces' water legislation, according to Beerling (1984, p. 48), "The word 'undertaking' is [typically] a reference to a project to develop, transport, distribute or use water or water power. It encompasses any means of storing water or stopping its flow. It covers channelling or changing the flow of water." La Forest (1973, p. 54) suggests that the determination by the courts of whether an undertaking comes under provincial or federal jurisdiction depends on whether the undertaking is "in pith and substance" of a provincial or of an interprovincial or national nature. Some water diversions, and certainly water-export undertakings, would seem to fall into the national or interprovincial category and so to be subject to federal powers.

Other relevant heads also support a claim for federal authority over water exports. Section 91(2), "The Regulation of Trade and Commerce," is one. Although the general influence of this section has over the past fifty years been circumscribed by a series of judicial interpretations, it remains central to any claim for federal jurisdiction on many subjects. For one thing, it "may help to extend federal legislation once it has been established under another head. . . ." (Emond, 1972, p. 669). Furthermore, it has been confirmed as the basis for federal controls over the export of logs and natural gas.

A third heading for federal jurisdiction over water exports can be found in the so-called "Peace, Order and good Government" clause in the preamble to section 91 of the *Constitution Act*, giving Parliament the authority "to make Laws for the Peace, Order, and good Government of Canada, in relation to all Matters not coming within the Classes of Subjects by this Act assigned exclusively to the Legislatures of the Provinces . . ."

In deciding whether legislation justified under this clause is within the federal Parliament's powers, the courts have used as a test whether the real subject of the legislation is beyond provincial interest alone and concerns Canada as a whole or has a national dimension. Recent Supreme Court opinions (1976) tend to confirm a view that water exports might well be treated, like aeronautics, radio and atomic energy, as being of distinct national concern.[5] Another test under this clause is the emergency test, which was applied in the 1976 Anti-Inflation Reference case (1976 2 S.C.R. 373). It is unlikely that federal water-export legislation could be justified under this test. However, other heads of power appear sufficient.

A fourth source of federal power is related to treaty making. Because of the international obligations that would arise as a consequence of large-scale water exports, Canada might wish to enter into a treaty-like agreement with the U.S.A. using the federal government's power to negotiate and conclude treaties with the United States. While such treaties may be binding on Canada (that is, on the *federal* government) under international law, their implementation in Canada would have to follow the constitutional division of powers between the federal and provincial levels of government (La Forest, 1973, p. 12). The negotiations preceding the Columbia River Treaty, during which Ottawa was sandwiched between British Columbia and U.S. northwest power interests, illustrates this federal role.

A fifth pair of powers assigned to the federal government deals with authority over "Navigation and Shipping" (section 91(10)) and "Sea Coast and Inland Fisheries" (section 91(12)). These heads may give the federal government a virtual veto power over those water-diversion projects that interfere with navigation, shipping or fisheries. For example, construction of a dam on a river could have such an effect, and it would need approval under the federal *Navigable Waters Protection Act* or the *Fisheries Act* or both. These two powers "ensure that the federal government has a substantial lever with which it can ensure a measure of provincial cooperation [in the matter of interbasin water transfers]" (Percy, 1981, p. 7).

Finally, the federal government could have influence over development of a water-export project by exercising its spending powers. Funds generated through the broad federal taxation power (section 91(3)) could be used to extend Parliament's influence over subjects not specifically granted it by the *Constitution Act*. While the status of this power varies from decade to decade, Parliament has successfully used it for post-secondary education, health, regional development and other "provincial" functions. Its effectiveness depends on the extent to which Ottawa can attach conditions to its disposal of money and other property. When disposing of public funds, for example, Parliament has used conditional grants to regulate activities where it lacks clear jurisdiction. Today's thinking is, however, that "Parliament may not directly invade the realm of provincial authority under the guise of its spending power" (Emond, 1972, p. 667). The federal spending power will be less influential where funds for construction and operation of a water-export project are raised by the province or privately.[6]

This interpretation of six sources of federal government jurisdiction suggests that the federal government must always play some roles in setting up or approving a water-export project. Especially important are its (rather weak) Trade and Commerce powers, its "national dimension" powers, its foreign-affairs powers and its spending powers. But any combination of these powers confronts an even more formidable array of provincial powers. The combination of provincial ownership rights and powers is so comprehensive that, were a very large water-transfer project to be entirely within one province, virtually no federal role might be found. Indeed it may be claimed that even in a transfer of water between two provinces (where no disagreement was involved, and where both provinces were chiefly depending on their regulatory rights to water mentioned in the earlier discussion of private ownership of water) any federal involvement would go beyond what the strict satisfaction of federal constitutional responsibilities requires.

Perhaps the most important provincial legislative power is over allocation of water within the provincial boundaries, based in part on the provinces' proprietary interest and in part on the exclusive powers granted by section 92 of the *Constitution Act*. The three principle heads are:

92 (5) The Management and Sale of Public Lands belonging to the Province and of the Timber and Wood thereon,
   (13) Property and Civil Rights in the Province,
   (16) Generally all Matters of a merely local or private nature in the Province.

What does "belonging to" the province mean? We have seen that the provincial property interest in water amounts almost to outright ownership. This property right exercised by the legislature, combined with the province's other legislative powers, gives a province very comprehensive jurisdiction over water resources within its boundaries. But it is unclear whether this jurisdiction is comprehensive enough to allow the province to allocate water specifically for export. Since such an allocation could be construed as part of an "extra-provincial" venture or undertaking, it could be argued that doing so specifically for export falls under federal jurisdiction. This argument, however, is wholly conjectural. In a legal test the provinces could likely present a strong case based on their proprietary status and legislative powers in favour of provincial control of water-export allocation decisions — especially in the absence of specific federal water-export legislation. At present, any intending water exporter would certainly need to receive an allocation of water from the provincial government, and without federal legislation to the contrary, that allocation might be valid for exports as well.

The 1982 natural resources amendment to the *Constitution Act* (section 92A) confers on the provincial governments legislative authority over "development, conservation and management of sites and facilities in the province for the generation and production of electrical energy" (92A(1)(c)). If a hydro-electric power plant were to be a part of a large-scale water-diversion project, it would appear that it would now come under provincial jurisdiction. However, if this facility were viewed as an integral component of an export undertaking, which, it was argued above, could be partly subject to federal jurisdiction, conflicts could arise. This constitutional amendment seems to have been designed to enforce provincial control over hydro sites that were not part of the provincial public domain. In general, the federal-provincial implications of this constitutional amendment have yet to be tried for water management and for water exports.[7]

Summary: Canadian Legal Aspects

What powers would be exercised in a "typical" water-export project? Let us assume that an entity or agency exists or is created, such as a private firm connected with an American water agency or enterprise. The three words "water," "project" and "export" give us heads to show the bounds and overlaps of the two orders of government.

The agency would first have to obtain water. This would certainly require the permission, indeed the encouragement, of the province of origin or diversion. (If the works caused effects on levels and flows in other provinces, they too could become directly involved.) The provincial government's ownership claim could surely not be disregarded, nor could its existing laws and machinery to expropriate or deal with losses of waters suffered by persons holding private or provincial water rights.

Secondly, the "project" would lead the agency to seek rights over or to private lands, public lands, easements, building materials such as rock and fill, and clearances involving environmental effects, working conditions and allocation of water along the route to Canadian customers of the export project. All these powers or rights to take or undertake these things would come from the provincial government. The federal Northern Pipeline Agency (NPA) provides an example of a possible arrangement for facilitating the acquisition of the needed rights and powers. Under the *Northern Pipeline Act*, many powers and responsibilities from federal departments and agencies were delegated to the NPA to provide a "single window" for regulation and coordination of the pipeline's construction by Foothills. Included in the Act were provisions for intergovernmental (federal/provincial) coordination.

Only the word "export" conveys the agency's need for reliance on federal approval powers and encouragement. To start with, the project's canals or diversions might cross more than one province, and the diversion would almost certainly change the present flows in interprovincial streams and affect fisheries, navigation, railways and other means of communication. Since the federal government might well regulate or prevent such undertakings under its existing powers (for example, the powers in the *Canada Water Act*, the *International Rivers Improvement Act*, the *Fisheries Act* and the *Navigable Waters Protection Act*), its intimate involvement and approval would be required.

When the canals or diversions cross into the United States, Ottawa's participation is indispensable. A change in levels and flows at the border would probably necessitate approval by the International Joint Commission. Moreover, an "export" would draw in those government departments that are concerned with trade and payments. Furthermore, the day-to-day management of levels and flows within the project itself would require some special international oversight (such as that involved in the International Columbia River Power Board under the Columbia Treaty) even if the exporting agency and its customer in the United States were both private entities. Finally, international caution and the absence of a super-court to enforce any contract would demand a special agreement whereby the American customer was protected against arbitrary interference with water flows and the Canadian exporter given acknowledged freedoms to vary or stop the flows under specific conditions. Such an agreement would involve Ottawa in its diplomatic role, and also in agreements with the provinces concerned. The present arrangements for natural gas exports provide a useful analogy.

As a result, water-export proposals will not succeed without the support and cooperation of both levels of government. While "detailed legal planning" would be required before such a water transfer could go ahead (Percy, 1981, p. 11), it appears that there is sufficient flexibility in the division of powers under the *Constitution Act* to allow a joint federal-provincial approach to regulation and management of any water-export proposals that may arise.

Legal Aspects in the United States

The United States also has some jurisdiction in the matter of Canadian water exports, for it may be able to divert water that would otherwise flow into Canada (such as the Red River and Lake Champlain), and can draw on both boundary waters (such as Lake Erie) and waters that flow into boundary waters (such as Lake Michigan in the United States). The Canadian-American rules about such diversions have been settled somewhat in advance of the progress of general international law on the same subject (Bourne, 1974). In 1900, to take a convenient date, there was increasing uncertainty about jurisdiction over such waters, especially about who had rights to obstruct them for power and navigation purposes. Some uneasiness about diversions had cropped up in connection with the Chicago Diversion and irrigation and diversion projects on the St. Mary's and Milk rivers along the parched Alberta-Montana border, but Canada was especially thoughtful about the 1895 American rejection of Mexico's legal claims to Rio Grande waters diverted before they reached the Mexican border. These questions were dealt with in the negotiations that led to the Boundary Waters Treaty, 1909. With a number of particular exceptions, the two governments agreed that each had exclusive control and rights to divert waters in rivers *crossing* the boundary.

This was the "Harmon Doctrine" transferred from the Mexican

border, with the modification that parties below the border injured by such diversions should have the same rights and access to the same legal remedies as if such injury took place in the country where the diversion was made (Article II). This principle, however, applied only to rivers crossing the border. Another rule was applied to watercourses flowing along the border: the two governments in effect banned obstructions that would change boundary waters' levels or flows unless these were approved by the International Joint Commission (IJC) set up under the same treaty (Article III). Note that the treaty has nothing to say about diversions from rivers entering boundary waters; such diversions, therefore, were subject only to domestic law. In any case, the right of injured parties to access or remedy as if that injury took place in the country where the diversion was made has turned out to have little applicability in Canada. This is because, as we have seen earlier in this chapter, provincial laws covering levels, flows and diversions do not give, even to local parties, rights (such as riparian rights) to uninterrupted flows.

Finally, the interdependence of the two countries is not to be ignored. Each is downstream of the other on important streams, so that neither can afford to take the lead in making a diversion that might free the other to make a retaliatory diversion on another stream. This recognition of their mutuality is evident in several ways. One of these is the unofficial expectation that when water apportionment is an issue, the solution will be close to an even division of the natural flow. (See the section on "Organization and Machinery" for more details.) Nevertheless, international apportionment issues are typically the most bitterly fought matters to come before any tribunal. This is probably because, with no water price being charged, parties on each side have every incentive to get as much water apportioned to themselves as possible. The IJC, whose members rarely divide on national lines, has several times so divided in apportionment cases. Nevertheless, Canada-U.S. "comity" may be said, in the few diversion or apportionment cases that have been at issue, to have led the national parties from the 100 percent Harmon position to the present style of negotiation of solutions in the neighbourhood of 50 percent.

This North American trend has taken place while the global international-law community attempted to make general rules for settlement of international watershed disputes. These attempts culminated in the 1966 "Rules" drafted by the International Law Association (a non-governmental organization) in conference at Helsinki. For our purposes the essence of these Helsinki rules is that each nation is declared to have a duty to take its neighbours' needs for water into account before diverting (Article IV). The convention evidently refused to take the further step of saying that the waters in a basin should be used for the benefit of the basin as a whole, disregarding the frontier (Bourne, 1974).

More will be said about diversions and international apportionments.

By way of summary here it may be said that (a) the 1909 embodiment of the Harmon doctrine in the Boundary Waters Treaty gave each country powers to divert waters that would otherwise flow in their natural channels across the border; (b) in spite of this, large diversions have not taken place, and in most Great Plains watersheds, transboundary flows have been apportioned on a fifty-fifty basis; and (c) this tendency to share conforms to strengthening international opinion (as exhibited in the Helsinki "Rules" and subsequent formulations) that the upstream country has a duty to consider needs or benefits downstream before diverting transboundary waters. As for "boundary waters" proper (such as Lake Erie), the Boundary Waters Treaty is less clear. The general rule is that (d) neither country is to obstruct or divert water in such a way as to affect the natural level of flow on the other side without IJC approval. But in its latest report the IJC does not seem to believe that the treaty gives it complete guidance about when it should grant and when deny its approval (International Joint Commission, 1985).

We may put these four generalizations to hypothetical tests by asking whether Canada's rights to waters entering Canada are so clear that she could "export" simply by selling her consent to an increased U.S. diversion of waters that would otherwise flow into Canada. It would appear that they are not. Indeed, the United States conceivably might (without paying compensation or obtaining agreement) "import Canadian waters" by their prior diversion before they run north into Canada. However, if the waters would otherwise flow into *boundary waters* (such as certain of the Great Lakes), the U.S. treaty obligation not to affect their levels or flows would give Canada more power to demand a price or compensation for its agreement to the U.S. diversion.

American Water Demand

A prerequisite for water exports is, of course, a willing buyer. At this point, it appears an open question whether American water demand will reach a level where Canadian water could economically augment U.S. supplies. Several large regions in the U.S.A. are experiencing or anticipating water shortages if current usage trends persist. Three areas where demands for Canadian water could be generated are the Colorado River basin, High Plains and Great Lakes regions.

The arid Colorado River basin region relies heavily on groundwater and on withdrawals from the Colorado River for irrigated agriculture and urban uses. Because water is very scarce in the basin, a number of interstate court cases have contested allocation of the river's flows. The result is that, at present, withdrawals by each state (California and Arizona being the biggest users) are limited to court-ordered allocations. However, the total of these allocations actually exceeds the river's flow during dry years. Furthermore the groundwater overdraft is about 2 million acre-feet (about 2.5 billion m^3) per year (Powledge, 1982, p. 153).

The resulting scarcity and misallocation between uses would seem to cry out for a water-pricing scheme. But powerful interests, especially in agriculture, have resisted this approach and instead have proposed water imports from other regions, including Canada, in spite of the extremely high cost of transferring water such a distance.

In the High Plains region from Texas to Nebraska, groundwater from the great Ogallala aquifer has been exploited for the last five decades to make irrigated agriculture possible. A tremendous expansion in irrigated acreage has put the aquifer in such a situation that according to Peter Rogers, withdrawals from the aquifer exceed its recharge by an estimated 17 billion m^3, or about 14 million acre-feet, per year (Rogers, 1983, p. 41). To relieve this overdraft of the groundwater resource, water transfers have been examined. In 1982, the U.S. Army Corps of Engineers completed a fairly elaborate study of four possibilities for transferring water from the Mississippi/Missouri drainage to the High Plains. The cost of transferring this water could go as high as Cdn. $640/1,000 m^3 per year (about U.S. $600/acre-foot per year) (U.S. Army Corps of Engineers, 1982). To transfer the water all the way from Canada via the Mississippi would presumably cost even more. Therefore, Canadian water does not appear to provide a financially attractive alternative to a pricing system or to transfers from other U.S. regions unless it is subsidized to a very large extent. However, the region's powerful water-using interests will probably continue to press for water imports. The cost of projects bringing water to the region's urban and farm consumers has been heavily subsidized in the past, but projects to import more water may well be far too costly for the government to continue its old policies.

The third potential import-demand area is the Great Lakes region. Heavily industrialized and densely populated, the region already withdraws water from the Great Lakes for municipal, industrial, agricultural and thermal power-generation purposes. There are growing concerns about increased consumption of water: one study predicts that water consumption in 2035 could be almost 4.5 times the 1980 rate (Canada, Department of the Environment, 1983). This increased drainage of the Great Lakes could be compensated by diverting Canadian water from the James Bay drainages into the Great Lakes; this would be, in effect, a water export. Because the Great Lakes would be used to deliver the water to the U.S. consumers, the only major transport projects involved would be in Canada. Thus, the cost of Canadian water for the northern states might seem to Americans to be less than that for water exported all the way to the Colorado River basin or to the High Plains states. However, the border cost of Canadian water would probably be high enough to induce the United States to examine other means of dealing with the potential shortages, such as price or demand-management alternatives.

For all three regions most experts argue that the best candidate for change is the present system of nearly free sale of water. Peter Rogers, like the other experts, believes that the problem is not one of insufficient water supplies, but of inefficiency in the ways they are managed, rationed and used (Rogers, 1983, p. 80; Wilkinson, 1985; Powledge, 1982, p. 6). All advocate some system of paying for water.

In most regions with water districts there are already flat-rate annual water charges. These have little or no effect on consumption. Such charges can indeed be quite high, since their usual purpose is to enable the water district to service the initial capital costs of elaborate collection, storage and delivery structures, and also to pay for operation and maintenance. But sometimes they are absurdly low, having been subsidized at an early date by government water programs (Rogers, 1983). It is worth repeating that such *fixed* water rates, either high or low, have no important effect on total water consumption, for they are not linked to the amount the consumer takes.

A very few water systems do make this linkage. They are to be found in districts that meter their customers' consumption and charge them for the amount taken. One urban example is in the Washington, D.C., area, where the Washington Suburban Sanitary Commission in 1978 implemented an incremental block-pricing system (Baumann and Dworkin, 1978, p. 23). Typically, the rates charged vary, including extra cents per cfs or acre-foot for the distance the water must be carried and, more important, for the degree of water scarcity at the time it is consumed. Thus a farm's rate schedule may rise and fall with the time of day and the time of year.

Those who criticize the water-management systems in many parts of the United States are saying two things: too much water (especially well or ground water) is totally free or unpriced; and too many charge schedules are unduly low. Thus for a very large amount of the water consumed in dry regions and for consumers who are attached to city systems and irrigation systems or who pump their own water, there is no incentive to restrict the amount taken daily until falling pressure cuts them off, or until the well threatens to run dry. Consumers cannot gain by cutting down what they draw, because doing so will not lower their total water payments and will not help them to get more water when, in dry periods, they really need it.

Some U.S. experts go much further than this: what they ask for is an "efficient" system of management and consumption. This word describes a water-delivery set-up by which the water is divided among the customers in a manner that will maximize the economic benefit from its use. To achieve this, water should be priced so that every consumer's marginal unit of water taken brings in a uniform final value of product, as measured by the amount that the consumer is willing to pay for it. In an "efficient" system this uniform marginal value will just equal what it costs to obtain the water from its alternative uses or consumers elsewhere, plus what it costs to deliver it.

Such an efficient system utilizes marginal-cost pricing. In many areas the marginal cost of water may be lower than the annual charge, full price or water tax now paid by members of water systems that have no government subsidy. But it is appreciably higher than the average price paid throughout the dry regions, for most users are not charged anything for their marginal acre-foot. The absence of any charge system (especially of a marginal cost system) is described by Rogers and others as evidence of lack of "political will" (Rogers, 1983, p. 80).

However much it might be, a marginal-cost charge for already-available water from neighbouring U.S. sources would fall well short of the per-user cost of sending water down from Canada (Wilkinson, 1985); see also the discussion of the "Benefits and Costs of Exporting Water" in this study. The impoundment, storage and delivery of Canadian water — not to mention the equally important costs of reimbursing Canadians for present and future economic and environmental water benefits forgone — would be a very unattractive alternative to developing the political will to make better use of the water supplies already available in the south and southwestern United States.

Any Canadian pondering a proposal to export water should take this into account. Even where there is an opportunity to export water, the U.S. buyer should be able to, and probably will, find a better bargain at home. The Canadian should bear in mind the history of the planning, financing and construction of the Foothills natural gas pipeline. This $40 billion project was half built when the U.S. importers belatedly discovered in the late 1970s that gas from the contiguous states would be less expensive than Alaskan or Canadian supplies. This discovery has led to financing difficulties and project delays so that it is now uncertain when, or even if, the pipeline will be completed.

Canadian Water Supply

Let us leave economics for a few paragraphs and consider where our water is. If the national statistics for average surface-water flows are compared to those for water use, it would seem that Canada has a great surplus of unutilized water. For example, the total Canadian monthly reliable flow (which is the lowest monthly flow experienced in ten years) was about 1,711 million m^3 per day, while total withdrawals in 1980 were estimated at about 120 million m^3 per day, about 7 percent of the monthly reliable flow (Environment Canada, 1983, p. 13). However, the distribution of water in Canada is not spatially or temporally uniform. Foster and Sewell point out that "much of the water is in the wrong place or is available at inappropriate times" (1981, p. 17). A study by the Canada West Foundation points out that, in western Canada, "over 80 percent of the natural water supplies are contained in an area populated by fewer than 10 percent of the region's people" (1982, p. 20), and that in the same region "over 60 percent of the total annual water flow passes through the prairies on its way to Hudson Bay during a three-month period" (1982, p. 24). As a result, local water shortages are foreseen by some in certain basins in southern Canada (Foster and Sewell, 1981, p. 17). Not all observers agree with this conclusion. Veeman argues that such a forecast has two "major economic difficulties": it assumes that water is a free good, and it ignores "economic alternatives" (demand management, for example) for coping with water shortages (Veeman, 1985, p. 18). Veeman suggests, therefore, that labelling these southern basins as "water scarce" may be premature (1985, p. 19).

Overshadowing the arguments and uncertainty about short-term water supply and requirements is the problem of the effect of long-term climatic change on Canada's water needs. A growing body of evidence suggests that Canada's climate may undergo what would be in a geological sense rapid warming. This warming would be a manifestation of the "greenhouse effect": increasing concentrations of carbon dioxide and other pollutants in the atmosphere — largely as a consequence of human actions — are thought to be causing the earth's surface temperature to rise (Hare, 1984, p. 73). If this warming trend continues, it could affect Canada's hydrologic cycles and could dramatically alter water supply and demand across the country (Hare, 1984, p. 81). There would probably be less water available to divert out of Canada to the U.S.A. if this type of climatic change occurred. Although, as Hare points out (p. 82), there is considerable uncertainty about the timing and severity of these climatic changes, their likely effects on Canada's water resources (increasing demand and reducing supplies) would have to be taken into account when attempting to establish whether Canada has an exportable surplus of water.

Proposals for large-scale exports from Canada likely would focus on three regions of origin: the Pacific, Great Plains, and James Bay/Great Lakes drainages. Although the Pacific drainages have about 21 percent of Canada's annual reliable flow (Environment Canada, 1983, p. 13), a number of factors militate against the use of this region as a source of exportable water. The present B.C. economy and society are based not only on urban and industrial water consumption, but also on other activities wholly dependent on continued water flows, such as the salmon fishery, hydro-power production and dry-belt agriculture. In addition, the distance to U.S. market regions and the difficulty of transferring water through Canadian and U.S. mountains would make most Pacific basins more expensive sources than the Great Plains or James Bay drainages.

A number of large rivers cross the Canadian Great Plains region, which extends from the U.S. border north to the Mackenzie delta. Most of them, including the Saskatchewan and Athabasca systems, are already apportioned among municipal, agricultural, power-generation and industrial users and could not, without considerable disturbance of existing consumers, provide much water for large-scale transfers to the

United States. The flows of these southern rivers would not be sufficient to support present domestic uses and large-scale exports. For example, a diversion of 2.5 billion m³ (2,000,000 acre-feet, enough to cover the annual groundwater overdraft in the Colorado River basin region) per year from the North Saskatchewan River would remove almost one third of that river's mean annual flow, which is approximately 7.7 billion m³ per year (Canada West Foundation, 1982, p. 58). It appears then that large-scale diversions would have to come from the Peace or Mackenzie rivers, transferred across the Prairies to the United States. Although diversion of 2.5 billion m³ per year would take less than 4 percent of the Peace River's mean annual flow of 65.3 billion m³ per year (Canada West Foundation, 1982, p. 58), serious downstream impacts could be created nonetheless, especially in the Peace-Athabasca delta. As we have already mentioned, this river plays a central role in the lives of many Indian and Métis peoples. Even this relatively small diversion could be seriously disturbing. And, of course, the network of canals, dams and pump lifts required to move the water through and across the southern prairie drainages to the U.S.A. would carry a much higher price tag than if the diversion were from the Saskatchewan system.

The third potential source of exportable water is the James Bay/Great Lakes region. Although some of the rivers draining northern Ontario and Quebec have been developed for hydro and other purposes, their waters remain almost unused in comparison to the intensity of use of Canadian rivers closer to the border. Construction of costly diversion canals across the Canadian Shield to the Great Lakes has been proposed. Once in the Great Lakes, the water could be moved to eastern and southern U.S. market regions through existing drainages (the Great Lakes/St. Lawrence River and the Missouri/Mississippi system) at relatively small additional cost.

More information on each of these three source regions is available, though little of it has been analysed from the point of view of massive diversions into other drainages or to the U.S.A. The capital costs have been assumed to be so heavy that most studies have concentrated on possible and relatively minor diversions *within* each of the three areas (such as the studies of opportunities to make diversions or control systems between parts of the Columbia River, the Saskatchewan rivers or the Great Lakes). Better supply-demand balances for each region are needed before we can say with confidence what would be the physical effect of large transfers on local flows. Such studies would also help us to measure the economic opportunity cost of the waters withdrawn from Canadian consumers.

Concluding Remarks

Seven important points arise out of this section. First, most water-export-caused effects of the change in water levels and flows would be experienced in the environment rather than in physical use.

Secondly, water is largely consumed privately, and private users have "rights" that can be changed only by major political interventions.

Thirdly, private rights are no longer closely linked to private property in land. They have been replaced by various systems of water law that more or less transfer proprietary rights to the provinces. Private use derives from provincial granting of water rights.

Fourthly, both the provinces and the federal government possess formidable powers under the Constitution to help or hinder a private water-export proposal. Undoubtedly, success in a water-export proposal would require cooperation from both governments.

Fifthly, there is considerable U.S. demand for more water, especially in the dry southern regions, where surface and groundwater flow more or less freely (without price) to private users. However this demand may not be adequate to justify investment in bringing water from Canada, given that water pricing could liberate large squandered flows from inessential uses today, and make water available at smaller real costs than would be exacted by water imports.

Sixthly, whether a "water surplus" exists in Canada also depends on economic considerations, among them the question of whether various scarcities in southern Canada do not also reflect the same "price-lessness" that afflicts American water consumption.

In the seventh place, any forecast of Canada's water supplies and demand should consider the long term as well as the short term. Large-scale water-export projects would probably be feasible only if water could be diverted over long periods — that is, decades — to the United States. This would require commitment of a large volume of Canadian water. Over the long term both U.S. and Canadian demand for water may increase due to economic growth and climatic changes. Although it will be difficult to estimate this long-term demand, the time frame for the supply (water surplus) forecast must be of about the same length.

Existing and Proposed Water Exports and Canadian Export Policies

The preceding discussion provided an introduction to the economic, environmental, legal and political issues associated with water exports in general. This section examines water exports at a less abstract level, presenting a survey of existing and proposed water-export projects, a brief discussion of current Canadian policies for exports of certain other natural resource commodities, and an examination of past and present Canadian water-export policies.

Existing Canadian Water Exports

Although many Canadians may believe that water exporting is a new idea, small amounts of Canadian water have been diverted to American uses for a number of years. One example is in the Great Lakes region. In 1848, the United States unilaterally diverted water from Lake Michigan through two canals into the Illinois basin (Carroll, 1983, p. 126). This project, known as the "Chicago Diversion," provided water to dilute pollution entering the Illinois Waterway from Chicago and to improve navigation and power generation downstream in the Illinois Waterway and the Mississippi River (into which the Chicago Diversion ultimately drains) (Carroll, 1983, p. 126; International Joint Commission, 1982, p. 7). The flow of water through the Chicago Diversion has averaged 3,200 cfs (about 90 m^3 per second, roughly equal to 1.7% of the average flow of the Detroit River, which drains the same body of water) since 1970 (International Joint Commission, 1982, p. 2).

This water taken from Lake Michigan appears to be replaced to a limited degree by water diverted through the Long Lac Diversion from the Kenogami River basin, which drains into James Bay and is moved through Long Lake and the Aguasabon River into Lake Superior. In the Ogoki Diversion water from the Ogoki River, which drains into James Bay, is sent back through Lake Nipigon and the Nipigon River into Lake Superior (International Joint Commission, 1982, pp. 4, 7). The volume of water diverted averages about 5,600 cfs, or about 140 m^3/s (International Joint Commission, 1982). These two diversions were intended to increase Canadian hydro-power generation capacity along both the Nipigon and Aguasabon rivers and further downstream in the waterways connecting the Great Lakes. However, if some of the water diverted into Lake Superior from Canada compensates for the withdrawal at Chicago, this process could be considered a form of water export. Likewise, any increase in the volume of the Chicago Diversion, as has been proposed from time to time (Carroll, 1983, pp. 126–27), compensated by increased Canadian diversions into the Great Lakes thus maintaining water levels for navigation and power, may be construed as a water export. Carroll predicts that "proposals to increase the Chicago Diversion . . . will be a recurrent theme at various times in the future . . ." (1983, p. 127). The Chicago Diversion has the capability to handle much larger volumes of water. Flow rates through the diversion reached 10,000 cfs (283 m^3/s) in 1928 (International Joint Commission, 1981a, pp. 4–10). This diversion is a rather tenuous example of an export, and is not officially considered a water export.

This example illustrates how the pattern of North American drainages makes it comparatively easy to arrange water transfers or exports between *any* two points. "Minor" water transfers can be local or can cover thousands of miles. Another example of minor water transfers to the United States is that of small delivery systems that carry municipal water a few miles to adjacent towns across the border. Thompson, writing in 1982, mentions a sale of water by the town of Coutts, Alberta, to the neighbouring community of Sweetgrass, Montana. According to Thompson (1982, p. 53), Coutts charges Sweetgrass $1.90 per thousand gallons (about $0.42 per m³) for the water, exported by a pipeline. (Thompson does not indicate the volume of water exported to Sweetgrass.) In return for water from Coutts, Sweetgrass's power and natural gas utilities have been extended to serve Coutts (Thompson, 1982, p. 53). These small-scale water transfers have not received a great deal of public attention, even though they are, we have argued, types of water exports. However, they cannot be portrayed as precedents for large-scale exports, such as river diversions. The volumes of water and the costs involved in these examples are trivial in comparison to diversions of rivers.

Proposals for Water Exports

In the early 1960s, in response to predictions of water shortages in some areas of the U.S.A. (especially the southwest), a search for new sources of supplies was begun. To many of those searchers, Canada seemed an obvious source. This has led to a number of proposals for large-scale transfers of water from Canada to the United States. These proposals are summarized briefly in this section.[8]

The North American Water and Power Alliance (NAWAPA)
The most famous, or perhaps the most notorious, water-export proposal is NAWAPA. Proposed in 1964 by a private firm of engineering consultants, the Ralph M. Parsons Co. of Los Angeles, NAWAPA would divert massive volumes of water from Alaska and northern Canada to southern Canada, the southern U.S.A., and Mexico (Parsons Co., 1964). The plan would involve flooding an 800 km length of the Rocky Mountain Trench (primarily in British Columbia) and the construction of "at least 50 different diversion and control works, including dams, canals, tunnels and reservoirs" (Sewell, 1969, p. 356). Included would be one 190-metre-wide by 11-metre-deep canal to the southern U.S.A. and one 23-metre-wide by 9-metre-deep canal across the Canadian prairies to link up with the St. Lawrence Seaway (Sewell, 1969, p. 356). The total volume of water diverted could be as much as 250 million acre-feet (about 310 billion m³) per year, a volume roughly equivalent to the average total annual discharge of the St. Lawrence River. The cost of the project was estimated in 1964 to be approximately $80 billion to $100 billion (Parsons Co., 1964, p. 4), which would be $280 billion to $355 billion in 1984 dollars.[9] These estimates reflect only the cost of building the project, and include $16.6 billion (1964 dollars) for land acquisition and community

relocation. The proposal completely ignores the social and environmental costs of the plan, which would be astronomical.

It is not clear how seriously the Parsons company meant their elaborate project to be taken. Their public exposition of it was not extensive, and it was not submitted to any government. Discussion chiefly amounted to little more than text surrounding frequent reproductions of their map, across which new lakes and waterways were slashed until North America began to resemble Schiaparelli's depictions of the canals on Mars. Was it an integrated, indivisible illustration of man's new-found earth-moving technology, wealth and confidence? It is noteworthy that in the same decade other massive projects were suggested to divert Russian and Siberian rivers into the Volga River and the Black and Caspian Seas; to link the Nile with the western desert lowlands and the Mediterranean; to harness the tides of the Bay of Fundy and the English Channel; and to link France and England by a multi-tube tunnel.

The very large St. Lawrence Seaway and Columbia River projects were just completed, the northern California irrigation canals and the Aswan Dam were just ahead. It was a decade of exciting mega-projects. With so many visions ahead and so many kites already flying, the Parsons people must have been taken aback by the vigour of the reaction to their brainchild. Thanks to this proposal, water exports now not only seemed a tangible possibility but appeared, more so than had been suggested by the Columbia, St. Lawrence or Fundy projects, sprawling and indivisible; their construction seemed to be based on indifference to Canadian wants or needs and to newly awakened environmental ideas. The title of Richard Bocking's book, *Canada's Water: For Sale?*, by an author who had already, in TV productions, chronicled the comparatively minor upsets of the Columbia Treaty projects, clearly signalled the hostile reaction that NAWAPA evoked. The disconcerting reception a few years later of Energy Minister J.J. Greene's reliance on a "continental" pattern of petroleum distribution was surely a symptom of this new hostility.

All this reaction was healthy, encouraging wide-spread discussion. It probably was responsible for the decided view of many Canadians that all water exports should simply be "banned." It is, however, unfortunate that the proposal's introduction as an indivisible hundred-year-long conquest of North American watershed geography should have obscured the essential divisibility of smaller projects and their high potential to make technically significant contributions with relatively small volumes of water. This inflated image was only partly remedied by a succeeding wave of other proposals for water transfers to the U.S.A.

The Central North American Water Project (CeNAWP)
The Central North American Project was developed by Dr. E.R. Tinney in response to NAWAPA, which he believes "does violence" to basic

engineering precepts of minimizing environmental impacts and using natural features as much as possible (Tinney, 1967, p. 23). The proposal would transfer water from Canadian basins as far north as the Mackenzie, via a series of pumping stations and canals, along natural prairie drainages to Lake Manitoba and Lake Winnipeg. From these, water would be diverted to Lake Superior through Lake Nipigon, and thence to the southern U.S.A. through the Missouri/Mississippi basin. Even though the CeNAWP project would rely on natural drainages wherever possible, as much as 4,000 km of canals would be needed (Bryan, 1973, p. 160). No cost or water-volume estimates were made, as the project was intended only as a conceptual alternative to the NAWAPA project. According to Bocking, Tinney's CeNAWP project "was put forth only to show that a much better scheme than NAWAPA could be devised if necessary" (1972, p. 74). It was not intended to advocate water exports from Canada.

The Kuiper Diversion Scheme

The Kuiper Diversion scheme, first published in 1966 by Professor E. Kuiper of the University of Manitoba, shares a number of features with the CeNAWP proposal. It, too, would divert water from the Mackenzie drainage into rivers across western Canada to Lake Winnipeg. From there, water could be diverted east to the Great Lakes or, by reversing the Souris River, south to the Great Plains region of the United States. Kuiper's plan involves a number of stages, first transferring water within Canada from basins progressively farther north, then an export component that would see a distribution network extended southward into the U.S.A. in three stages, using existing drainages where possible. The diversion scheme would have delivered water to central Texas at an estimated transfer or construction cost of $35 per acre-foot, or about $97/1000 m^3 in 1984 dollars (Kuiper, 1966, p. 15). Again, this figure does not include opportunity costs or environmental costs.

Western States Water Augmentation Concept

This water-transfer proposal, first suggested by L.G. Smith in 1968, would use the western Canadian drainages and the Rocky Mountain Trench to move water to the southern United States. Although this plan does not include NAWAPA's 800 km reservoir in the Rocky Mountain Trench, it does call for diversion of waters from as far north as the Liard basin, south through the Trench, where the water would be transferred through tunnels or canals through the Fraser, Columbia or Kootenay rivers to the U.S.A. Some of this route would thus redirect or pre-empt storage and channels now dedicated to the existing Peace and Columbia River schemes. A second component of the project involved transferring water from the Smoky, Athabasca and Saskatchewan Rivers through the Qu'Appelle or Souris River to Lake Winnipeg, from which, presumably, water could be diverted south.

According to Quinn (1973, p. 16), the Western States Water Augmentation Concept would yield about 47 billion m³ per year, and would cost approximately $75 billion to construct (about $295 billion in 1984 dollars) plus costs within the U.S.A. Like the Kuiper project's costs, this amount does not include opportunity or environmental costs.

The Magnum Diversion Scheme

The Magnum Diversion Scheme, first proposed by Knut Magnusson in the late 1960s, is another western Canada diversion project that, Bryan says, "was put forward more as a suggestion for further consideration than as a detailed plan" (1973, p. 164). The proposal would divert water from the Peace River basin via the Athabasca, North Saskatchewan, Battle, South Saskatchewan and Qu'Appelle drainages to the Souris River, through which the diverted water would be exported to the Great Plains region of the U.S., and then further south through the Missouri River. The plan included no estimate of project costs nor of deliverable water volumes, and "it does not appear to offer significant improvements on the Kuiper scheme" (Bryan, 1973, p. 165). It should not be considered in isolation, but as part of a growing interest in Alberta in long-distance water transfer.

The Great Recycling and Northern Development (GRAND) Canal

While the five preceding proposals for water diversions have been partly cancelled by other water projects in the same basins and are, in any case, largely matters of historical interest (retrieved from time to time for studies of water exports), the GRAND Canal concept is still being actively advocated by its originator, Thomas Kierans. Kierans first proposed the concept in 1959 (Quinn, 1973, p. 16). In 1984, he presented a new version of his project in writing to the federal Inquiry on Water Policy (Kierans, 1984). Recently, the project has been supported by a growing number of public figures who view water exports as a source of revenue or as a bargaining chip for free trade with the United States (Newman, 1985). Kierans' project was initially intended to provide a source of fresh water that could be used to regulate the *levels* of the Great Lakes (a gigantic problem with which the two governments, the IJC and millions of lake riparian owners and users continually wrestle); water exports were a by-product (Kierans, 1965). Kierans' solution was originally an extension of the existing elements in the Great Lakes level-management system. His diversion, however, would also permit greater withdrawals from the Great Lakes by both Canada and the United States, so that it eventually became known as a water-export project. The proposal calls for James Bay to be turned into an immense freshwater reservoir by building a dike across the Bay where it meets Hudson Bay; the water from the reservoir would be pumped and diverted south through a series of canals and the Ottawa River to the Great Lakes (Kierans, 1984, p. 3). Because the water would not be diverted out of natural drainages, but would be collected after the rivers drain into James Bay, Kierans refers to his plans as water "recycling," not diversion. Water would be transferred to the U.S.A. through the Chicago Diversion and possibly other diversions as well. In 1984, Kierans estimated that the project would cost about $100 billion to construct over a period of eight years (Kierans, 1984, p. 7). This figure does not appear to include other than construction costs (no opportunity costs, environmental costs, etc.), nor are water transfer volumes indicated.

Freil Lake Tanker Proposal

This water-export proposal, developed by Colin Beach of Coast Mountain Aquasource Limited of West Vancouver, is currently in the planning and approvals stage (Anonymous, 1984). It differs from the previously described water-export proposals in several important ways. First, the amount of water involved in the project would be trivial in comparison to a large-scale, overland, river diversion. Secondly, very little permanent infrastructure would be necessary, as the proposal is for potable water to be shipped by tanker to the southern U.S.A. and Mexico. The only major infrastructure requirements would be for some moorage facilities in Hotham Sound, where water will be taken on; for a water-control structure on Freil Lake, about 90 kilometres up the Sunshine Coast from Vancouver; and for a road to the dam. Finally, the environmental impacts of the project would be few and small, especially in comparison to inter-basin water transfers. As Freil Lake empties into the ocean through a waterfall, there are no fish movements to be affected by construction of the dam at the lake's outlet (Beach, 1984). The chief opportunity cost of the export project would seem to be that its approval might prevent more valuable *potential* engineering and environmental uses yet to be proposed.

Perhaps the most important aspect of the project from an exports-policy perspective is the flexibility and interruptibility of the water deliveries. An often-expressed concern about overland water transfers, with their apparent long-term commitments of water to justify tremendous infrastructure requirements and costs, is that it may be very difficult to "turn off the tap" if increases in future Canadian demand or water scarcity suggest this course. Water exports by tanker, however, could be interrupted much more easily, in that a policy decision to export water by tanker would be less costly to *reverse*.

Canwex 2000 International Tanker Proposal

A more recent export-by-tanker proposal is that of Canwex 2000 International, a private firm based in Quebec. The proposal is for the export of drinking water from Sept-Iles, Quebec, to a number of Arab states (Carvalho, 1985). At present, the water-purification plant in Sept-Iles has excess capacity of about 1,700 million litres per month, of which 1,500 million litres per month would be shipped by super-tanker to the United Arab Emirates. The project could bring revenue of up to $15 million over 10 years and create 14 to 20 permanent jobs. Because of the project's small scale, its environmental costs would be small (Carvalho, 1985). The project could be increased in scale to 3.7 billion litres per month (equivalent to only 1.4 m³/s, or about 44.4 million m³ per year) if other countries also placed orders for water from Sept-Iles (Carvalho, 1985). This project is unique in that it would involve the export of purified water from Canada, water that could command a higher price than unprocessed river water.

Summary of Water-Export Proposals

Although the various proposals for large-scale water transfers from Canada to the United States have generated controversy and debate over the last 20 years, it appears that Canadians need not expect the imminent diversion of Canada's rivers to the U.S.A. Most schemes were proposed primarily to stimulate discussion of alternate engineering means of transporting water and were not closely linked to particular water-short regions or users. On that level they appear to have been successful. None of the large-scale diversions described above has ever approached the multi-million-dollar stage of detailed planning. The proposals may, in general, be technically feasible, but their economic feasibility has hardly even been suggested. Their extensive environmental and socio-economic consequences received only passing attention during the 1960s. Containerized water exports (such as the Freil Lake proposal) appear to be much more feasible, primarily due to their much smaller scale and greater interruptibility. Of course, containerized exports may not be feasible means of meeting large demands for water in the U.S.A.

Many of the water-export proposals have been put forwarded by Canadians, not Americans. While some private Americans have expressed interest in importing water from Canada, Shaffner et al. (1980, p. 564) point out that the U.S. government has never officially supported long-distance large-scale water transfers from Canada.

Current Federal Export Policies for Other Resource Commodities

Canada's economy is based to a large extent on the production of natural resource commodities — both renewable and non-renewable — for export markets. The federal government's export policies for the various commodities range from a hands-off approach to close scrutiny and regulation of exports. This section briefly outlines current federal policies for exports of electricity, natural gas, forest products, minerals and grain, to illustrate the range of federal export policies.

Electricity Exports

Canada has a long history of trade in electrical power with the United States. The first notable trade in electricity began at the turn of the century (1900) when hydro-electricity generating stations were built at Niagara Falls, Canada (Miller, 1970, p. 10). Energy from these stations, besides serving Canadian customers, was exported across the Niagara River to Buffalo, Lockport and Syracuse. The Canadian market was small, and the early developers were chiefly interested in serving U.S. industry and industrial towns.[10] Although the Ontario government passed export-regulatory legislation, and the newly formed Ontario hydro agency attempted to limit the commitment of firm power to the U.S. market, the amount exported increased steadily. Ottawa established an export regulatory regime, and the U.S. Congress and interests in New York state, alarmed by the possibility that Canada might uni-laterally switch off exports, also undertook to use their powers to limit imports into the U.S. market. Nevertheless exports continued to grow, both from Quebec and from Ontario. Grauer and Davis (1961) estimate that by 1910, one-third of the energy from Canadian central generating stations (i.e., energy not tied to particular users) was exported, and the amount licensed and exported increased up to 1917.

During the war the situation became tense. Canada was advanced in plans to manufacture electro-chemicals for munitions, and power was needed. It turned out that all Canadian capacity was either used or committed to exports. Negotiations between Canadian generating firms, the U.S. government, the U.S. coal industry (for fuel to supplement Niagara hydro generation) and the Ontario government eventually enabled the Canadian war-power controller to scrape together and apportion enough for all users, and the crisis ended in 1919.

But the power-export "issue" became more acrimonious over the next 20 years. In Ottawa, Quebec and Ontario successive debates revealed that the war experience had suggested to many Canadians that licensed exports, in spite of their explicit terms, had been treated by the exporters and their customers as irrevocable and permanent. Sir Henry Drayton, who had been power controller, expressed the sentiment that "power exported is power lost." The matter came up repeatedly in all capitals in connection with new power projects, and it became usual not to license "firm" power exports.

Large-scale exports of electricity to the United States again became an important issue during the negotiation of the Columbia River Treaty. To obtain provincial support for the treaty, the federal government announced that it was prepared to authorize power exports to the U.S.A. for the following purposes, among others: "to provide for sales of surplus interruptible energy; . . . [and] to provide for exports of firm power for limited periods [up to 25 years] to make possible the step by step construction of the most economical generating facilities on either side of the boundary" (Miller, 1970, p. 251).

Since 1959, the export of power has been regulated by the federal National Energy Board (NEB); this specialist body (partially modelled on the U.S. Federal Power Commission, which exercises jurisdiction over *imports*) has replaced the necessity for legislative debates on each proposal. According to Perlgut, before electricity may be exported to the U.S., "the NEB must determine that the export quantity is in surplus in relation to foreseeable Canadian electricity needs and that the price is just and reasonable in relation to the public interest"; and the NEB expects export prices for electricity to be at least as high as domestic prices, and preferably higher (1978, p. 37). Moreover, although the NEB is authorized to issue long-term licences for power exports, Perlgut says that export licences are "frequently" limited to five years (1978, p. 37).

To the extent that much of the power Canada exports to the United States is produced by hydro-electric generators, we are exporting a renewable resource. Since the Great War years, the various U.S. and Canadian power-distribution systems have become almost completely intertied, primarily to provide back-up sources of power and to increase efficiency of power supply, with the result that we now have, in essence, a continental power grid. This development means that further exports of power from Canada do not require the construction of new infrastructure to handle the exports. This is an important difference between exports of electricity and water from Canada, as capital costs for transporting new electricity exports would be very small in comparison to those of new water exports.

Natural Gas Exports

The export of natural gas from Canada is closely regulated by the federal government.[11] Again, the National Energy Board is the principal federal regulatory body. Under section 83 of the *National Energy Board Act* of 1959, the NEB is authorized to grant licences for exports of natural gas (as well as for oil and electricity) as long as it is satisfied that:

- the quantity . . . to be exported does not exceed the surplus remaining after due allowance has been made for the reasonably foreseeable requirements for use in Canada having regard to the trends in the discovery of gas in Canada; and
- the price to be charged by an applicant for gas or power exported by him is just and reasonable in relation to the public interest (R.S.C. 1970, c. N-6, s. 83).

In its deliberations the Board relies to a large extent on information supplied by the industry it regulates. This includes information from the provinces owning the resources to be exported. It has also exercised a considerable degree of discretion in its calculations of surpluses. The NEB since its creation has treated oil and natural gas "simply as trade products" (Lucas and Bell, 1977, p. 8), and has not been reluctant to authorize the export of any gas that it has deemed surplus: "the Board has always taken the position that any surplus gas or power is *prima facie* exportable" (Lucas and Bell, 1977, p. 22).

In addition to allocating gas for export, the NEB also regulates individual export projects. For example, in the second phase of the 1982 Gas Export Omnibus Hearing, the NEB examined and reported on the economic, contractual, regulatory and other aspects of the 29 applications the Board had at that time received for new or altered gas exports (National Energy Board, 1983, p. 2). The Board is also involved in the ongoing regulation of these (and other) gas-export projects.

Presumably because of the economic importance of the natural gas industry in western Canada and its contribution to revenues and the balance of payments, the federal government's policy toward natural gas exports has been, in recent years, more supportive than restrictive. Parliament has even negotiated cuts in the price of exported gas to maintain or increase the penetration of Canadian gas into American markets.

Exports of Forest Products
The Canadian forest industries export logs, chips and manufactured lumber, pulp and paper, and finished wood products. The federal government's policy on these exports is, generally, to permit exports of manufactured products while restricting the export of primary and intermediate products. In exercising its authority under the *Export and Import Permits Act*, it follows the lead of the provincial governments when issuing permits for primary and intermediate wood products. (The provinces have long exercised their landlord's power to control the export of logs cut on provincial Crown lands.) Such export controls are intended to stimulate manufacturing in Canada: "Both the federal and provincial governments restrict exports of unmanufactured timber . . . with a view toward promoting the domestic manufacturing industry" (Pearse, 1976, pp. 305 and E2).

Exports of Minerals
Since World War II, the federal government has encouraged the export of Canadian minerals, as long as the minerals to be exported are surplus to Canada's domestic needs. It uses the same law to control mineral exports as log exports: the *Export and Import Permits Act*. Under this Act, "Canadian producers were [and are] still required to meet domestic needs before export licences could be obtained" (Wojciechowski, 1979, p. 55). This Act has been used to control exports of copper, nickel and lead during periods of shortages in the last two decades (Wojciechowski, 1979, p. 56). A similar policy has been followed since the war for exports of uranium (Wojciechowski, 1979, pp. 53–54). The provincial governments can control mineral exports by setting the terms of leases of mineral rights, following their practice with log exports. Precedents for

this do exist (e.g., in encouraging the setting-up of intraprovincial smelting and refining plants), but they are infrequent.

Exports of Grain

According to Wilson (1979), "Seventy-five percent of the grain handled by the licensed elevator and transportation system is exported from Canada. Export markets are therefore of vital significance for Canadian grain" (1979, p. 327). The federal government has actively regulated these exports.

The federal government's main instrument in its grain-exporting activities is the Canadian Wheat Board. Other countries have established agencies that are responsible for importing grain; these "usually purchase Canadian wheat, oats, and barley directly from the Canadian Wheat Board" (Wilson, 1979, p. 344). Private Canadian dealers are also involved in the international grain trade, although to a lesser degree (Wilson, 1979, p. 344). The Board is involved in virtually all aspects of grain exports, including negotiating prices and volumes for Board grain exports and developing export markets (Harvey, 1981, p. 32). It can, and has, forbidden the export of both its own wheat and that of private dealers.

Summary of Export Policies for Other Resources

Three lessons emerge. The first is that the federal government has set up agencies for controlling the exports of several natural products. The second is that it has developed fairly complex policies to guide its export-control agencies, sometimes intended to promote foreign sales and their prices and sometimes to protect Canadian consumers and processors. The third is that these agencies share power over most exports with provincial departments. Given these general terms of reference, the agencies rely on the economic climate, not electoral factors, to play the primary role in determining how much of each commodity should be exported. As we shall consider in the next section, this has not been the case in Canada's export policies for water.

Current Canadian Water-Export Policy

As was shown above, Canada has not failed to export its natural resource commodities — ranging from renewable resources such as grain and lumber to non-renewable, strategically important resources such as oil and natural gas — when the opportunity has presented itself. Canada's water, however, has in general been an exception to this rule.

One reason for this is primarily economic: export proposals have not been vigorously promoted. Another reason is that export permission might well have been refused, for water has not been regarded as an economic commodity. Water, in the form of rivers, lakes and streams, has great cultural importance in addition to its physical importance to human life and activities. Quinn (1969, p. 245) writes that water:

> is an integral element of the environment . . . Because the river or lake has always been there, because it permeates so many aspects of their daily lives, directly and indirectly, small wonder that the people of a region or country perceive water as their heritage, to which they have first, if not exclusive, right.

This emotional dimension to water may have had an important effect on government water-export policies. Over the past 20 years, the stated policy of both the federal and provincial governments has been one of "no water exports." At the federal level, Thompson (1983, p. 53) says that water exports to the United States have been "rejected . . . as a possibility." In August 1984, Charles Caccia, then federal Minister of the Environment, stated that:

> Canada's position to oppose the export of water hasn't changed . . . We reject the contention that water is available for export. This will be a very important commodity for Canadians in the decades ahead. We therefore reject any such notion whether it comes from provinces, municipalities or regions in the north . . . Our position on that is clear and consistent. (Anonymous, 1984)

While the federal policy may be clear, it is not entirely convincing, for no serious campaign has been launched to test the government's firmness.[12]

At the provincial level the declared situation is the same. Alberta's official position is "water not for export." In Alberta "priority of water use and allocation is based firstly on Provincial, secondly on interprovincial, and finally on national considerations, and will not be influenced by international considerations" (Alberta Environment, n.d., p. 14).

The one exception to this stricture is the sale of water by Coutts, Alberta, to Sweetgrass, Montana, which was outlined in the description of existing Canadian water exports. British Columbia's policy has been softening. In June 1985, the B.C. government published a price schedule for bulk exports of water by tanker (Anonymous, 1985). The federal and provincial export policies are such that large-scale water-export proposals are, in general, "not being considered by either the federal or provincial governments" (Canada West Foundation, 1982, p. 87). But neither are such proposals being advanced.

The role of the emotional dimension in statements of our water-export policies in Canada cannot be overestimated. In fact, that dimension appears to have been more important than all others. Exports have been opposed as a matter of principle, an *ad hoc* principle unrelated to ecology, economy, comity or future need.

Types of Water-Export Policy

Introduction

A country may be said to have adopted a policy about water exports when it has prepared itself in advance to deal with new situations. Looking backward, the word "policy" is often used merely to describe the sequence of actions that the government took in a particular area, as in "Canada's mineral policy, 1945–1985." But when used to apply to future actions, policy refers to the government's preparedness: its published readiness to deal with new proposals or opportunities in a particular way, as in the Liberal administration's 1970s policy toward foreign investment.

Preparedness is a quality that comes in three sizes, of which policy is the middle one. The least-prepared government is one that is passive. It responds to each new problem or issue in an *ad hoc* manner. That is perhaps how Canada responds to new problems of foreign emergency aid or reception of refugees. Each time, the authorities must attempt to obtain information, weigh the various choices, set up a special administration or agency, and, following events very closely, attempt to learn whether the manner and amount of its actions were appropriate to Canadian political reactions.

The extreme opposite to this minimal state of preparedness is what might be called a "program." When a program exists, the government is set to take specific actions. Indeed, in a fully programmed governmental area, there may be contingency plans available for each future situation foreseen. In any event, a water-export program might be just as elaborate as a government's activism suggests: its plans might approximate a dated schedule of activities to be undertaken when the word is given, activities to obtain technical, meteorological and environmental information; to construct works, to raise finances, to liaise with other agencies and so on. (Of course, if prior thinking had induced the government never to export water, the program's many activities would be zeros.)

To have a policy is to have avoided both the unpreparedness of being purely passive and reactive, and the super-preparedness of having an active program in place for every contingency. To have no more than a policy is to recognize that in our mixed economy, many of the challenges and opportunities that may be presented for public choice are unforeseeable. The wise government neither walls itself up behind the Maginot Line of complete negation, nor does it keep its door on the latch to every approacher. Instead it compiles a certain amount of information in readiness for any initiative, and it clarifies its own reactions to typical proposals; it tests the powers and jurisdictions of citizens and of all orders of government. These preparations made, it may be said to have a policy, for the implementation of which it may even set up certain agencies and procedures.

Has Canada had a water-export policy up to now? Using our definition of policy from the preceding paragraphs, it has not. Government has simply *reacted* to the export projects proposed over the last two or three decades. Perhaps this record echoes the history of government responses to earlier water-resource issues. Many irrigation, water-power and water-supply impoundments and diversions originated as private or municipal promotions. Government typically reacted to these initiatives in a host of ways. One way of reacting was to set up a legislative framework, such as we see now in provincial water and irrigation Acts and in the international Boundary Waters Treaty. But these responses were made *after* private proposals had twisted themselves into public problems; they were not the embodiment of policies or programs thought out and implemented *in advance* of the private initiatives. Today, though, government is better prepared for water-resource issues such as hydro development and domestic supply management: policies have been stated, and in some cases government programs and review processes have been implemented.

Our position is that the same policy preparedness is required to cope with new initiatives for water exports from Canada.

Let us, then, concentrate on what policy should be. When a government has obtained some information, tested its powers and clarified its general attitudes, it is ready to take two essential steps that may be said to confirm the existence of a policy. First, it signals: it publishes a *message* so that all who would propose water-export projects will understand what kind of political reception they are likely to meet. Just as important, it sets up a *procedure* so that all who would propose action will know what steps they should take, what information they should present, and what payments they should offer.

When, eventually, government has constructed some statutory mixture of message and procedure for handling further water proposals, it has usually assigned itself two roles stemming, respectively, from its proprietary and its regulatory powers. Provincial water acts, for example, are primarily useful for handling private proposals to utilize or transport government-owned water. Other legislation, however, such as that governing the obstruction of boundary rivers or the setting up of irrigation districts, is an exercise of more general governmental powers not relying on public water proprietorship.

The *message* in such policies conveys government's general attitude on questions of national advantage or interest. Imports must pay a duty unless they are of a class or kind not made in Canada; investors must pay attention to ownership and control by non-Canadians; broadcasters must see that their productions have Canadian content; employers must not attempt to bring in talented outsiders when Canadians are available.

There is also a narrower category of export policies in which the message is that only when particular conditions are met will government permit electricity, uranium, oil, gas, logs and certain other goods or services to be exported. Occasionally, it is proposed to add to this list: that students may not take their talents abroad until or unless they have repaid the state for their education; that Canadian technology should be kept for the benefit of Canadian industry; and so on. Perhaps the unfamiliarity of these suggestions will illustrate how much more inclined Canadians are to proclaim their intention to restrict imports of goods and services than to restrict exports. But export-control messages are easy to signal and have proved not too costly to enforce.

Enforcement of a policy message requires a policy *procedure*, probably involving an agency to which applications may be made. For example, the applicants might be required to furnish a prospectus like that for the launching of a new public utility, including information about prospective ownership, finances and "public necessity and convenience"; they might also be required to provide something like an environmental impact statement. The governments, in their turn, would be required to hold hearings on these statements, as well as to create an agency to test the applicant's statements and a commission or political process to decide on the application. Procedures may be *ad hoc*, such as most of those that were followed in dealing with some recent megaprojects: the TransCanada Pipeline, the Mackenzie Pipeline and the James Bay power development. When it is believed, however, that the "message" about the policy is clear, and when the applicants are fairly numerous, a procedure may be formalized under a statute and given its own administrative routine, such as that available for setting up a bank under the federal *Bank Act* or for acquiring water rights in most provinces, or even for creating an irrigation or water district.

Thus, the quest for a water-export policy can be said to be a quest for a standing government "message" to those who would put forward water-export proposals, and to those who would be affected, along with a standard "procedure" to be followed by all who become involved. The next section outlines three kinds of message-procedure combinations among which Canadians might choose in deciding how to move from their present state of unpreparedness to consenting to and promulgating a policy.

Three Kinds of Policy Message

If Canada is to develop a water-export policy, it must publish a message. What should it say? That question must involve a prior question: What should it be *about*? Of course, if the policy is like that advocated in 1911, "no truck or trade with the Yankees," the signalling task would seem to be pretty simple. But history has shown that even though that message was clear and triumphant, it was little more than a slogan and did not convey at all what were to be Canada's economic relations with the United States. Railways were not pulled up, shipping continued, exports and imports went on, foreign investment proceeded.

So it is with water exports. Those who oppose a permissive policy make exceptions for certain kinds of water shipment or diversion. Indeed, it turns out that like the 1911 slogan, their remarks are intended to signal to the government their *generally* disapproving attitude to a kind of policy they imagine someone else might advocate. Their feelings could perhaps be expressed in a poem like this:

> Our running water that now flows
> Down from our lakes and springs,
> Supports our trees and wildlife,
> O'er waterfalls it sings.
>
> It sustains us in field and town,
> It joins our regions wide.
> Our Canada would not endure
> Were e'er our rivers dried.
>
> Not just another traded good
> Supplied for price or fee,
> Our water is our own lifeblood
> And flows to keep us free.
>
> Let those whose rivers they have stained
> With wastes insulting to the eye
> Whose water tables they have drained
> Let them now hear our cry:
>
> "O tempt us not with deals or wealth,
> Talk not of desperate need
> Nor threaten us with force or stealth.
> Our rivers we'll not cede.
>
> "Not if your coins to us are poured
> Nor if with drought you fail
> Not for your aid nor for export
> No drop is up for sale!"

Such verse may convey people's feelings, but it falls far short of "policy." Like earlier attempts to solve public decision problems by an absolute prohibition of all actions within an unduly wide general class, such a prohibition is weak and vulnerable to change and evasion. (We need only consider the fate of well-known general prohibitions of the past to realize that something better is needed here. Closing the economy to imports and immigration and refusing to allow certain exports or emigration or travel are the best examples. Although known as "policies," such ideas are soon in tatters everywhere as voters, pressure groups, administrators, governments and the courts relax them or make broad exceptions. The same is true of book-banning, censorship, liquor prohibition and drug control. These approaches to economic or social policy have become unenforceable.) Its history will be marked by successful attempts to avoid it by redefinition and exemption, so that where it seems best enforced and obeyed, one finds the apparent success is the result of large-scale exceptions to the general rule. In the process, the general spirit behind a worthy policy may have become distorted or frustrated.

In short, water-export policy must be specific. It may turn out that the application of such a specific policy will later reveal a generalization such as that "Water-export permissions are rarely granted." But such a result, if it stems from patient application of general procedures to individual cases, will be accepted and enforceable.

To be specific, a water-export policy message must distinguish among projects and proposals according to their geography, their economic and social profitability, and their timing. Each element must be examined on its own merits. The scrutiny of each project proposal should be rigorous enough so that it can be shown to be *without* sufficient merit; that it is not worth its costs or sacrifice to Canada; and that for such a project, exports should be zero.

The general policy should make it clear that when merit is missing, permission will not be granted and water exports will not take place. The policy should, in announcing how applications will be handled, concentrate on three important dimensions along which every application will be measured:

- conditions to be met;
- payments to be received; and
- timing or period of approval.

What conditions for water export?   Along this direction are ranged policy messages setting forth progressively less demanding conditions that must be met by an applicant following a water-export procedure. The zero position is, of course, that the total conditions are prohibitive, and that no export application can succeed. Moving away from this extreme are policy positions that set out the total conditions to be met in a sequence that is increasingly permissive. The conditions include those to do with demonstrating that there is a water surplus at the source, that changing water levels and flows will not harm the environment, that water users will not suffer, that employment will not decline, and so forth. A "permissive" policy message might set forth a procedure under which applicants had only to show that there was a water surplus in the average year or in almost all years; that environmental damage would be limited; and that producers and communities displaced by the water diversion works would be relocated.

What payments for water export?   Along this policy continuum are ranged payment messages that become steadily less demanding. At the zero end, the payment requirements are prohibitive and no exports result. Progressing along this dimension the demanded compensation is reduced. At its remote end, therefore, compensation has tapered off until water exporting has become essentially free and uncontrolled. To illustrate, four policy positions along this dimension might be: first, no exports; second, exports only on discriminatingly monopolistic terms whereby every scrap of advantage to the water importer is converted into cash gain to Canada; third, fair compensation only for actual cash and opportunity costs incurred by Canada; and fourth, no compensation as long as the water exporter pays for all the works along the water-diversion route.

What timing for water export?   Along this policy continuum are ranged policies that vary with respect to the period in which water-export applications may succeed. The initial or zero position is, of course, that no water exports will *ever* be allowed. A less prohibitive position might be that applications, if they are ever to succeed, must be *postponed*. Another position on this dimension, one less onerous perhaps, would be the message that applications can *sometimes* succeed. At the permissive extreme, the policy message would be that water-export proposals are welcome now and *always*.

The questions raised along each of these dimensions are recognizable. In our broadcasting-licence policy, for example, the CRTC screens out applicants by a conditions procedure. The prize goes to the broadcaster proposing and accepting the most onerous conditions. The payment dimension, too, is in actual use. For example, the provinces can be said to grant permission to log in Crown forests or to drill for oil on the basis of competitive stumpage or bonus bidding. Failing competitive bidding, the policy is to set Crown payments (and private compensation to farmers and others) high enough to meet the policy objectives. The timing dimension is less formally recognizable, but it is certainly in use. Some Canadians have said that export of raw materials should never be allowed; Mr. Justice Berger held that the Mackenzie Valley pipeline should be postponed for at least 10 years; various inquiries have recommended that Crown resources should not be disposed of at once, but spaced out over many years for sustained yield or steady revenue; and some advisors of Secretary Watt in the U.S.A. suggested that the public lands' resources should be sold out immediately.

What are the advantages of selecting just one of these three policy dimensions and placing Canadian water-export policy at a given position along it? They are obvious. Applicants and opponents know where they stand: there is certainty. Those who have projects can begin to plan on the basis that general policy is settled, and that only the conditions or the payments or the timing are a barrier to their proceeding. Similarly, those who oppose water export will understand what it is that under a hearings or application procedure, they must show. (Of course, if the policy position is a prohibitive one, there is *complete* certainty for both applicants and their opponents.) Much more might be said on the advantage of this definite selection of a policy, recalling the criteria once listed as the characteristics of a good tax: yield, justice, certainty, economy in collection, and compliance. However, the disadvantages of this one-dimensional approach to water-export policy are overwhelming. If such a policy is adhered to, it is inflexible, unrealistic and wasteful.

As to its inflexibility, one-dimensional policy has the fault of committing the country to a future policy stance on the basis of today's incomplete knowledge. Those who believe that the purpose of policy is to guide government actions so that they will add to the general benefits received from all sources, private and public, recognize that new problems and new opportunities come along with time. It is unrealistic to commit one's country to a water-export policy, knowing that future events could cause the policy, whenever it is invoked, to reduce public welfare rather than to increase it. Such events can be predicted to lead to a campaign to evade or abandon the policy completely.

A third disadvantage of adopting a one-dimensional water-export policy is that it is wasteful. To adopt any policy there must be a prior investment in information about technology, ecology and economic and environmental preferences. Such information is costly, as was shown by the number of inquiries into the Mackenzie Valley pipeline, the Columbia River and St. Lawrence River treaty-water management projects, and the proposed construction of the Site C dam on the Peace River. (All of these projects have much in common with a typical water-export project.) The waste occurs because if the specific policy investigated does not succeed, the fact-finding and attitude-shaping investments go down the drain. Furthermore, there is the waste or the misdirection of public interest and the distraction of political energy from other government functions.

The costs of inflexibility, unreality and wastefulness are all real enough. It is true that they can be exaggerated because they are not strictly additive to one another. They are three aspects of one undesirable characteristic of specific policies drafted to deal with only *one dimension* of water-export proposals. The lesson is that both policy and policy making should be clear, and should also be flexible and adaptable, available for application to proposals in continually changing circumstances. This aim can be accomplished most economically by setting out a well-understood and robust "procedure," the heart of any policy.

The procedure, in turn, should make it possible for governments, tribunals, applicants and opponents to bring forward evidence about specific water-export proposals that is germane to a decision along *any* of the policy dimensions: conditions, payment or timing. Indeed, each proposal should not only be investigated in detail for its ecological, environmental, economic and social effects, but also experimentally varied to redefine it so as to examine the most attractive combination of the three aspects that we have called "the three policy dimensions."

This procedure is the comprehensive project-review process outlined below under the heading of "Benefit-Cost Analysis."

An Economic Test of Water-Export Policies

In this section are presented three brief arguments that lead to our favouring an economic approach to the making and implementing of a water-export policy.

First, as has already been argued, each proposal should, broadly, be evaluated on its own merits. The reason is that the domain of possible proposals is so extensive that it would be difficult to draft a useful policy that covered all possible projects. This is because it would tend to have either of two serious defects. If, on the one hand, it were to consist of a general message to cover all future proposals, it would be so unspecific and empty that it would leave future governments unassisted in working out particular decisions as if the original policy had never been made. This would be so even if the message were completely prohibitive or completely permissive. On the other hand, a policy conveying to future governments and applicants *all* of the conditions that must be satisfied by every possible water diversion-and-sale project, would be so time consuming and costly to develop and so inflexible in application as not to be worth attempting.

It follows that a water-export policy "message" should inform everyone about what must be taken into consideration and weighed, and who must be consulted, and how their preferences are to be assessed. The procedure would consist of a set of fairly firm but general rules for those who prepared the information on each proposal and, more important, for those entrusted with making decisions.

An important objection to this kind of policy would be that if every proposal were judged separately, the total, nation-wide water-export situation would be neglected. Canada might decide efficiently and fairly on every case, yet in the end wind up with too much or too little diversion and sale of water. This is a reasonable fear. It implies that the procedure must state that in each decision the authorities must take into account not only the immediate good and bad effects of the proposal, but also the cumulative consequences of the proposed project as an addition to the total amount of water exported from that region, from that river or source, and from Canada as a whole. Thus this objection is not fatal to our argument for an economic, project-by-project, implementation of water-export policy.

Secondly, whatever the policy, the procedure must be one that is capable of weighing or balancing a variety of effects from a single project. This conclusion follows from the assertion underlying the previous proposition that diversion projects will be unlike one another. The additional presumption here is that they will differ in their good effects or benefits, and in their bad effects or costs. Furthermore, it may be argued that from a Canadian point of view the *real* effects of diverting water to the United States are all undesirable. Some may be fairly tolerable, and some may be seriously disturbing. But it is hard to think of any Canadian river having levels and flows such that we would positively wish for its stages to be lowered or its volume reduced. If it were so, we might even be willing to pay the United States to drain some of our excess water away. Nothing like this has been suggested.

It follows that nearly every conceivable water-export proposal will be acceptable to Canadians if, and only if, the importers offer compensating payment in some form. The payment may be in the form of a reciprocal water import into Canada, cash (permanent or annual), debt cancellation, lowering some barrier to trade (or migration or investment) or some other favourable U.S. foreign-policy action.

It also follows that the procedure that is part of our water-export policy must be one that is capable of balancing the almost inevitable real losses to Canada from diversion and transfer against the gains that are offered in return. Each export proposal will have its own special costs and will attract its own proffered rewards or gains. It is not unreasonable to define national advantage as a situation where the expected gains sufficiently exceed the expected costs. The point here is that the procedure for determining whether there is a national advantage must be able to weigh all the effects. That points to an economic benefit-cost analysis of the kind favoured here.

Our third argument for favouring an economic method of implementing policy is that the procedure must be one that is capable of "optimizing" each water-export proposal before it is decided on. Optimization is a process of adjusting the design and timing of and the payments for a project until it is reconstituted in its most attractive form.[13] There are several reasons for doing this. All come down to the proposition that it makes no sense to evaluate a second-rate proposal when extra preparation would make it possible to determine whether a better variant was worth permitting.

For example, it is wasteful to study only whether to direct water from point A on a river when further study would suggest a more benign environmental impact and lower construction costs if diversion were made from point B. Why would private promoters propose a less-than-optimum project? They may wish to put to work some specific asset of their own: land already owned or a canal or dam already in existence. The process of project evaluation should detect this and propose the substitution of the socially better variant before a final decision is made. Another example also involves social as contrasted with private costs. A promoter may argue that energy to lift water over a mountain divide is costless because the total project will generate energy as a by-product. From a social point of view this contention would be incorrect if such energy has an alternative market. Consequently, the procedure that evaluates the project should enter the energy used at its real or opportunity costs. Other examples involve timing. A promoter may be forced to propose rapid construction because of the interest costs during construction. This pace may not accord with public priorities, however, because a smaller and slower project might have a more desirable impact on the local labour market or the high financing costs pressing the promoter might not be as serious from a social point of view. This example recalls the debates between the proponents of "megaprojects" and "small is beautiful." Boosters and promoters of water-resources projects are correct when they argue that the costs they perceive call for high-pressure coordinated-construction activity, for high dams, wide canals, and for other sources of economies of scale. The evaluation procedure should review their plans, however, to obtain the social best from a series of projects producing different social, environmental and economic effects.

To repeat, there are three dimensions of questions to be dealt with in every policy message: the conditions that a project should satisfy; the benefits in the form of payments that it should produce; and the timing and duration of the project. In optimizing each project, the authorities should consider these as *variable* and consequently as capable of being moulded and shaped to improve a proposal beyond its initial specifications. However, to replace such platitudinous conditions as that the project must involve minimum environmental impact, minimum construction cost, and minimum social disturbance, that it must attract a maximum cash-or-kind payment from the water importer, and that the projects must be installed in a present-value-maximizing sequence, the policy procedure might be built around a series of calculations that enables decision makers to understand the advantage to the total project to be had from small adjustments along each of these dimensions.

Each small improvement along any dimension will, when the project is in near-optimal shape, cause a small loss along another dimension. For example, an improvement in the scheduling of the project might lead to a predictable environmental loss. The relationship between these small gains and losses is what is referred to technically as the "trade-off" of timing-induced gains for environmentally oriented losses. Such trade-offs can be calculated between changes along all pairs of dimensions. The details of data requirements and procedures are tedious, but we believe that the lesson should be clear. An economic approach is needed for the decision makers to shift their consideration from scattered proposals to "the best" project.

To summarize, this section has attempted an orderly arrangement of the case for an economic evaluation. First, it has been argued, as it was in the preceding section, that a policy message about water exports will be valueless unless it consists mostly of terms of reference and detailed instructions for a procedure for separately judging individual export projects. Next, it was argued that the evaluation of each proposal should take into account all its various kinds of effects — environmental, economic and social — and that this conclusion leads to the need for an *economic* framework for evaluation. Finally, it was argued that the procedure should not take proposals as they are offered, but should optimize them by observing the change in overall value as experimental changes are made in their characteristics along three dimensions: physical characteristics, payments and timing. It was urged that this optimization process would give decision makers trade-off values for judging marginal or incremental effects along one dimension as another aspect is altered.

We believe that an economic procedure is needed to obtain these three important qualities of water-export policy implementation, and we shall now proceed to illustrate such a procedure.

The Benefits and Costs of Exporting Water

Introduction

The purpose of this section is to outline how an economist might evaluate water-export proposals. A method of economic analysis is presented that allows for the identification and measurement (in dollar values) of the benefits and costs of a water-export project. An economist asked whether a particular water-export proposal should be adopted might answer, "If Canada is on balance made better off — that is if the benefits to Canada exceed the costs imposed on Canada when both are measured properly — then the project should be approved."

The rationale for this type of analysis is that water in Canada is a scarce resource with many competing uses. Its scarcity gives it value, and competition among its potential uses implies that allocating water to one use (e.g., diverting it to irrigate North Dakota farms) carries the cost of not having the water for other uses (e.g., irrigating Saskatchewan farms). The following analysis of water-export projects is based on the general assumption that economically valuable resources should be allocated to maximize the benefits they can provide to Canada. This sentiment applies as much to the allocation of water as it does to the allocation of labour or capital.

To avoid impatience with an economic approach to export projects, the reader must understand how the word "economic" is being used here. The word is not intended to mean that only commercial or market valuations will be used. On the contrary, these valuations make up only one part of the recommended approach. Also to be taken into account are important non-commercial values, such as those measuring losses or gains of an environmental or social nature. Examples of the latter might even include the international prestige gained from the completion of a large-scale water-diversion project. If, therefore, the "economic" nature of the benefit-cost analysis of a project causes uneasiness, it should not be because of its narrowness but because of its ambition.

It is argued in this paper that a comprehensive economic analysis that includes all the consequences of a water-export project is the best way of organizing data and opinions for the Canadian decision-making process.

There are two very important objections to benefit-cost analysis. First, no decision is acceptable that simply weighs gains against losses without taking into account that they may accrue to quite different groups of Canadians. It never has been Canadian policy to presume such an intense national organic unity that it does not matter who suffers for others to gain. Nevertheless there are advantages to starting with a nation-wide point of view. For example, it is arguable that a benefit-cost analysis that is national in scope will be better able to differentiate between factors affecting the distribution of incomes and those affecting the rural scale of economic activity. At the same time, the analysis can be constructed to give appropriate weight to changes in the distribution of income to the degree felt necessary by Canadians.

A second possible objection is simpler: it is impossible to use economics or any other discipline to weigh different kinds of benefits and costs against one another. Some are immeasurable, and all are incommensurable. The section below on the Canadian costs of exporting water examines this objection in depth. At this stage it need only be commented that decision makers must already weigh unlike effects against one another; that economic terms is a modest effect; and that it is a good and flexible method of integrating and comparing dissimilar concerns.

Canadian Benefits of Exporting Water

This section describes the benefits that Canadians might garner from a water-export project. These include all results that can be classified as additional goods or services enjoyed, cost savings in the provision of any other goods or services, or both. The potential gains from a water-export project might include payments to Canada for the water it has exported, increased employment during the construction phase of the project, indirect cost savings made possible by the installation of the water-export project, recreational gains and political benefits. Each of these will be considered in turn.

The largest potential benefit is the payments Canada will receive for its exported water. Payment might be expected to be based on the volume of water transported and might also reflect the seasonality of the water's value. To compare this benefit with various initial costs if payments are received over the lifetime of the project (rather than as a lump-sum payment at its inception), future payments must be converted into present dollars. This is a straightforward operation, but it involves choosing an appropriate discount rate and allowing for future changes in the domestic foreign value of the dollar.

In addition, the successful completion of a water-export project might lead to political gains for the Canadian and provincial governments. These gains could include increased goodwill and cooperation from foreign governments and the achievement of federal and provincial policy goals made possible by the project. Examples of the latter include assistance for regional development projects and decreased reliance on exhaustible fossil fuels.

Another potentially significant benefit might stem from increased employment during the construction phase of the water-export project. If the project's construction draws labour (or other factors of production) from demonstrably less productive uses, especially if the project were undertaken in a region of chronic underemployment, the value of the increase in employment can justifiably be included as a benefit. If, on the other hand, employment during the operation of the project involves the use of skilled labour having a high probability of employment elsewhere, we must conclude that the project is displacing skilled labour from alternative productive employment. As a result, little or no net benefit is generated from this assignment to the water-export project.

Cost savings in Canada made possible by a new water-export project may also be included among its benefits. Let us consider how these might come about. A scheme to transport water to the United States is likely to have substantial effects on the water-supply patterns in adjacent Canadian regions. It might be possible for those regions to benefit from the water exports to America. For example, local water supply might be made more reliable or less expensive if the water export works were designed to serve Canadians as well. Alternatively, local flood control might be made less costly by a water-diversion project.

There are other potentially significant benefits stemming from water-export projects. These projects might create new recreational opportunities. For example, a water-diversion project might lead to the creation of a lake attractive for recreational boating. Such a benefit is real enough, though hard to measure. Its value can be approximated by public willingness to pay for its use.

These are the benefits that might be expected to arise from a water-export project. Before turning to the costs of such a project, two important and often controversial aspects of any benefit-side calculations warrant consideration. These are the income-redistributional effects of a water-export project and the problem of uncertainty in the measurement of the benefits (and costs) of a water-export project.

Usually, the redistributional effects on incomes of a water-export project are not incorporated into a benefit-cost study because they reflect nothing more than dollar-for-dollar transfers among Canadians. The gains to some are exactly balanced by the losses of others. How to treat these gains and losses is given considerable space in the official Canada Treasury Board *Benefit-Cost Analysis Guide* (1976, chap. 2). The general rule is that such redistributions should be considered as a benefit (or cost) only to the extent that they also influence the allocation of resources, or that they reflect the achievement (or failure) of governmental policies. For example, a water-export project might inadvertently bring larger federal compensation payments to a region than the foreign payments received in Ottawa. Thus, the project would effect a general income and welfare transfer to the region from the rest of Canada. Whether this interregional transfer should be treated as a benefit of the project is a question to be answered by reference to political policy. If it helps to achieve what Parliament would attempt to bring about in any case, some fraction of it may be counted as among the project's benefits to Canada as a whole. Of course, to the favoured region all of the transfer may be treated as a benefit.

Finally, it is more than likely that future benefits accruing from the water-export project will be known imperfectly, or at least that there will be uncertainty regarding their extent. These informational problems could arise from uncertainty about future forecasts of American demand for our water, or if the future supply-demand balance of Canadian water is not well understood. Benefit-cost analysis can usually be extended to allow for these considerations. By considering the probability of alternative future water scenarios and finding the weighted average of future benefits from these separate scenarios, decision makers can benefit from benefit-cost analysis in the face of uncertain or imperfect information.

Canadian Costs of Exporting Water

The previous section discussed the benefits that might be generated by a water-export project. Carrying out such a project, of course, will not be without its costs, against which the benefits must be assessed. In general terms these costs equate with the value of the real resources to be employed in the project that are displaced from other uses in the economy. The purpose of this section is to identify those resources and consider how they are valued.

The main cost component of a water-export project will probably be for construction of the water-transportation facility. As mentioned earlier, diversion canals, dams, levees and other works will be needed. In the United States, water-diversion projects moving water across flat desert areas have had annualized capital-cost projections of $60/1,000 m^3 per year for a 600 km pipeline (Howe and Easter, 1971, p. 110). As most of the capital costs must be incurred before operation can begin, there may be a considerable accumulation of interest costs during the construction period and early life of the project. The reason for including interest charges with the direct cost of capital is that interest charges are a measure of the annual return to the economy as a whole that the capital employed in the project could have earned in profitable opportunities elsewhere. (These costs lead to a pronounced compression of the construction phase. It is costly to construct a water-export project in distinct phases over a number of years unless the project has other purposes, such as water supply for irrigation at intermediate points along its route. If the project were intended solely for carrying water to export, its construction would cost least if it were continuous, with its numerous components begun concurrently. This is chiefly because most costs of export projects are incurred at the outset, and the interest expense of any extension of the construction phase accumulates into prohibitive carrying costs later on. However, analysts must watch for the extra social costs of unduly rapid construction.)

Operating and maintenance (O & M) costs must be added to the project's annualized capital costs. Once operation has begun, we might expect these costs to be more or less constant. A major part of O & M costs will be the project's annual wage bill. The extent to which the cost of labour is included as a cost of the project will depend on the state of employment locally. If labour (or another resource) employed during the life of the project would not have been employed otherwise, then in an economic sense the cost of its use is zero, for nothing is forgone in using its services on the project. A more likely scenario is that labour is underemployed only to a degree. Some workers might have had jobs at least part of the time. Also, even in a region with high unemployment some of the workers hired must be drawn from a labour market of skilled experienced employees with good alternative employment opportunities. The extent to which labour costs may be "marked down" is often a difficult and controversial topic in benefit-cost analysis (Canada Treasury Board, 1976, chap. 2).

A second major component of operating and maintenance costs will stem from the energy required to pump water. Because of the substantial increases in energy costs during the 1970s and 1980s and because of the mountainous topography of much of western North America, the costs of pumping and raising water may be quite significant (see Christensen et al., 1982).

While the other resources used in a water export project will usually be valued at something close to their market prices, their cost to the project may, in some instances, have to be corrected by imputation. For example, if publicly owned land is used in the construction of a water-diversion canal, no market transaction will occur to reflect the value of its use. Yet that area may have valuable alternate uses (as farmland or parkland, for example). In this situation a value must be imputed to the land for the purpose of measuring the full costs of the project.

A more important example concerns the benefits we will forgo by having less water available to Canada as a result of water exports. If water is to be sold or exported to the United States, and if that water could have been used in Canada, then we must net out from the project benefits the value of its use had it remained in Canada. This value would stem from its use in irrigation, industrial, recreational or domestic consumption. We shall refer to this too-often neglected value as the "opportunity cost" of exporting water. A subtle point needs to be considered in computing the opportunity cost of the water exported. Expanded supplies of irrigation water to American farms may allow that industry to increase its output. If American agricultural output is large relative to the world market, the expansion in American production could lower world agricultural prices. In turn, the prices received by Canadian farmers might fall, thereby lowering their income. The impact of this rather indirect effect certainly would have to be included in any computation of the opportunity costs of exporting water.

A potentially significant but often neglected cost is that of decommissioning the project. Dams and canals have finite lifetimes. In many cases at the end of the project's lifetime efforts will be made to return the project site to its original state (for example, through tearing down capital structures, landscaping and reforestation). For some large public projects these costs can be expected to be substantial. As for construction, operating and maintenance costs, the calculation of decommissioning costs will depend on the time pattern of expenditures and will require the choice of an appropriate discount rate to convert remote future expected costs into current dollar values. As most water developments have been relatively recent, we have little experience with the need, the process or the costs of decommissioning dams and canals.

The final set of costs related to water exports stems from the potential impact on the natural environment. We have already insisted that both land and water used in the project should be costed at at least the value of their best alternative use. In addition to the removal of land, the project may cause environmental degradation during its construction or operation phases. Examples of this type of impact include the following: lowered river levels causing higher mortality among fish populations; stream diversions leading to decreased wildlife habitats; and accelerated rates of stream erosion. Although these effects are difficult to identify and quantify, any environmental damage from a water-export project should be recognized in the benefit-cost analysis.

There are three ways of handling the difficulty that human valuations of hydrological and ecological changes are rarely stated in money terms.

One way is to attempt direct estimates, emulating market valuations; a second is to measure the cost of mitigative measures and compensation payable to those who suffer from the changes, minus the gains to those who benefit; a third is to abandon the measurement attempt and treat environmental damage as a physical and subjective concept to be valued as a residual in benefit-cost calculations. Each of these is touched on below.

Direct Estimates   There are well-known techniques available for estimating parts of the environmental damage sustained when water quality is changed. Peter Victor, for example, is the author of studies of the value of fisheries damaged by acid rain in Ontario; estimates like this have been made in several regions (Dewees et al., 1975). Other studies, including one by Peter Pearse, made earlier estimates of the damage stemming from mercury released into the Great Lakes basin. Some of these techniques are applicable to changes in water flows. Another set of studies has accumulated over the years, demonstrating the possibility of measuring the human valuations of changed water levels. The best examples are, once again, those made for the Great Lakes, usually for IJC references. In other sources attempts are made to value the effects of lake-level changes on fisheries. Another source of estimates is the damages sought or awarded in legal cases. The Alberta action brought by the Town of Peace River against B.C. Hydro concerning the change in the regime of the Peace River due to the Bennett Dam is especially useful here because the alleged damage was part of a more extensive change in river-basin ecology. In the Garrison Dam and Poplar River dockets of the IJC, too, will be found testimony concerning the damage from ecological changes. Some of these imply orders of magnitude in the minds of the speakers or writers. Another approach is in its infancy: bidding games by recreational users or even by outsiders in which a method of consistently eliciting valuations of a recreational area is attempted (see Kneese and Brown, 1981, pp. 170–78).

Mitigation and Compensation   Some of the more serious environmental effects of construction can be reduced or prevented altogether by adding other features to the diversion works. The expenditure necessary to mitigate the damage is then used as a proxy for a measurement of the environmental cost. Examples and discussions are to be found in the Berger Report (1977), the Site C Report of the B.C. Utility Commission (1984), and the IJC's Garrison Report (1977). Most of these have to do with environmental quality; however, the IJC's Poplar River report also deals with the *amount* of water needed for power-plant cooling and waste-heat disposal. There is a very large literature on the costs of environmental mitigation, especially reclamation and rehabilitation of open-pit coal mines (Kneese and Brown, 1981).

A good example associated with water transfers is to be found in the High Plains report. The authors devote a long chapter to the environmental impact of the four optional canal projects and include a methodology for estimating mitigation costs. For the one canal to which the estimating procedure was applied, mitigation costs averaged about 5 to 6 percent of expected capital costs. One such cost would be acquisition and improvement of wildlife-habitat lands to compensate for other habitat losses.

Closely related to mitigation costs are those arising from the acquisition of information about environmental impacts by attenuation and monitoring. At several places in this study we have mentioned the opportunity to slow down construction work and space out its components over an extended period. Such attenuation permits decision makers to learn at first hand how projects may hurt or enhance their natural surroundings. A closely related idea is monitoring. As Keith Henry, the chairman of the major Site C hearings, commented, "Many decisions might be delayed if an adequate system of monitoring impacts were to be set up, including a method of making sure that impacts so measured would be mitigated or compensated for. This solution would allow an opportunity to see what really does happen and provide specific remedies" (Henry, 1983, p. 75). This approach is costly, though not necessarily more so than any alternative. Building smaller versions of eventual works produces information without much damage, but it also misses the technical economies of scale of full-sized works. The waiting time before full operation is likely to be considerably longer and so more costly to finance. Monitoring itself is difficult to organize and expensive. Furthermore, if it is successful in detecting serious environmental harm, it points to further costly mitigating works, compensation, removal or indeed abandonment of the whole project. But this is the point: it may be less costly to go ahead and experience bad impacts than to delay and study them using too little data. Jane Austen's character Charlotte Lucas put well the unprofitability of some advance measures of study and mitigation: "I wish Jane success with all my heart; and if she were married to him to-morrow, I should think she had as good a chance of happiness as if she were to be studying his character for a twelvemonth" (*Pride and Prejudice*, chap. 6).

When there is little information to be pondered, environmental harmony and matrimony are both matters of chance, as Charlotte later observes. It follows that the extra costs of keeping components small, building slowly, monitoring new effects, and being receptive to using the project itself as a study device may be the least wasteful of the components building up the environmental cost category.

Residual valuation   The methods mentioned above may fail. There may not be enough information about citizens' valuations of the changes in the environment brought about by a water-export project. If not, politicians and their assistants must do without scientific investigations. Then, under the third method, benefit-cost analysis expression must be stood on its head. The question whether a project's benefits are greater than its construction costs plus water-opportunity costs plus environmental costs must be restated, and becomes the question whether its perceived or feared net environmental effects (costs) are serious enough to exceed its expected net benefits (that is, benefits minus construction costs and water-opportunity costs). This "Is it worth it?" approach to estimating an amount has been used in some actual environmental studies. Here it side-steps the dollar-measurement problem by putting the emphasis on a comparison of total benefits (net of construction and water-opportunity costs) with what is objectively known and subjectively felt about what would happen to the environment at the source and along the course. The burden of estimation, in other words, is placed more heavily on benefits. Knowledge of how much the promoter is willing to pay helps the resource owners to think through not only how much the water is worth but, more important, how much the consequent net damage to the environment is worth.

How should a decision be reached, once both benefits and costs have been estimated? The basic idea is to make sure that the present value of benefits exceeds costs. The precise details of this general criterion are a subject for debate: for a review of various criteria and their respective pros and cons, see the Treasury Board's 1976 *Benefit-Cost Analysis Guide*, pp. 26–32. The most commonly employed criterion states that if the benefits exceed the costs, completion of the project will contribute to the wealth of Canada; and if the net benefits are greater than any other scheme designed to achieve the same goals, the project should be undertaken.

There are situations in which this decision-making rule should be modified. The presence of uncertainty regarding important costs and benefits requires that we compare the *expected* present value of benefits and costs. This procedure was discussed in the section of this chapter on the Canadian benefits of exporting water.

Alternatively, the project may involve making decisions that are in some way irreversible. For example, a water-export project may become so much a part of the way of life of the importing region that it would be politically or diplomatically unthinkable to end it. A river diversion (with its attendant impacts on agricultural and industrial development) may be treated as irreversible if the diversion can be undone only at a prohibitive cost. In such situations economic analysis calls for modification of the benefit-cost decision rule. It has been shown that adding a certain sum to the value of the forgone environmental asset will prevent over-investment in irreversible projects. The needed sum has been called an "option value" and can be thought of as an insurance premium paid to make sure that the asset (or equivalent compensation) is available if and when wanted.[14] Of course, as taking out insurance does not prevent a fire, so adding an option value to a project's costs does nothing real to increase the probability of the project's reversibility. That must be part of the project's optimization.

Some Illustrative Calculations

The preceding sections have outlined the major difficulties encountered in the measurement of the costs and benefits of any water-export project. The purpose of this section is to present some more specific calculations, drawing on evidence from past water-transfer projects and current proposals. Thus, this section will provide some "real world" estimates of the capital costs of transporting water and will illustrate the types of calculations surrounding the analysis of a hypothetical diversion project. This exercise should give some clarity to our theoretical discussion and should provide some feeling for the "ball park" in which cost-and-benefit figures rest. Unfortunately the available information is sparse.

We should need to know how much Canadians and Americans are willing to pay for various amounts of fresh water. The key parameter for these data is the "elasticity of demand," stating how much consumption would fall if the per-litre water charge to them increased slightly. Second, and almost as important, is the elasticity of substitution, a statistic revealing the relative importance of water compared to other inputs in farming and other water-intensive activities. Thirdly, we ought to know the cost economies of scale with respect to volume and distance for water-canal and pipeline construction.

There may be several reasons for paucity of information about these parameters. Perhaps most important, until recently the perceived abundance of water in Canada (and to a lesser extent the lavish subsidization of water in the United States) has stifled econometric research. Furthermore, the topographical conditions among water-diversion routes may have differed enough to make generalizations regarding project costs difficult or uninformative.

Despite these problems, some ball-park figures such as would be relevant to the study of a specific Canadian water-export proposal can be estimated. We first consider estimates of *capital costs* of past water-diversion projects.

Costs   Howe and Easter (1971, pp. 107–111) report amortized capital-cost figures for several proposed and operational water-diversion projects in the western United States. These costs (converted to 1984 dollars) range from $70/1,000 m³/year for a Colorado-based project designed to transport 9 billion m³/year over a distance of 500 kilometres to $250/1000 m³/year for a complex scheme to divert 2 billion m³/year in the

TABLE 2-1 Increasing Unit Costs of Water Transfer in California

Annual Yield or Delivery (billion m³/year)	Amortized Capital Cost (1980 U.S. $/1000 m³ yield)
0	30
1	35
2	40
3	45
4	60
5	80
6	120
7	150
8	250–300

Source: Wallace et al., 1982, p. 201.

American South West over 1500 kilometres. These figures are based on a 5 percent discount rate and an assumed project lifetime of 50 years. More recent capital-cost estimates are available from Wallace et al. (1982, p. 201). Their results are presented as Table 2-1, showing how capital costs rise as the amount of water to be pumped and transferred increases. The numbers are drawn from seventeen actual and proposed California projects to bring water various distances from outside the state, for, say, at least 300 km.

The most important point to notice from the table is that in order to increase the annual yield of water diverted into California, the water authorities there would find capital cost growing at an increasing rate, because of the need to draw upon successively less productive (and, therefore, more expensive) sources. This is relevant for the possibility of importing Canadian water, as such a project would likely enjoy cost economies of scale with respect to the distance the water was transported.

Such economic studies of alternative proposed (or existing) Canadian water-diversion projects within Canada are scarce. Those available are usually engineering cost estimates: that is, the cost of a particular design, approved on engineering or geological grounds. Consequently, unlike Table 2-1, they convey little about the relationship between size of scale (or market) on the one hand and construction costs on the other. Moreover engineering evaluations usually do not incorporate measures of implicit costs such as the opportunity costs of water and land or the costs of environmental degradation. Nonetheless the available studies do carefully delineate expected capital and operating costs and are therefore valuable starting points for the examination of the feasibility of Canadian water exports.

One such engineering cost study was undertaken by the Saskatchewan-Nelson Basin Board (SNBB) (1972). The Board considered several possible water-diversion projects in the southern Canadian prairie provinces. For our purposes a particularly interesting proposal concerns the

TABLE 2-2 Qu'Appelle River Diversion

Item[a]	Cost (million 1984$)[b]
1. Channel Improvements	
Qu'Appelle Dam to Buffalo Pound Lake	42.0
Buffalo Pound Lake to Craven Control Station	56.7
2. Lake Control Structures (two)	0.75
3. Craven Pumping Plant	56.0
4. Canal: Craven to Rafferty	210.0
5. Boggy Creek Dam and Reservoir	1.8
6. Wascana Diversion Canal	1.5
7. Sidley Dam and Reservoir	2.8
8. Moose Jaw Creek Diversion Canal	8.3
9. Rafferty Dam and Reservoir	18.4
Total	398.25
Annual Cost (approximate)[c]	36.0

Source: Saskatchewan-Nelson Basin Board, 1972, Appendix 3, pp. 84, 92.

a. A detailed discussion of the nature of the project and its components can be found in Saskatchewan-Nelson Basin Board, Appendix 3, pp. 84–85 and 92–93.

b. The Qu'Appelle project was designed in 1970. The cost of items 1, 3 and 4, originally expressed in 1970 dollars, has been updated to 1984 dollars using the engineering-cost estimates in the six-state High Plains study (1982, Appendix E, Figures 22 and 24). The original cost estimates for the other items found in Saskatchewan-Nelson Basin Board, 1972, were simply updated using the Non Residential Building Construction Input Price Index (Statistics Canada Cat. No. 62-007).

c. Annual costs were computed by adding discounted annualized capital costs, including depreciation to estimated discounted annual operating and maintenance costs (see Saskatchewan-Nelson Basin Board, 1972, Appendix 2, pp. 125–30 for details).

diversion of water from the South Saskatchewan River through the Qu'Appelle River north of Regina, southward to the Souris River in the southeastern corner of Saskatchewan. We chose this example because it transfers water from an "all Canadian" river to one that flows into the United States. The project would have the capacity to divert some one billion m³/year of water over the 300 kilometre distance. This amount is probably not feasible from a water-supply point of view, as it would require the diversion of almost 15 percent of the mean annual flow of the South Saskatchewan River. Water would probably have to be diverted from the Peace River drainage if exports of more than one billion m³ per year were anticipated. This extra distance would make the total cost of the project very much higher (and would therefore raise the necessary payment for the exported water substantially). Consequently we emphasize that in the following detailed cost breakdown we are presenting an illustrative calculation, using available numbers, of a rather hypothetical project. Nevertheless the figures are illuminating.

Spread over the intended billion cubic metres per year the construction cost of $36 million per year comes to $36/1,000 m³/year at 1984 prices. This unit cost lies in the same order of magnitude as the Auburn project in California's Sierra foothills, with capital costs of around

$50 (U.S.) per 1,000 m^3 (Rogers, 1984). Although this is considerably less than the $400–$800/1,000 m^3 per year for the other four possible High Plains projects studied in 1979 by the U.S. Army Corps of Engineers, these projects differ so drastically from Canadian plains conditions that comparisons may not be useful. Whereas the Canadian SNBB project involves lifting water out of the Qu'Appelle watercourse into another until the Souris River is reached at a lower altitude, the American projects would transfer water about the same distance, uphill most of the way, until the High Plains area is reached, in some places 3000 feet above sea level. Installation of dams and pumps to make this possible would account for much of their higher cost. In any case, the SNBB study suggests an initial cost in Canada, for construction only, of approximately $400 million in 1984 dollars.

To this capital cost must be added first the opportunity cost of the water and then the environmental costs. The main opportunity cost is the alternative use of the water for irrigation. Its value can be approximated from the contribution of this flow to agricultural output at the source, the Qu'Appelle River basin. This now has approximately 7800 hectares of irrigated farmland (Prairie Provinces Water Board, 1982, Appendix 3, pp. 75–76). Unfortunately, no study of irrigation's contribution to the net value of agricultural output in Saskatchewan has been conducted. However we may draw on recent estimates compiled by Muller (1985) for the value of irrigation water in Alberta. Muller reports an average value of $19/1,000 m^3 per year for contribution of irrigation water to the net value of agriculture.

This may be determined to be the basic opportunity cost of the water, to be added to the $36/1,000 m^3 per year construction cost previously estimated. This suggests that works and water together would cost any exporter from the South Saskatchewan drainage about $55/1,000 m^3 per year.

We must pause to ask if we have found the right value for the water. Some of it, if not exported, would be used for urban and industrial purposes. If municipalities had to develop new supplies of water to replace the exported water, this would be the source of another type of opportunity cost. Gysi (1981) indicates that present urban water rates are about $0.25/1,000 m^3 (p. 50) and that in Calgary the cost of adding new capacity (through a new water-treatment plant) to the system is about 10 times as much (p. 48), or about $2.50/1,000 m^3. As it would likely cost even more to bring in entirely new supplies (and treat the water), the opportunity cost may be as much as $10/1,000 m^3 too low. If so, the combined cost of works and water may be closer to $65/1,000 m^3.

A second question is whether the calculated yearly irrigation value today is representative of future years. There are two general but conflicting trends here. On the one hand it may well be that for economic and climatic reasons land cultivation will be moving north within North

TABLE 2-3 Economic Benefits or Costs of Water Withdrawal from Lake Superior

	Millions per year[a]
Shore property valuations	$ +11.0
Lake navigation values	−20.0
Hydro power values	−78.0
Total Effect	$ −87.0

Source: Decooke et al., 1984, p. 13.
a. Effects of 10,000 cfs (285 m³/s) withdrawal in both Canada and the United States are in 1979 U.S.$.

America (Hare, 1984). If this happens, the value of water for irrigation in the Alberta-Saskatchewan region will increase so that water exports will impose a future opportunity cost larger than today's.[15] On the other hand, there are forces at work to reduce the need for water. The frontier of cultivation on the Canadian plains is no longer expanding, and the water needs of the agricultural sector should also decline. Furthermore, it is to be expected that other inputs can increasingly be substituted for water, should it become more valuable. Intensive research is necessary, therefore, before we may judge whether our $55–$65 cost estimate so far is high or low.[16]

The final category of costs is the environmental costs. The three techniques outlined above can be used to estimate these costs. For example, Decooke et al. (1984) make a direct estimate of the economic effects of a 10,000 cfs (285 m³/s) withdrawal from Lake Superior, as summarized in Table 2-3. The $87 million/year cost would be incurred in the annual diversion of 10,000 cfs (285 m³/s). This works out to be about 9 billion m³ per year and gives an environmental cost from these three effects of about $10/1,000 m³ per year. Although this number may not be directly applicable to the Qu'Appelle example, we shall use it as a rough "order-of-magnitude" approximation. This suggests that a figure of, say, $15/1,000 m³/year to represent other aesthetic and biotic environmental costs is not out of line, again as an indicator of the possible range of actual costs.

Benefits   Earlier in this study we observed that it is not completely clear who in Canada has the right to the various aspects of flowing and standing water. The owner of the rights is the party who ultimately suffers loss if the water is diverted away, for the owner has the right to consume its services, give them away, leave them unharvested or sell them. When we speak of water exports we speak of sale. The owners can be assumed to be entitled to the proceeds of the sale, whether in kind or cash. We shall refer to these proceeds as payments or "benefits."

How much are Americans willing to pay? Let us consider a significant block of water, one billion m³ per year, carried from, say, the valley of the

TABLE 2-4 Summary of Direct Marginal Benefits per Acre-foot and 1,000 m³

Area		1984$ per acre-foot	1984$ per 1,000m³
California		52	46
Colorado		9–24	7–19
Arizona	Central (short run)	63	51
	Central (long run)	39	32
	Pinal County	27	22
Texas	High Plains (1970)	81	66
	High Plains (1990)	108	88
Utah		36–45	29–36

Source: Howe and Easter, 1971, pp. 38–48, esp. Table 11, p. 47. All studies were made in the late 1960s.

North Saskatchewan River to Colorado. An agreement is made dealing with the seasonality and steadiness of flows, storage, quality, short-run fluctuations with or without notice or compensation, and long-run revocability of the whole agreement with or without compensation. Although each of these aspects of the deal affects its value, we must cut through these details here to ask about what sort of price the Americans would be willing to pay.

Immediately we ask this, we run into another conceptual problem: Who are the Americans? As we have said, little or no irrigation water is distributed in the United States (or Canada) at its cost. The information problem is far worse than that confronting North American energy-demand analysts in the early 1960s. It seemed then that no important fuel was being sold at its true cost; instead regulatory regimes had rationed oil-import permits, held down gas prices, subsidized hydro electricity, and distorted coal-transport charges. Using some ingenuity, however, it was possible for experts to calculate what American industry and consumers were willing to pay for increased supplies of gas, oil, coal and electricity. Our reading of the water literature suggests that these experts will have a far more difficult time deciding what, if available U.S. water were sold in a water market, farmers and industry would, in equilibrium, be willing to pay. As Bain et al., (1967) showed, even the state of California with its network of intersecting and connecting canals and laterals has nothing that could be called a water market. This is the state where appropriative, transferable, water rights originated!

Table 2-4, which is drawn from various sources, shows what some American water users were estimated to gain from marginal acre-feet and m³ supplied in the 1960s.

Other data are in the same range, let us say $100 (Cdn. 1984$) per 1,000 m³. But this is almost certainly an overestimation of the value of water, since farm prices are supported, and the water already in use is subsidized. If the farmers and other users had to pay the full construction,

FIGURE 2-1 The Demand for Water

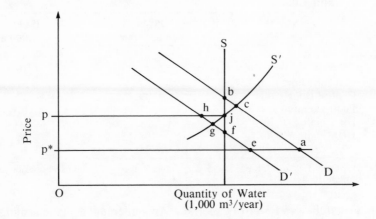

FIGURE 2-1 The Demand for Water

financial and opportunity costs of their water, the amounts already taken would fall.

Consider the illustrative supply-and-demand curves in Figure 2-1. S is the amount of water supplied to an irrigation district by an existing system. p is the hypothetical water price that would pay for the supply system and the opportunity cost of the water. p* is the actual subsidized amount paid by water users. With farm products at protected and supported prices, the derived demand curve for water is D. Farmers would like to consume amount a but only S is available. Hence the marginal demand price, such as that reported by Howe and Easter, is as high as b. If all users were charged b, water would be diverted from other American users, and the supply system would be expanded to S'. The relevant marginal demand price for water transported from long distances would then be higher than j, the existing cost of water supplies, but less than b, the reported marginal demand price.

Even this may be an overestimate. If the price supports and protection for foods and fibres produced under irrigation were removed, the demand curve would slip down to D'. With existing supplies, the stated marginal demand price would be f. If this is less than p, as shown, an abandonment of subsidies on water supplies would eventually return the water-demand price to the neighbourhood of g (or h or j, depending on whether the local system is expanded or contracted in the long run). These are all lower than b, which is therefore still to be considered an overestimate of the marginal local U.S. demand for water carried from Canada.

This demand would be estimated at k in Figure 2-2 if the U.S. continued to protect and subsidize agricultural food production, but as low as m if this farm program were withdrawn or scaled down. The free market-demand price delivered to the local district might therefore be as low as

FIGURE 2-2 Effect of Canadian Exports

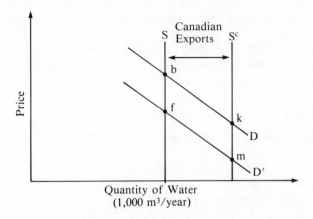

Quantity of Water
(1,000 m³/year)

$75 (Cdn.), far too little to cover the $400–$800 transport costs from Canadian rivers or lakes. (This estimate of transport costs is based in part on figures in the U.S. Army Corps of Engineers' 1982 High Plains study.)

Unfortunately, all this free-market analysis does not serve to predict what the U.S. government will be willing to pay. It would be folly to assume that American governments will suddenly cease to attempt to provide water for the farm and semi-rural regions in the southwestern states. It is true that the present Reagan administration has not encouraged spending on large-scale water impoundment and transfers, and this may reflect a new hostility by voters to the water projects that have played such a role in American politics since the Great War. On the other hand, the Garrison Dam project continues to obtain some 1985 Congressional support, and there is no move to stop further investigation of the High Plains project. On balance, Canada should assume that the U.S. thirst for dramatic reclamation and irrigation projects is still unsatisfied, and that in the future the states and the federal government will resume their quest for new supplies. This seems even better advice if future climatic change reduces U.S. precipitation.

The government's or the official offer price may therefore be much higher than the individual marginal demand prices discussed in Table 2-4. A U.S. government that will contemplate U.S. $600/acre-foot per year (about $640/1,000 m³ per year [$ Cdn.]) to bring some of the existing flows from the Mississippi-Missouri system to the High Plains might readily agree to pay $200/1,000 m³ at the Canadian border to firm up this flow and avoid taking water from existing U.S. users. But will it contemplate such sums? If the Canadian water price to cover diversion construction and opportunity and environmental costs in Canada were in the $50-$100/1,000 m³ per year range, and if this were added to the U.S.

transportation cost of $640, the resulting delivered cost to water districts would be so high that the magnitude of the necessary subsidies from the U.S. government would appear to imply that the project could not be politically feasible.

A definite conclusion is difficult. A tentative conclusion therefore is that the U.S. government might offer Canada over $100/1,000 m³ per year *if* the water is available in large amounts from locations where pumping near the border would not be a serious cost. American price offers may even exceed that level to the extent that:

- the Canadian supplies are available at a high altitude or in the west (to reduce U.S. transfer costs);
- Canada is willing to export large volumes (to reap economies of scale in canal building); and
- alternatively to the preceding possibility, Canadian supplies are marginal to new large U.S. diversions to the southwestern states (to obtain a premium for firming up fluctuating supplies already paying for new diversion works).

The price paid per unit would not be the only source of benefits from Canadian water exports. For instance, a water diversion that lowers regional water flows in Canada might also serve to regulate water levels and flows and thus lower the frequency of flooding during peak-flow seasons. We have seen that the stabilization of Great Lakes levels would bring benefits to the owners of shoreline properties. Less well studied, in the Qu'Appelle River diversion project the installation of four dams and reservoirs is expected to moderate changes in river levels. If the value of crops in the areas subject to flooding and the change in the probability of flooding were known, a dollar value of the benefits from the reduced likelihood of flooding could be estimated.[17]

The final category of benefits stems from the likelihood that the construction of a water-export project will provide employment for some otherwise underemployed factors of production. Little can be said now regarding the magnitude of this class of benefits without knowing the particulars of the project proposal, its timing and the regional economic context in which it was to be undertaken.

To pull together the discussion in the previous sections, Table 2-5 is presented. The derivation of some of the numbers has been discussed in the text, but several are largely hypothetical to illustrate the benefit-cost calculation and to suggest the order of magnitude they have in the authors' estimation of the situation.

To take the benefits in turn, the U.S. payment number is derived from the text. Incidental benefits to Canada are undoubtedly small and include regional employment benefits as well as possible benefits from reducing river fluctuations and providing irrigation water en route.

The costs to Canada are even more uncertain. The $65/1,000 m³ figure

TABLE 2-5 Summary of Hypothetical Costs and Benefits of Export of 1 Billion m³ per year

Benefits		Costs	
	(1984$ per 1,000 m³)		
Payments from U.S. (no transportation)	$100	Diversion, transport pumping, operation & maintenance	$36
Incidental real Canadian benefits	$ 25	Water opportunity cost	19
		Environmental costs	
		Great Lakes items	10
		Aesthetic and biota	15
Total benefits	$125	Total costs	$80

Source: Data are largely hypothetical, as discussed in the text.

is considerably below the probable construction and maintenance expense of the best-known modern project, the GRAND diversion, which passes through rocky country and involves a good deal of pumping. It may, however, be closer to the cost of a Great Plains diversion. The present opportunity cost of water in Canada is small, although none of the authors who have discussed the deceptiveness of this belief have stated a number to support their discussion. We suggest $19 for the Great Plains. We recognize that our estimates for environmental costs are even less substantiated. The first figure (for the Great Lakes) is taken from Decooke et al. (1984), and consists mainly of the effects on power production of a change in lake level. The second figure labelled "aesthetic and biota" is not based on any research or investigation. A good check would be to discover whether it is compatible with the sum for which the James Bay Natives sold some of their right to object to present diversions in northern Quebec. If acceptable calculations of environmental damage cannot be made, the procedure must depend on the "residual" method mentioned earlier in the chapter.

We hope that our foray into illustration will bear fruit by provoking others to supply better estimates of the elements of a representative water-export calculation. The purpose here is almost entirely illustrative. It was argued earlier that a good water-export policy for Canada would be built around a benefit-cost analysis of particular proposals. This example has suggested the possibilities and difficulties of undertaking this kind of economic evaluation. (Alternatively, the items in the table might be re-assembled to construct Canada's necessary "price" for export of plains water: at least $80 per thousand cubic metres. But our purpose is to show what benefit-cost analysis can do.)

There is no denying the difficulties. The chief advantage of such an approach is that it provides a method of giving weight to each of the great variety of factors that must be taken into account in making a decision on concrete proposals. For example it gives those who feel strongly about the environmental (and especially aesthetic) costs of any water diversion or transfer the opportunity to suggest numerically the strength of their feeling. Citizens do this implicitly all the time. In their private lives they must decide how much to spend on the appearance of their home and its furnishings, apart from the costs of simply keeping out the weather. In their public lives they support or oppose various politicians who make even more complex choices about expenditures on the environment, music and art as against spending on public works, social services, defence and R&D. These choices are made routinely, and they obtain the consent of the voters. An economic analysis of the kind illustrated here merely makes explicit and numerical the choices, the weights and the values.

Organization and Machinery

This section examines possible organizational arrangements that could be used to implement the procedure that we have just proposed.

Administration of Existing Diversions and Apportionments

The purpose of this section is to describe briefly the existing administrative arrangements for permitting, setting up and controlling some Canadian and international (Canada-U.S.) water diversions and apportionments. These are important to our study not because we are reporting on stream regulation, but because of the precedents they give for intergovernmental arrangements for coordination of water use.

The Columbia Treaty System
The sinuous Columbia-Kootenay system has been harnessed since the turn of the century by an increasing number of hydro-electric dams and reservoirs in Canada. As the Columbia River is part of an international drainage, both Canada and the United States are restricted by the Boundary Waters Treaty of 1909 in the extent to which each can construct works that raise water levels in the other country. The 1955 *International Rivers Improvement Act* allows the federal government to regulate provincial or private international diversions, by providing a licensing procedure.

The two nations entered into the Columbia River Treaty in 1964. In it Canada and the United States agreed not to make any diversion of the (regulated) natural flow of the Columbia-Kootenay waters for 20 years, until 1984; and after that to make limited diversions *within* the Columbia basin. The Treaty involved Canada, the U.S. government, the British Columbia government, B.C. Hydro and the Bonneville Power Administration. Day-to-day management governing upstream water releases and related power and energy-transmission questions is by the two latter power companies, under the supervision of a permanent Engineering Board created by the Columbia River Treaty. The existence of this structure notwithstanding, a new international diversion would probably require negotiation at the highest diplomatic level and full provincial participation.

Kitimat and Kemano

The Alcan (Aluminum Company of Canada) Kemano project, another British Columbia river development, diverts water out of the Nechako-Fraser drainage, through central B.C., into channels and tunnels to the coastal Kemano generating station. The Kemano project began in 1949, when the B.C. government passed the *Industrial Development Act*, which gave the Lieutenant-Governor in Council the power to grant Alcan the right to use those waters for its project. In December 1950, the B.C. government and Alcan entered into a written agreement for the project, and in 1954 the Alcan aluminum smelter began operating. Although not directly involved in the original agreement, the federal government can be involved in day-to-day management of the diversion as a result of its mandate under the *Fisheries Act*. A recent court case illustrates the strength of the federal government's powers: an application by the federal government under section 20(10) of the *Fisheries Act* for an injunction that required Alcan to release a certain minimum volume of water into the Nechako River, to protect salmon migrations and spawning grounds, was granted by the B.C. Supreme Court.[18] This injunction specified the actual minimum volumes to be released, and in a subsequent case,[19] Mr. Justice Berger, who granted the initial injunction, stated that "the Minister [of Fisheries and Oceans] should be able to vary the directions to Alcan regarding the discharge of waters as the need arises." Clearly, while this sort of water-resource development is primarily a provincial matter, federal power and legislation give the federal government a permanent voice in the operation of such developments.

Prairies

There are a number of dams on the Saskatchewan-Nelson system, described in detail in the 1982 report of the Prairie Provinces Water Board. One of these involves an international diversion. An old irrigation system in Montana takes water out of the St. Mary River into the Milk River; this might be regarded as a diversion from the Saskatchewan-Nelson basin into the Missouri basin. Under Article VI of the Boundary Waters Treaty, the two rivers are treated as one for the purposes of apportionment, and the waters are apportioned equally between the two countries. The apportionment is supervised by the International St. Mary-Milk River Board of Control, created by the IJC in 1921 (Carroll, 1983, p. 202).

In southern Alberta, several dams and canals serve irrigation districts. Irrigation causes a minor, indirect, inter-basin water transfer when water withdrawn from the Bow River basin is transferred to the Oldman River or Red Deer River basin as run-off from the irrigated fields (Canada West Foundation, 1982, p. 73). In 1977, 1978 and 1979, the volume of water transferred out of the Bow basin averaged only about 445,000,000 m^3 (about 361,000 acre-feet), with just over 80 percent of that volume ending up in the Red Deer River basin (Canada West Foundation, 1982, p. 73). Of course, this transfer occurs only during the crop season. The Alberta government, primarily through Alberta Agriculture and Alberta Environment, is involved in these irrigation developments in Alberta, along with the Irrigation Districts and the individual farmers. Joint federal-provincial action led to the construction of the Qu'Appelle Diversion in Saskatchewan, which diverted water from the South Saskatchewan River to the Qu'Appelle River, primarily to improve municipal water supply to Regina and Moose Jaw (Canada West Foundation, 1982, p. 192).

On the prairies at present, water apportionment is a more important issue than are diversions. There are two categories of apportionment (interprovincial and international), and administrative arrangements exist for each. (Earlier we suggested that international reapportionment can be viewed as a form of water export.) In 1969, the three prairie provinces and the federal government signed the Prairie Provinces Master Agreement on Apportionment. The agreement allows Alberta and Saskatchewan to use 50 percent of the water flowing through or rising within the boundaries of each province, thus ensuring that Manitoba receives a share of those flows. The agreement is administered by the Prairie Provinces Water Board, a joint federal-provincial body. The Board makes recommendations on questions from or disputes between any of the four parties. If the Board's recommendations do not satisfy the parties, the Master Agreement makes the Exchequer Court of Canada the deciding body. We have no information to suggest that this machinery has ever been severely tested.

Along the Saskatchewan–U.S. border there are two examples of international apportionment, both the subject of some international tension. A large lignite coal-burning power station, owned by Saskatchewan Power Corporation, stands just north of the Montana border on the Poplar River, which flows south into the Missouri River system. The power plant's construction has led to disputes not only about its effects on water and air quality in Montana, but also about water apportionment, as Saskatchewan's plans called for using water from the Poplar's three forks for cooling. As we have seen, under the Boundary Waters Treaty, upstream diversions may be made without U.S. or IJC approval — indeed, without notification. (However, Canadian federal approval *is* needed under the 1955 *International Rivers Improvement Act*.) The IJC was called on to make a definitive apportionment of Poplar River flows. When the three forks of the Poplar are considered as a whole, the Commission's decision could be said to have divided the flows into roughly real national shares (International Joint Commission, 1981b). This allotment, not called for by the Treaty nor by the spirit of the Helsinki rules in international law (which suggest that water be apportioned in accordance with benefits), is in the emerging "tradition" of equal apportionment. The IJC's earlier Pembina River recommendations, which had used water apportionment as the foundation for a joint irrigation scheme straddling the border, were never implemented. But its water-sharing decision was historically significant for such later cases as Poplar River. An IJC board watches the Poplar for the Commission.

The second example occurs slightly further east, where the Souris River in the Assiniboine system winds out of Saskatchewan through North Dakota into Manitoba. Flows, once the occasion of vigorous transborder friction, are small. Today, under IJC rulings, half the natural flow must pass into the United States, while the rest may be used upstream. When the Souris River meanders back into Manitoba, a minimum flow must be guaranteed. But neither North Dakota nor Manitoba has any substantial works depending on this river's levels and flows: the extensive Lake Darling near Minot, North Dakota, is a wildlife refuge; floods have recurred in recent years. An IJC control board makes recommendations concerning year-to-year decisions within the previous IJC rulings.

Great Lakes

The waters of the Niagara River, the St. Mary's River at Sault Ste. Marie and the St. Lawrence River, which run through hydro-electric stations, have been apportioned by various agreements and treaties. Under these agreements the hydro entities themselves keep track of the flows they are using and report to a "control board" under the IJC. The IJC thus ensures that the flows are apportioned in accordance with the original agreements. It has also been assigned a responsibility to various interests to see that navigational channels have enough depth, and that the levels of the Great Lakes themselves do not rise to an extent that will damage shore properties. These long-standing arrangements have given the two countries unparalleled day-to-day experience in international freshwater apportionment and management.

Chicago Diversion

As mentioned earlier, the original Chicago Diversion was constructed in

1848. By 1929, the average flow annually was as much as 10,000 cfs. Wisconsin and other lake states disputed in the courts the right of Illinois to divert such a large volume of water. Between 1925 and 1980, a series of decisions and orders by the U.S. Supreme Court forced Illinois to reduce the diversion, which is now of the order of only 3,200 cfs.

The chief reason for judgment of the Supreme Court has been the injury suffered by other lake states, chiefly with respect to navigation, caused by the lowering of lake levels by the diversions. The injury suffered by Canada from the same cause seems not to have been a reason for judgment. In vetoing a bill by which Congress would have authorized increased diversions at Chicago, then President Eisenhower did say that it seemed to him "that the additional diversion is not of such national importance as to justify action without reference to the views of Canada" (United States Congress, 1968, p. 644). Apart from remarks such as this, the Chicago-Michigan diversions have been treated chiefly as a domestic issue between American states.

In 1977, the two national governments referred to the IJC the question of the effect on the levels and flows of the Great Lakes basin of the existing diversion at Chicago (and of other diversions around the lakes). In September 1981, a report was submitted to the IJC by its technical board; recently, the IJC itself reported to the governments (International Joint Commission, 1985). Truly this is a mammoth and intricate question, one that dwarfs the IJC's previous complex levels-and-flows management references. Although the Board's report is difficult to understand and seems somewhat evasive, two points stand out. First, only a small fraction of the present 3,200 cfs flow through the Chicago diversion can be reduced further if the port of Chicago and the navigation canal are to be kept in business. Secondly, any further reduction of the diversion would have only a small effect on the level of Lake Michigan and the other Great Lakes (International Joint Commission, 1981a, pp. 7-1 to 9-8).

Therefore, the Chicago Diversion has importance for water exports only if present limitations and constraints are changed. For example, the U.S. Congress might decide to override the objections of the lake states and to increase flows down the Mississippi watershed, and thus release flows upstream in the Missouri system for irrigation and water supply. In this way the Chicago Diversion could not only carry present Great Lakes boundary waters to U.S. consumers, but also other waters diverted into them from the James Bay or Ottawa River systems. Such U.S. action would require Canadian participation in determining a new regime of Great Lakes boundary-water levels and flows (and new IJC controls). Furthermore, it would be of little practical importance unless not only Canada, but also Ontario and Quebec actively entered into the roles of water exporters.

SUMMARY

The foregoing discussion, although by no means all-inclusive, demonstrates that Canada has had considerable experience dealing with a wide array of intergovernmental water quality and quantity issues. For water exports, nine key points should be stressed:

1. Transfers in Canada have required provincial participation.
2. However, the existing federal legislation on various points is not to be ignored, notably the Boundary Waters Treaty, the *International Rivers Improvement Act* and various *ad hoc* statutes.
3. The Harmon doctrine allows Canada and the United States to cut the flows of streams entering the other country.
4. This has not been done on any stream, though it did come up in connection with the Poplar water division.
5. Rather, the rule on prairie-water divisions has been to cleave closely to a 50/50 split.
6. These have involved private parties, provincial governments, the federal government, and the IJC.
7. The most important diversions into the Great Lakes system, the Long Lac-Ogoki diversions into Lake Superior, involved the Ontario Government, Ontario Hydro (as consumer) and the federal government.
8. The most important diversion out of the Great Lakes system, at Chicago, is presently restrained by (a) a domestic decision on a U.S. interstate legal action and (b) presidential deference to ongoing agreements and cooperation with Canada.
9. The Chicago Diversion could become an important route for Canadian water exports. If so, its use would require cooperation and consent from a long list of authorities and governments on both sides of the border.

Administration and Procedure

Water exports are an emotional subject. Government has dealt with this tricky matter by running for safety, by making declarations that our water is not for sale. So far this has been a safe strategy because there are few influential and articulate interests in favour of water exports. Now however, anticipating that activists in the U.S.A. or Canada may soon make more concrete proposals, government must have policies and procedures ready to meet the pressures.

Compared to U.S. governments, which have been dealing with vigorous proponents of ever-increasing water-transfer projects for at least a century, our Canadian governments' warehouse of ideas is nearly bare. This is serious because our laws, constitution, climate and geography differ so drastically from those in the United States that we do not know whether we can safely borrow practice, traditions or procedures. Nor are our professional or academic resources yet prepared with the familiarity and expertise necessary. Our water supply and hydro-power engineering professionals have contributed much of the knowledge and experience behind the mechanisms and procedures reviewed at the beginning of this section. But what mechanisms and procedures are to define the main water-export questions and frame the main decisions? In what sort of administrative, fact-finding, evaluative, legal and monitoring arrangement are our experts to work?

In this section we explore these questions by identifying necessary qualities or characteristics of the mechanism or complex of agencies.

Economic   This first characteristic recommended follows from everything said so far in this study. The policy message suggested was that each water-export proposal should be looked at on its economic merits. Further, it was asserted this could best be done by formally evaluating its benefits and costs so that such aims as regional growth, environmental protection and ecological continuity were given weight from the outset. In short, around the economic evaluation of each water-export proposal should be constructed the whole procedure of decision making.

Provincial and Local Point of View   A second characteristic recommended is that the project-appraisal procedure should, from the outset, adopt the point of view of those most affected. In the case of water-export proposals, this means that federal, provincial and local participation in the evaluation and decision-making procedures should be built in. To make this clear it should be emphasized that our survey of the legal, constitutional and regional realities in Canada has not indicated that it is safe to depend on either a "national" or a narrowly localized point of view. The provinces have an overwhelmingly strong proprietorial interest in water resources, and they have, as well, almost unchallengeable legislative powers to transfer waters among their own regions, cities and industries, subject only to their responsibilities to neighbouring provinces.

However, because personal interests in water use are customarily regarded almost as private rights (whatever provincial law may say), the provincial governments are not, in fact, free to meddle with existing river-basin flows without a strong political mandate arising from well-understood, if implicit, regional consent. Consequently local and regional districts and councils administering waters affected by exports will eventually be involved and should, for economy of information dissemination and information gathering, be involved from the beginning. Obviously, however, the provinces and their components are not competent alone to handle water exports. Their approval, if it were forthcoming, might still injure those goals and interests entrusted to the federal government, ranging from parks, fisheries and boundary waters to policies concerning international relations and the economy.

Nevertheless, it is recommended here that so far as possible the agencies and mechanisms involved should have a predominantly provincial and local viewpoint. In the jargon of foreign affairs, the procedures and decisions would have so far as feasible a "transnational" (group to group) rather than an "international" (External Affairs to State Department) orientation. This recommendation cannot be pushed to an extreme limit, for Ottawa's experience with and responsibility for national identity and sovereignty in the face of U.S. determination, and its explicit constitutional responsibilities, demand that no thought be given to its exclusion. But the public must be relieved of the suspicion that Ottawa favours (or detests) projects for which the main benefits and costs would be incurred regionally, not nationally. Thus water-export evaluation must have a predominantly provincial and regional point of view, embedded in a procedure in which all levels of government are adequately represented.

To undertake a benefit-cost analysis from several viewpoints is not impossible. But overly firm rules or principles must usually be adopted in advance, and these can militate against decisions that might benefit all parties (see Jones et al., 1980). Analysis of these problems suggests that Canada's goals with respect to water-export proposals would be best served if the first and strongest voice were at the provincial level.

Individual compensation   A third recommendation is that the policy should make full provision for individual compensation. This extends the previous "viewpoint" characteristic to the level of the individual water user, the Canadian whose property is acquired or damaged in the carrying out of a water-export project, or whose welfare is reduced thereby. Existing policy on megaprojects is ambivalent about this, for government's role as promoter has often conflicted with its role as protector of property and individual rights. That this should be remedied is indicated by what every researcher soon learns: great water projects of the past are perhaps best remembered today by the manner in which they dealt with those whose lands were flooded. The displacement of Iroquois villagers on the St. Lawrence and of Arrow Lake riparians under the Columbia treaty; the flooding of Tweedsmuir Park without replacement; and the buying-out of Native rights for the James Bay project: all are recalled when the engineering, strikes and construction booms are forgotten. Most of these arrangements involved circumvention of normal provincial expropriation procedures, which in some provinces have yet to be modernized. Since water exports can hardly be disguised as anything but money-making schemes for the governments, it is obviously important that those who are forced to move are generously compensated. The same is true of those who lose jobs or markets.

It is particularly important that the procedure give due weight to the compensation of those who hold provincial water rights. These are legally licences or permits and, as outlined earlier, are not evidence of users' full water "ownership." Today's provincial laws make private compensation for transfer of these rights difficult, and even seem to contemplate that holders could be deprived of their water at govern-mental discretion. At the very least, such rights should be turned over to a water-export project only with compensation, as if they were rights to land.

It is unlikely that this discretion will be forgotten, since in every previous railway, canal, pipeline and transmission project, the acquisi-tion of private rights has been the most conspicuous politics-ridden aspect of the institutional arrangements. It would be pleasant if now, before a proposal is before us, the land- and water-expropriation and compensation-provision procedures could be settled so that other aspects of the proposal would get more attention; for compulsory land acquisition is inevitably an individual, distasteful, strategic matter of appraisal and hard bargaining business mixed with sporadic generosity.

Project design optimization   This characteristic is related to the first: that the machinery should make provision for prior optimization of the proposal and subsequent learning by doing. Any benefit-cost procedure, if properly carried out, should be able to detect and develop proposals that will make everyone better off, that will be a part of economic growth. This aspect of an acceptable project is not important if it is a small project. But if it is large, it is worth investing in a dynamic process of evaluation that starts with the development of the proposal before final selection and approval and continues with its subsequent shaping by management, monitoring and modification.

In the case of water-export proposals this means that an agency must not waste time on an ill-thought-out project, but must be free and able to substitute one or more superior variants. It should look not just for positive net benefits, but for maximum net benefits. Furthermore, it should, as far as possible, be able to recommend that projects be approved in small or "attenuated" versions capable of doubling or filling-out later as information accrues.[20] Since the development of the projects and the decisions about this development may thus be stretched out, there is much to be said for a two-stage procedure, one concerned with the general acceptability and suitability of the project as a concept, and the second concerned with the construction timetable, project refinement, impact modification, re-routing, mitigation, compensation and so forth.

An optimized project design will have the flexibility to cope with the uncertainty of future water supplies and demands in both countries, particularly to reduce the burden of an irreversible commitment to supply water. This is discussed further under the heading "Flexibility and Reversibility" below.

Information acquisition and learning   This characteristic reminds us that the procedures should provide for the informing of both the formal decision makers and of all who are concerned. As Thompson and co-authors (1981) point out, there are many kinds of combinations of:

(a) initial information collected and provided by the proposal's promoter;

(b) information about the attitudes and actions of all levels of government and their departments. Many effects of the project will stem from how local, provincial and national health, school, social, agriculture, water, housing, transportation, fisheries and environmental agencies will behave as part of their bureaucratic mandate — if the project proceeds. Obviously such agencies must be kept informed. Better, they should contribute information about the effects of their own actions.

(c) expert evaluation of documentation;

(d) hearings on (a), (b) and (c): these can be judicial and adversarial; informal and repetitive; consultative of neutral experts; and so on.

The best sequence of these proceedings and the role of hearings in the sequence depend in part on the degree of responsibility the authorities are willing to take for the final decision. The procedure can be used to educate the public and to mobilize opinion, as well as to obtain specific data for its own purposes. The point here is that the way information is disseminated and acquired is a main characteristic of a water-export evaluation procedure.

Prior and subsequent information   This characteristic has to do with the timing of information, and the role of monitoring. Any procedure imposes heavy costs of documentation, data, hearings and bargaining and may deter applicants from advancing flexible and unfinished proposals. The requirement for initial information cannot, however, be waived. Since information is necessary under any policy or institutional arrangement, it is efficient that information costs be charged against the claimed benefits of a project by being added to the other private and social costs.

Note that the best arrangement would seem to be for the promoter to start the informational wheels turning. If the provincial governments wish to sell water, they can anticipate demand by putting together a prospectus on exportable flows. But their doing so is not called for here. Nor do we see an extended "prior information" role for the federal government.

What information should the applicants furnish? Any who have observed environmental impact hearings in recent years will agree that some appraisal systems do seem to call for, and produce, excessive amounts of data, often with little notion of how they are to be used (Olynyk, 1984). Not surprisingly, such broad demands are often met by the provision of an encyclopaedic bounty of facts, poorly classified and analysed, and a stubborn resolution to provide no more information or to discuss how different project designs might have different environmental or social consequences.

Thompson et al. (1981) suggest that this relevance problem can be partly dealt with through a two-stage procedure. The promoter would provide enough information at the first stage to support the general justification of the proposal, leaving to a second stage (after project approval-in-principle) a more educated request for that specific information which would be required for consent to the project's various effects. At stage two, current immediate information costs can be traded off against future monitoring costs, envisaging later optimizing of both the design and the operation of the original version of the project.

Centralization   This characteristic has to do with the extent of "centralization" of the decision-making procedure. How shall the various kinds of agreement to, and approval of, a large-scale water-export proposal be coordinated?

Various administrative devices can be imagined here. At one extreme there is a "one-window" approach. A single designated agency may act as the applicant's agent in ascertaining the requirements of all parties under their various statutes and policies. It may even deal with other levels of government, and with U.S. agencies.

However simplifying this procedure may appear, it is doubtful if anyone can name one department or bureau that can represent all governments' interests in such a complex business as water export. The provisions of some legislation call for the exercise of discretion on the part of a minister: this cannot always be delegated to another body. The problem is even more serious when, as here, the departments are of different orders of government. Furthermore, bureaus' traditions and jealousies may prevent centralization. Neither the NEB nor the Northern Pipeline Agency has successfully replaced all other bodies.

Nevertheless, quite apart from the time and costs of compliance with dozens of departments, there is one very good reason for some form of centralization. It can be stated in two ways. Centralization can be sought as a means of avoiding the "tyranny of small decisions." By this is meant that faulty arrangement whereby, when every administrative hurdle has been leapt, and every environmental and social safeguard has been met, there is still the feeling that the main theme of the object has not been fully examined, or that no decision maker has been made to glimpse the proposal in all its broad economic, environmental, ethical, political and social dimensions. Alternatively, centralization can be sought as a means of "internalizing" the final decisions about the proposal so that instead of requiring a flat approval on every aspect, the governments would be able to trade off less important for more vital characteristics.

Flexibility and reversibility　　These characteristics are essential in every procedure governing projects that endure for many years. The size or route of the water transfers, the water quality, or the mere fact of export may become more or less onerous in the future. The payment for water may seem excessive (to the U.S. importer) or deficient. The need here is for both parties to be able to enter into discussions to alter the arrangement, and eventually to implement their changed preferences. Presumably an agreement that meets this criterion will call for the parties to give notice and for one to compensate the other party.

Earlier chapters have shown that the problems of inflexible arrangements have been encountered before, in connection with hydro-electricity exports. With this experience in mind, Canadians will be concerned about keeping powers to revoke or reverse a water-export agreement. We can think about a "real" solution to this problem and a financial instrument which, while not correcting it, will make it more acceptable.

The "real" solution is to make sure now that when future conditions change, water exports can be stopped or even be reversed. There are no technical difficulties in the way: works can be designed that contemplate an eventual end to diversion and transfer. The problems of adjustment in Canada are more serious. The economy would have to be prepared for more water to be used, or it would have to be able to adjust to new water availability. At the same time, the treasuries of the various jurisdictions would have to be ready for the flow of international compensations to end. Most serious of all would be Canada's diplomatic and political difficulties of "depriving" some region of the U.S.A. of an accustomed flow of Canadian water. A real solution to this problem is to make sure that no U.S. group is wholly deprived of water by the end of the water transfer, and more generally to make sure that the exported water makes only a small contribution to the consumption of many water users so that its withdrawal will have only a marginal effect on anyone. This could be achieved if Canadian policy were such that exports could be approved only if they augmented existing flows, rather than serving as the basis for new U.S. projects opening up new cities or irrigated areas. This would be a difficult policy to enforce, but if successful it would reduce significantly the political and diplomatic problems attendant on ending water exports in the future.

The "financial" solution is to sell that water on a strictly non-firm or interruptible basis. While both these solutions reduce the amount that U.S. users are likely willingly to pay for Canadian water, both also give Canadian drainage regions security in the face of uncertainty about future climatic and economic states of the world. Flexibility is a characteristic that can be built into any procedure. Too much of it, however, makes both countries (Canada especially) vulnerable to unpredictable political changes in the other's domestic policies regarding its water-providing and water-consuming regions. All attempts to achieve flexibility are more costly (or less remunerative) than firm commitments.

Conclusions: A Water Export Council

The eight qualities or characteristics of the recommended economic procedure ought to be embodied in machinery. Can we find an existing agency or bureau that can perform the functions implied in these requirements? "One-window" procedures installed in the various provinces have given us some experience of agencies that are charged with decisions and with administration of projects that impinge on the mandates of more than one government branch. These systems are still being perfected. Their existence does suggest that it is possible for a government concerned with a water-export decision to be represented by a small number of officers qualified to speak and act in pursuit of all those goals entrusted to separate agencies. Whatever it is called, an agency to coordinate the talents and missions of these officers should make it possible to see the project as a whole, to escape the tyranny of segmented small decisions, and to adhere to an orderly benefit-cost evaluation, optimization and monitoring of a water-export proposal.

The problem is that more than one order of government is involved. In spite of the primacy of the provinces today, it is unlikely that we can find a single provincial bureau or agency that can act on behalf of its own government and the national government as well. Although the problem of machinery is a federalistic rather than an international one, the Canadian experience with the International Joint Commission may suggest how the governments might, at minimal transaction costs, work together on the implementation of the necessary procedure.

The required characteristics reviewed in the previous section might be assigned to a high-level federal-provincial council composed of "sections" respectively appointed by each Canadian government involved. The U.S.A. would not be involved. The council, like the IJC, would have a small expert secretariat. Like the IJC, it would be able to appoint subsidiary-expert boards to report to it on specific questions. These boards' members would normally be seconded from federal and provincial public services. The governments at both levels could refer to this council, *at an early stage*, water-export proposals made to any of them. The council could then proceed to obtain information and receive reports. At an early stage it would be necessary to check the *general* premises on which the proposals before it were based. Independent analysis is essential. The existence of its boards would help and so would public airing, hearings and criticism. It is important to avoid professional

unanimity based on unquestioned assumptions. The council would analyze the proposals, optimize and refine them, and report for or against
them to the parent sponsoring governments.

Should its report be unfavourable, its non-partisan procedure will
have helped to alert and educate citizens and governments to the value of
water to the Canadian environment and to potential future users.

On the other hand, should its report be favourable and should the
parent governments accept the report, the council could, at a second
stage, be entrusted as a consultant to Canadian diplomats and provincial
officers officially charged with negotiating the best possible agreement.
Two types of negotiation can be foreseen. One would be between Canadian governments, and between them and private or Native interests
claiming rights to land or water in the project area. The other level of
negotiation is that between Canada and the United States. Ad hoc teams
would be needed for the many discussions necessitated by the intergovernmental nature of the project. The proposed council would not
negotiate in any of these senses. After giving its approval, it would be
available to assist those directly involved. It is important that the events
and drama of negotiation be guided away from excessive salesmanship
or excessive caution. The council should be able to offer a sober understanding of what conditions are essential for each water-export project,
and assist the many parties in seeking and interpreting these conditions.

There are several arguments favouring continuing council involvement after the negotiations. First, the council would by that time be well
informed, it would be able to provide continuity, and it would know well
the opportunities and reservations perceived by all orders of government. Secondly, the Columbia Treaty negotiations showed the possible
impotence of federal international negotiating teams that failed to carry
an explicit mandate from the province involved. Thirdly, flexibility
requires that the agreement contain safeguards that will probably be
more keenly desired by the provinces than by Ottawa. Finally, the
commission, more than the federal government, would understand the
value of "learning by doing": monitoring effects of large-scale projects
that might lead to recommended changes, including either possible
expansion or complete discontinuation and abandonment of the project.
The IJC provides a pattern in connection with monitoring and the
enforcement that may go with it.

The council would therefore be involved at a third (operation and
monitoring) stage. Like the International Columbia Engineering Board,
it would be responsible to the Canadian governments for ensuring that
the international agreement was adhered to, reasonably. Like the Great
Lakes Water Quality Board, it would carry out research, monitor
ongoing environmental and social impacts, and recommend changes
that carry out the "flexibility" characteristic discussed in the previous
section.

Further detail would be inappropriate here. For a contrasting arrangement, the reader may look up the failed U.S. Water Resources Council (Johnson, 1984). This study has emphasized the need for a "policy" of examining water-export proposals on their merits, coupled with a procedure. Most of this section has been concerned with emphasizing eight rather abstract characteristics that the total procedure should possess, given that its main purpose is to conduct an examination of particular schemes. It has suggested that in the absence of a single government department currently available to harmonize this examination procedure, a new council should be set up even before any project is proposed, to conduct the examination, advise the governments in any subsequent interjurisdictional and international negotiations, and represent them all to check on continuing monitoring and enforcement.

Conclusions and Recommendations

This study has proposed that water-export projects be separately assessed by a government review process, using economic criteria for determining desirability. The particular approach recommended is the use of benefit-cost analysis on a project-by-project basis. The idea of project-by-project assessment of potential water transfers is not new. For example, it is not unusual for a government to declare that "the waters in each major drainage must be fully and efficiently utilized before inter-drainage transfers are considered." We support this pragmatic approach, but we question its usefulness as a practical policy. Expressions such as "fully and efficiently utilized" raise many questions that can lead to endless and acrimonious debate.

We believe that with the very broad definition of the word "economic" employed in this paper, we have shown that an economic approach to present and future uses is practical. No other approach can weigh competing uses against one another. The particular economic approach favoured, benefit-cost analysis, provides a comprehensive framework giving due weight to the financial, environmental and social effects of water-export projects. Earlier in this study we demonstrated how this economic approach can be applied to a water-export project, though our information base is incomplete and the economic values uncertain.

For many people, one of the most important issues is who controls water exports. The water within their boundaries belongs to the provinces, to the extent that the law recognizes ownership of such "fugitive" resources. This proprietary role gives the provinces the lead in managing water resources, including water exports. However, the division of other powers between the federal and provincial orders of government under the *Constitution Act* gives each level a virtual veto over water exports.

The obvious consequence of this situation is that both orders of government must participate in applying the proposed economic analysis to Canadian export projects. The provincial governments, in addition to their proprietorship over water, have responsibilities to look after most affairs in the exporting region and along the diversion route. At the same time, the federal government must be involved to ensure that national impacts — including, for example, the cumulative effects of a number of export diversions from different provinces — and international impacts — such as the potential political problems of halting exports should the need arise — are considered. In addition, the federal government has some local responsibilities such as those for fishing, for agriculture and for the North. Our study provides a brief description of one possible arrangement that could coordinate federal and provincial powers in a water-export council and that would reflect the eight "necessary qualities" outlined in the previous section.

Water exports are a contentious issue in Canada. Many Canadians rebel at the thought of water as an economic commodity, especially in interregional or international affairs. Others view it as an exportable resource like any other. The policy proposed in this study for water exports would be flexible enough to allow full scope for these and other divergent viewpoints. The proposed procedure for reviewing water-export projects would provide a consistent and comprehensive framework for evaluating the benefits and costs for Canada, but it is not intended to override whatever values people place on their water resources.

In a long digression, we emphasized our belief that neither a simple "permissive" nor a "prohibitive" policy is good enough. Both policies would be too inflexible to deal with all possible situations that might arise in the various Canadian regions. Hence a more open policy is required. But its procedures would give weight to the views of those who feel strongly on the issue.

For those who are reluctant ever to sell water, the procedure provides a niche for their objections and also lets them express in terms of forgone dollars the intensity of their feelings. For those who are neutral or favourable, the procedure saves them from endorsing socially profitless or inferior projects. For those who are concerned about our water resources as national wealth in itself, the procedure gives promise of preventing ignorant and careless water allocations.

Notes

This study closely follows the text of a "research paper" prepared for the Inquiry on Federal Water Policy by Anthony Scott, assisted by John Olynyk and Steven Renzetti: "The Economics of Water Export Policy." In their preparation of that earlier version and in their revisions for this extended version, the authors received useful suggestions from anonymous referees and generous and substantial comments and suggestions from Professor Bruce Wilkinson of the University of Alberta, Professors Irving Fox and Andrew Thompson of the University of British Columbia, Mr. William Harland of Crippen Consultants Limited, Vancouver, Professor Kent Olson of Oklahoma State University, Professor Chad Day of Simon Fraser University, and Professor Dixon Thompson of the University of Calgary. Dr. Frank Quinn, Director of Research for the Inquiry, an expert in his own right, has helped us to obtain valuable material, and the members of the Inquiry have been helpful. Finally, they wish to thank Ms. Audrey Moroz and Mrs. Jerry Pladsen of the Westwater Research Centre of the University of British Columbia for their enthusiastic, rapid and accurate typing of the manuscript.

The study was completed in April 1985.

1. The study cited is Taylor (1967). By way of comparison, the mean annual flow of the North Saskatchewan River at Edmonton from 1912 to 1975 was about 7,725 cfs (218.8 cubic metres per second) (Canada West Foundation, 1982, p. 109).

2. Detailed discussion of social costs of pipeline construction may be found in the Report of the Berger Commission on the Mackenzie Valley pipeline (Berger, 1977).

3. This section is influenced by Campbell et al. (1974).

4. The excerpts from the *Constitution Act* quoted in this section were taken from: Canada, Department of Justice (1982).

5. These opinions are;
   Anti-Inflation Reference, [1976] 2 S.C.R. 373;
   Reference re Regulation and Control of Aeronautics in Canada, [1932] A.C. 54 (Privy Council);
   Reference re Regulation and Control of Radio Communication in Canada, [1932] A.C. 304 (Privy Council); and
   Denison Mines vs. A.-G. Canada, [1973] 1 O.R. 797 (Ontario High Court) (re atomic energy).

6. Another potential source of federal authority is the "declaratory" or emergency clause of section 92(10)(c) (working with section 91(29)). Section 92(10)(c) excerpts from provincial legislative jurisdiction:

   > 92(10)(c) Such works as, although wholly situate within the Province, are before or after their Execution declared by the Parliament of Canada to be for the general Advantage of Canada or for the Advantage of Two or more of the Provinces.

   > Such a declaration would not empower Parliament to forever remove certain classes of projects from provincial jurisdiction, it could only be applied to existing or contemplated works and undertakings. Neither would it give Parliament complete control over all aspects of water export, but only over "works" with the provinces retaining other powers. In view of the federal jurisdiction that could be established under other heads, it does not appear that the federal government would gain much additional control over exports through an emergency declaration.

7. In a 1981 case (*Fulton v. Energy Resources Conservation Board*), the Supreme Court of Canada held that Alberta had powers to regulate and approve a transmission line to interconnect with a B.C. line and so, indirectly, with the United States. Lucas and Saunders (1983, pp. 10–11) summarize the Court's judgment as follows (footnotes omitted):

   > The Court held that the province had jurisdiction to regulate electrical transmission facilities that were wholly within its boundaries. That the transmission facilities are intended to be connected with those of an agency outside the province did not bring the matter within exclusive federal authority. The provincial legislation is valid so long as it does not purport to regulate the interconnec-

tion. It is a matter within provincial authority in relation to local works and undertakings under s. 92(10). The situation was particularly clear in the absence of federal legislation to regulate interprovincial power lines. Had such legislation existed, it is possible that a direct conflict with the provincial legislation could have been found that would have given the federal government jurisdiction on the basis of paramountcy.

There are implications of Chief Justice Laskin's judgment that the result might have been different had the proposed transmission line interconnected with a line owned and operated by the same utility in another jurisdiction. This would be consistent with cases that have found operations such as railways and motor transportation systems to be single interprovincial or international undertakings and, therefore, subject to federal jurisdiction under s. 92(10)(a). This part of the Supreme Court's opinion suggests that interconnected transmission facilities spanning several provinces and U.S. jurisdictions are not likely to be characterized as single works or undertakings. Systems are put together by provincial utilities through construction of system components within provincial boundaries. This fact is likely to exclude full federal regulatory control of both energy development and construction of facilities for interconnected systems which are developed through coordinated planning.

Additional discussion of current water law and policy issues in Canada, including international issues, is presented in Rueggeberg and Thompson (1984).

8. A more detailed review of these proposals (with the exception of the Freil Lake project) can be found in Bryan (1973, pp. 151–68). Day (1985) provides a more current review of these and other diversion projects.

9. Cost estimations were converted to 1984 dollars using Statistics Canada's Non-Residential Construction Input Price Indices (Catalogue #62-007). Unless specified as 1984 dollars, the costs given in this section are in current dollars (that is, the value of the dollar at the time each proposal was first presented).

10. The next three paragraphs are derived from a pioneering study by Grauer and Davis (1961).

11. The provincial government can indirectly regulate gas exports by regulating gas production at the wellhead.

12. The most recently published federal water policy statement (in 1978) makes no mention of water exports (Canada, Department of Fisheries and Environment, 1978).

13. Optimization also applies when choosing the type of project needed to meet the given public goals, as well as to the optimal dimensions of a given project. This higher level of optimization is discussed in greater detail in: Sewell et al. (1965); British Columbia Environment and Land Use Committee Secretariat (1977); and Canada, Treasury Board (1976).

14. See Dasgupta and Heal, 1979, pp. 397–400.

15. For example, David K. Elton (1983) and the Canada West Foundation (1982) forecast a doubling of prairie irrigation by the end of the century. This optimistic forecast requires far less water than if "maximum use of available water" were undertaken, and still less than if all irrigable land were supplied with water transferred from other river basins. Elton summarizes official and Canada West Foundation "demand" forecasts; by "demand" he appears to mean political demands by Alberta farmers for water at present (subsidized) prices. See also Canada West Foundation, 1982, p. 25.

16. See Canada West Foundation (1982) for the downward revisions of irrigation water withdrawals from Lake Diefenbaker. See also Veeman (1985); this is one of the few water studies that take value or cost into consideration.

17. For a more detailed example, see Canada Treasury Board, 1976, pp. 56–62.

18. *Attorney-General* v. *The Aluminum Company of Canada*. Unreported judgment, Aug. 6, 1980, Supreme Court of British Columbia.

19. *A.-G. of Canada* v. *the Aluminum Company of Canada (2)*. Unreported judgment, Aug. 11, 1980, Mr. Justice Berger (in Chambers).

20. The building of canals and dams generates economies of scale. It is the loss of these economies that is one of the main costs of "starting small." The arguments for and the

extra costs of this "learning by doing" have been investigated by H.F. Campbell and Anthony Scott in such articles as Campbell and Scott (1979). The idea is carried in other directions by A.R. Thompson and various co-authors in Westwater Research Institute publications (see Thompson, Bankes and Souto-Maior, 1981) and by C.S. Holling (1978) in a continuing campaign for "adaptive" environmental assessment theory and procedures.

Bibliography

Alberta. Department of the Environment. N.d. *Water Resource Management Principles for Alberta.* Edmonton: The Department.

Anonymous. 1984. "B.C. Water Sale Promoter Stirs Federal Action." *Vancouver Sun.* August 15, 1984, p. A12.

Anonymous. 1985. "B.C. Approves Water Export." *Globe and Mail.* June 7, 1985, p. 10.

Bain, J.S., R.E. Caves, and J. Margolis. 1967. *Northern California's Water Industry.* Baltimore: Johns Hopkins University Press.

Baumann, D.D., and D. Dworkin. 1978. *Water Resources for Our Cities.* Resource Papers for College Geography No. 78-2. Washington, D.C.: Association of American Geographers.

Beach, C. 1984. Submission by Coast Mountain Aquasource Ltd. to the Federal Inquiry on Water. November 22, 1984, Vancouver, B.C.

Beerling, C.W. 1984. "Water Allocation Law: Potential Impacts on Economic Development." *Canadian Water Resources Journal* 9 (1): 46–58.

Berger, Justice T.R. 1977. *Northern Frontier, Northern Homeland.* Report of the Mackenzie Valley Pipeline Inquiry. 2 vols. Ottawa: Minister of Supply and Services Canada.

Boadway, R., and N. Bruce. 1984. *Welfare Economics.* Oxford: Blackwell.

Bocking, R.C. 1972. *Canada's Water: For Sale?* Toronto: James Lewis and Samuel.

Bourne, C.B. 1972. "Procedure in the Development of International Drainage Basins: The Duty to Consult and Negotiate." *Canadian Yearbook of International Law* 10: 212–34.

_____. 1974. "Canada and the Law of International Drainage Basins." In *Canadian Perspectives on International Law and Organization,* edited by R.St.J. MacDonald et al. Toronto: University of Toronto Press.

British Columbia. Environment and Land Use Committee Secretariat. 1977. *Guidelines for Benefit-Cost Analysis.* Victoria: Queen's Printer.

British Columbia Utilities Commission. 1983. *Site C Report.* Report and Recommendations to the Lieutenant Governor-in-Council on Disposition of British Columbia Hydro and Power Authority's Application for an Energy Project Certificate for Peace River Site C Hydroelectric Generating Station. Vancouver: The Commission.

Bryan, R. 1973. *Much is Taken, Much Remains.* North Scituate, Mass.: Duxbury Press.

Cail, R. 1974. *Land, Man, and the Law.* Vancouver: University of British Columbia Press.

Campbell, H., and A.D. Scott. 1979. "Alternative Policies Towards Frontier Mining Projects with Adverse Social Consequences." *Journal of Business Administration* 11 (1 and 2): 241–64.

Campbell, R.S., P.H. Pearse, A.D. Scott, and M. Uzelac. 1974. "Water Management in Ontario — An Economic Evaluation of Public Policy." *Osgoode Hall Law Journal.* 12 (2): 475–526.

Canada. Department of Energy, Mines and Resources. 1982. "Mineral Policy." Discussion Paper. Ottawa: Minister of Supply and Services Canada.

_____. Department of the Environment. 1983. *Canada Water Year Book 1981–1982.* Ottawa: Minister of Supply and Services Canada.

_____. Department of Fisheries and Environment. 1978. *A Vital Resource — Federal Policy Statement on Inland Waters.* Ottawa: Minister of Supply and Services Canada.

_____. Department of Justice. 1982. *Consolidation of the Constitution Acts, 1867–1982.* Ottawa: Queen's Printer.

_____. Treasury Board. 1976. *Benefit-Cost Analysis Guide*. Ottawa: Minister of Supply and Services Canada.

Canada West Foundation. 1982. *Nature's Lifeline: Prairie and Northern Waters*. Canada West Foundation and Devonian Group of Charitable Foundations. Calgary.

Carroll, J.E. 1983. *Environmental Diplomacy*. Ann Arbor: University of Michigan Press.

Carvalho, P. 1985. "Montreal Company Prepares to Sign Water Deal with Arabs." *Globe and Mail*. June 4, 1985, p. 4.

Christensen, M. et al. 1982. "Competition for California's Water: The Role of Energy." In *Competition for California's Water: Alternative Resolutions*, edited by E. Englebert. Berkeley: University of California Press.

Council on Foreign Relations. 1984. *Canada and the United States*. Proc. 68th American Assembly, November 15–18, 1984. Harriman, N.Y.: Arden House.

Dasgupta, P., and G. Heal. 1979. *Economic Theory and Exhaustible Resources*. Cambridge, England: Nisbet-Cambridge University Press.

Day, J.C. 1985. "Canadian Interbasin Diversions." Inquiry on Federal Water Policy. Research Paper No. 6. Ottawa: Minister of Supply and Services Canada.

Decooke, B.G., J.W. Bulkley, and S.J. Wright. 1984. "Great Lakes Diversions — Assessment of Economic Impacts." *Canadian Water Resources Journal* 9 (1): 1–15.

Deener, D.R., ed. 1963. *Canada-United States Treaty Relations*. Durham, N.C.: Duke University Press.

Dewees, D.N., C.K. Everson, and W.A. Sims. 1975. *Economic Analysis of Environmental Policies*. Toronto: University of Toronto Press.

Economic Council of Canada. 1985. "Water Resources." In *Western Transitions*, chap. 6. Ottawa: Minister of Supply and Services Canada.

Elton, D.K. 1983. "Managing the Water Resources of the Prairies." In *Water Policy for Western Canada: The Issues of the Eighties*, Proc. 2nd Annual National Resource Conference September 9–12, 1982, Banff, Alberta, edited by B. Sadler, pp. 137–57. Calgary: University of Calgary Press.

Emond, D.P. 1972. "The Case for A Greater Federal Role in the Environmental Protection Field: An Examination of the Pollution Problem and the Constitution." *Osgoode Hall Law Journal* 10 (3): 647–80.

Foster, H.D., and W.R.D. Sewell. 1981. *Water: The Emerging Crisis in Canada*. Toronto: James Lorimer.

Gallagher, D.R. et al. 1981. *Methods for Forecasting Urban Water Demands*. Technical Paper 59. Canberra: Australia Department of National Development and Energy, Water Resources Council.

Gibson, D. 1969. The Constitutional Context of Canadian Water Planning. *Alberta Law Review* 7: 71–92.

Grauer, A.E. Dal, and J. Davis. 1961. "The Export of Electricity from Canada." In *Canadian Issues: Essays in Honour of Henry F. Angus*, edited by R.M. Clark, pp. 248–85. Toronto: University of Toronto Press for University of British Columbia.

Gysi, M. 1981. "Measuring the Needs for Interbasin Transfer." *Canadian Water Resources Journal* 6 (2): 43–53.

Hare, F.K. 1984. "The Impact of Human Activities on Water in Canada." Inquiry on Federal Water Policy. Research Paper No. 2. Ottawa: Minister of Supply and Services Canada.

Harvey, D.R. 1981. *Government Intervention and Regulation in the Canadian Grains Industry*. Economic Council of Canada Technical Report E/16. Ottawa: The Council.

Henry, K.A. 1983. "Major Water Projects: How Governments Decide." In *Water Policy for Western Canada: The Issues of the Eighties*, edited by B. Sadler, pp. 68–76. Proc. 2nd Annual National Resource Conf. Sept. 9-12, 1982, Banff, Alberta. Calgary: University of Calgary Press.

Holling, C.S. ed. 1978. *Adaptive Environmental Assessment and Management*. Toronto: John Wiley.

Howe, C.W. 1979. "Economic Issues Related to Large-scale Water Transfers in the U.S.A." In *Interregional Water Transfers: Problems and Prospects*, edited by G.N. Golobev and A.K. Biswas, pp. 127–36. Oxford: Pergamon Press.

Howe, C.W., and K.W. Easter. 1971. *Interbasin Transfers of Water: Economic Issues and Impacts*. Baltimore: Johns Hopkins University Press for Resources for the Future.

Howitt, R. et al. 1982. "The Economics of Water Allocation." In: *Competition for California's Water: Alternative Resolutions*, edited by E. Englebert. Berkeley: University of California Press.

International Joint Commission. 1977. *Transboundary Implications of the Garrison Diversion Unit*. Washington and Ottawa.

_____. 1981a. *Great Lakes Diversions and Consumptive Uses*. Report to the IJC by the International Great Lakes Diversion and Consumptive Uses Study Board. Washington, D.C.: U.S. Government Printing Office, 1981-72-402.

_____. 1981b. *Water Quality in the Poplar River Basin: An International Joint Commission Report to the Governments of Canada and the United States*.

_____. 1982. *Great Lakes Diversions and Consumptive Uses — Executive Summary of the Report to the IJC by the International Great Lakes Diversions and Consumptive Uses Study Board*. Ottawa: Minister of Supply and Services Canada.

_____. 1985. *Great Lakes Diversions and Consumptive Uses*. Report to the Governments of the United States and Canada under the 1977 Reference. Washington, D.C.: U.S Government Printing Office.

Johnson, R.W. 1984. "Multi-State Management of Rivers: The Colorado and Delaware." Unpublished manuscript, University of Washington, Seattle.

Jones, R.A., P.H. Pearse, and A.D. Scott. 1980. "Conditions for Cooperation on Joint Projects by Independent Jurisdictions." *Canadian Journal of Economics* 13 (2): 231–49.

Kierans, T.W. 1965. The GRAND Canal Concept. *Engineering Journal* 48 (12): 39–42.

_____. 1984. "The Great Recycling and Northern Development (GRAND) Canal." Notes for a Submission to the Inquiry on Federal Water Policy in Canada. Presented September 24, 1984 at St. John's, Newfoundland.

Kneese, A.V., and F.L. Brown. 1981. *The Southwest under Stress: Natural Resource Development Issues in a Regional Setting*. Baltimore: Johns Hopkins University Press for Resources for the Future.

Kuiper, E. 1966. "Canadian Water Export." *Engineering Journal* 49 (7): 13–18.

La Forest, G.V. 1973. *Water Law in Canada: The Atlantic Provinces*. Ottawa: Information Canada.

Laskin, B. 1969. *Canadian Constitutional Law*, 3rd ed. rev. Toronto: Carswell.

Lucas, A.R., and T. Bell. 1977. *The National Energy Board: Policy, Procedure and Practice*. Ottawa: Minister of Supply and Services Canada.

Lucas, A.R., and J.O. Saunders. 1983. "Canadian Electricity Exports: Legal and Regulatory Issues." Working Paper No. 3. Calgary: Canadian Institute for Resources Law.

Miller, J.T. 1970. *Foreign Trade In Gas and Electricity in North America*. New York: Praeger.

Milliman, J.W. 1963. "Policy Horizons for Future Urban Water Supply." *Land Economics* 39 (2): 109–32.

Muller, R.A. 1985. "The Socio-Economic Value of Water in Canada." Inquiry on Federal Water Policy. Research Paper No. 5. Ottawa: Minister of Supply and Services Canada.

National Energy Board. 1983. *Reasons for Decision in the Matter of Phase II — The Review Phase — Of the Gas Export Omnibus Hearing, 1982*. Ottawa: Minister of Supply and Services Canada.

Newman, P.C. 1985. "Bargaining with Fresh Water." *Maclean's* 98 (17): 37.

Olynyk, J. 1984. "Environmental Impact Assessment: Effects on Corporate Mega-Project Planning." Unpublished M.Sc. Thesis. University of British Columbia, School of Community and Regional Planning, Vancouver.

Ortolano, L. 1979. "Environmental Assessments in Water Resources Planning." In *Inter-*

regional Water Transfers: Problems and Prospects, edited by G.N. Golobev and A.K. Biswas, pp. 159–76. Oxford: Pergamon Press.

Parsons Co., Ralph M. 1964. NAWAPA — North American Water and Power Alliance. Brochure 606-2934-19. Los Angeles.

Pearse, P.H. 1976. *Timber Rights and Forest Policy in British Columbia — The Report of the Royal Commission on Forestry Resources* 2 vols. Victoria: Queen's Printer.

Percy, D.R. 1981. "Legal and Jurisdictional Aspects of Interbasin Transfers." *Canadian Water Resources Journal* 6 (2): 1–12.

Perlgut, M. 1978. *Electricity Across The Border: The U.S.-Canadian Experience.* Montreal: Canadian-American Committee.

Powledge, F. 1982. *Water: The Nature, Uses, and Future of Our Most Precious and Abused Resource.* New York: Farrar Straus Giroux.

Prairie Provinces Water Board. 1982. *Water Demand Study — Historical and Current Water Uses in the Saskatchewan-Nelson Basin.* 8 vols. Ottawa: Department of the Environment.

Quinn, F.J. 1969. "Is Water Different?" In *Water Balance in North America*, pp. 243–46. Proceedings of the Symposium on Water Balance in North America. Banff, Alta. June 23–26, 1969. Sponsored by American Water Resources Association.

———. F.J. 1973. *Area-of-Origin Protectionism in Western Waters.* Study prepared for Environment Canada. Inland Waters Directorate. Social Science Series No. 6. Ottawa: Department of the Environment.

Rogers, P. 1983. "The Future of Water." *The Atlantic* 252 (1): 80–92.

———. 1984. "Fresh Water: Issues and Opportunities for Resource Development." Paper prepared for the Conference "The Global Possible: Resources, Development and the New Century." Wye Plantation. Maryland. May 2-5, 1984.

Rueggeberg, H.I., and A.R. Thompson. 1984. *Water Law and Policy Issues in Canada.* Vancouver: Westwater Research Centre.

Saskatchewan. Nelson Basin Board. 1972. *Water Supply for the Saskatchewan-Nelson Basin.* 9 vols. Ottawa: Queen's Printer.

Sewell, W.R.D. 1969. "Pipedream or Practical Possibility?" In *Water*, edited by J.C. Nelson and M.J. Chambers. Toronto: Methuen.

Sewell, W.R.D., J. Davis, A.D. Scott, and D.W. Ross. 1965. *Guide to Benefit-Cost Analysis.* Ottawa: Queen's Printer.

Shaffner, R., F.J. Quinn, and J.E. Carroll. 1980. Other Replenishable Resources. *Natural Resources in U.S.-Canadian Relations*, edited by C.E. Beigie and A.O. Heroite, Volume 2, pp. 541–73. Boulder, Colorado: Western Press.

Statistics Canada. *Construction Price Index.* Cat. No. 62-007. (Monthly). Ottawa: Statistics Canada.

Stephenson, D. 1981. *Pipeline Design for Water Engineers.* 2d ed. New York: Elsevier.

Taylor, G.C. 1967. *Economic Planning of Water Supply Systems.* Giannini Foundation of Ag. Ec. Research Report No. 291. Berkeley: University of California Press.

Thompson, A.R., N. Bankes, and J. Souto-Maior. 1981. *Energy Project Approval in British Columbia.* Vancouver: Westwater Research Centre.

Thompson, D. 1983. "Water Allocation Systems and Their Implications for Management." In *Water Policy for Western Canada: The Issues of the Eighties*, edited by B. Sadler, pp. 46–64. Proc. 2nd Annual National Resource Conf. Sept. 9-12, 1982, Banff, Alberta. Calgary: University of Calgary Press.

Tinney, E.R. 1967. "Engineering Aspects." *Bulletin of the Atomic Scientists* 23 (7): 21–25.

United States. Army Corps of Engineers. 1982. *Six-State High Plains Ogallala Aquifer Regional Resources Study.*

United States Congress. 1968. *Documents on the Use and Control of the Waters of Interstate and International Streams: Compacts, Treaties and Adjudications.* (T. Richard Witmer, compiler.) House Document No. 319, 90th Congress. Washington, D.C.: U.S. Government Printing Office.

Veeman, T.S. 1985. "Water and Economic Growth in Western Canada." Discussion Paper. Ottawa: Economic Council of Canada.

Wallace, R. et al. 1982. "Economics." In *Competition for California's Water: Alternative Resolutions*, edited by E. Englebert. Berkeley: University of California Press.

Wilkinson, B. 1985. "Canada's Resource Industries: A Survey." In *Canada's Resource Industries*, volume 14 of the research studies prepared for the Royal Commisson on the Economic Union and Development Prospects for Canada. Toronto: University of Toronto Press.

Willoughby, W.R. 1979. *The Joint Organizations of Canada and the United States*. Toronto: University of Toronto Press.

Wilson, C.F. 1979. *Canadian Grain Marketing*. Winnipeg: Canadian International Grains Institute.

Wojciechowski, M.J. 1979. *Federal Mineral Policies, 1945 to 1975: A Survey of Federal Activities That Affected the Canadian Mineral Industry*. Working Paper No. 8. Kingston: Queen's University, Centre for Resource Studies.

John Olynyk is a Research Associate with the Westwater Research Centre, University of British Columbia, Vancouver.

Steven Renzetti is a graduate student of the Department of Economics, University of British Columbia, Vancouver.

Anthony Scott is Professor in the Department of Economics, University of British Columbia, Vancouver.

Bruce W. Wilkinson is Professor in the Department of Economics, University of Alberta, Edmonton.

THE COLLECTED RESEARCH STUDIES

Royal Commission on the Economic Union and Development Prospects for Canada

ECONOMICS

Income Distribution and Economic Security in Canada (Vol.1), *François Vaillancourt, Research Coordinator*

Vol. 1 Income Distribution and Economic Security in Canada, *F. Vaillancourt* (C)*

Industrial Structure (Vols. 2-8), *Donald G. McFetridge, Research Coordinator*

Vol. 2 Canadian Industry in Transition, *D.G. McFetridge* (C)
Vol. 3 Technological Change in Canadian Industry, *D.G. McFetridge* (C)
Vol. 4 Canadian Industrial Policy in Action, *D.G. McFetridge* (C)
Vol. 5 Economics of Industrial Policy and Strategy, *D.G. McFetridge* (C)
Vol. 6 The Role of Scale in Canada–US Productivity Differences, *J.R. Baldwin and P.K. Gorecki* (M)
Vol. 7 Competition Policy and Vertical Exchange, *F. Mathewson and R. Winter* (M)
Vol. 8 The Political Economy of Economic Adjustment, *M. Trebilcock* (M)

International Trade (Vols. 9-14), *John Whalley, Research Coordinator*

Vol. 9 Canadian Trade Policies and the World Economy, *J. Whalley with C. Hamilton and R. Hill* (M)
Vol. 10 Canada and the Multilateral Trading System, *J. Whalley* (M)
Vol. 11 Canada–United States Free Trade, *J. Whalley* (C)
Vol. 12 Domestic Policies and the International Economic Environment, *J. Whalley* (C)
Vol. 13 Trade, Industrial Policy and International Competition, *R. Harris* (M)
Vol. 14 Canada's Resource Industries and Water Export Policy, *J. Whalley* (C)

Labour Markets and Labour Relations (Vols. 15-18), *Craig Riddell, Research Coordinator*

Vol. 15 Labour-Management Cooperation in Canada, *C. Riddell* (C)
Vol. 16 Canadian Labour Relations, *C. Riddell* (C)
Vol. 17 Work and Pay: The Canadian Labour Market, *C. Riddell* (C)
Vol. 18 Adapting to Change: Labour Market Adjustment in Canada, *C. Riddell* (C)

Macroeconomics (Vols. 19-25), *John Sargent, Research Coordinator*

Vol. 19 Macroeconomic Performance and Policy Issues: Overviews, *J. Sargent* (M)
Vol. 20 Post-War Macroeconomic Developments, *J. Sargent* (C)
Vol. 21 Fiscal and Monetary Policy, *J. Sargent* (C)
Vol. 22 Economic Growth: Prospects and Determinants, *J. Sargent* (C)
Vol. 23 Long-Term Economic Prospects for Canada: A Symposium, *J. Sargent* (C)
Vol. 24 Foreign Macroeconomic Experience: A Symposium, *J. Sargent* (C)
Vol. 25 Dealing with Inflation and Unemployment in Canada, *C. Riddell* (M)

Economic Ideas and Social Issues (Vols. 26 and 27), *David Laidler, Research Coordinator*

Vol. 26 Approaches to Economic Well-Being, *D. Laidler* (C)
Vol. 27 Responses to Economic Change, *D. Laidler* (C)

* (C) denotes a Collection of studies by various authors coordinated by the person named.
  (M) denotes a Monograph.

POLITICS AND INSTITUTIONS OF GOVERNMENT

Canada and the International Political Economy (Vols. 28-30), *Denis Stairs and Gilbert R. Winham, Research Coordinators*

Vol. 28 Canada and the International Political/Economic Environment, *D. Stairs and G.R. Winham* (C)
Vol. 29 The Politics of Canada's Economic Relationship with the United States, *D. Stairs and G.R. Winham* (C)
Vol. 30 Selected Problems in Formulating Foreign Economic Policy, *D. Stairs and G.R. Winham* (C)

State and Society in the Modern Era (Vols. 31 and 32), *Keith Banting, Research Coordinator*

Vol. 31 State and Society: Canada in Comparative Perspective, *K. Banting* (C)
Vol. 32 The State and Economic Interests, *K. Banting* (C)

Constitutionalism, Citizenship and Society (Vols. 33-35), *Alan Cairns and Cynthia Williams, Research Coordinators*

Vol. 33 Constitutionalism, Citizenship and Society in Canada, *A. Cairns and C. Williams* (C)
Vol. 34 The Politics of Gender, Ethnicity and Language in Canada, *A. Cairns and C. Williams* (C)
Vol. 35 Public Opinion and Public Policy in Canada, *R. Johnston* (M)

Representative Institutions (Vols. 36-39), *Peter Aucoin, Research Coordinator*

Vol. 36 Party Government and Regional Representation in Canada, *P. Aucoin* (C)
Vol. 37 Regional Responsiveness and the National Administrative State, *P. Aucoin* (C)
Vol. 38 Institutional Reforms for Representative Government, *P. Aucoin* (C)
Vol. 39 Intrastate Federalism in Canada, *D.V. Smiley and R.L. Watts* (M)

The Politics of Economic Policy (Vols. 40-43), *G. Bruce Doern, Research Coordinator*

Vol. 40 The Politics of Economic Policy, *G.B. Doern* (C)
Vol. 41 Federal and Provincial Budgeting, *A.M. Maslove, M.J. Prince and G.B. Doern* (M)
Vol. 42 Economic Regulation and the Federal System, *R. Schultz and A. Alexandroff* (M)
Vol. 43 Bureaucracy in Canada: Control and Reform, *S.L. Sutherland and G.B. Doern* (M)

Industrial Policy (Vols. 44 and 45), *André Blais, Research Coordinator*

Vol. 44 Industrial Policy, *A. Blais* (C)
Vol. 45 The Political Sociology of Industrial Policy, *A. Blais* (M)

LAW AND CONSTITUTIONAL ISSUES

Law, Society and the Economy (Vols. 46-51), *Ivan Bernier and Andrée Lajoie, Research Coordinators*

Vol. 46 Law, Society and the Economy, *I. Bernier and A. Lajoie* (C)
Vol. 47 The Supreme Court of Canada as an Instrument of Political Change, *I. Bernier and A. Lajoie* (C)
Vol. 48 Regulations, Crown Corporations and Administrative Tribunals, *I. Bernier and A. Lajoie* (C)
Vol. 49 Family Law and Social Welfare Legislation in Canada, *I. Bernier and A. Lajoie* (C)
Vol. 50 Consumer Protection, Environmental Law and Corporate Power, *I. Bernier and A. Lajoie* (C)
Vol. 51 Labour Law and Urban Law in Canada, *I. Bernier and A. Lajoie* (C)

COMMISSION ORGANIZATION

Chairman
Donald S. Macdonald

Commissioners

Clarence L. Barber	William M. Hamilton	Daryl K. Seaman
Albert Breton	John R. Messer	Thomas K. Shoyama
M. Angela Cantwell Peters	Laurent Picard	Jean Casselman-Wadds
E. Gérard Docquier	Michel Robert	Catherine T. Wallace

Senior Officers

Executive Director
J. Gerald Godsoe

Director of Policy	*Senior Advisors*	*Directors of Research*
Alan Nymark	David Ablett	Ivan Bernier
	Victor Clarke	Alan Cairns
Secretary	Carl Goldenberg	David C. Smith
Michel Rochon	Harry Stewart	
Director of Administration	*Director of Publishing*	*Co-Directors of Research*
Sheila-Marie Cook	Ed Matheson	Kenneth Norrie
		John Sargent

Research Program Organization

Economics	Politics and the Institutions of Government	Law and Constitutional Issues
Research Director	*Research Director*	*Research Director*
David C. Smith	Alan Cairns	Ivan Bernier
Executive Assistant & Assistant Director (Research Services)	*Executive Assistant*	*Executive Assistant & Research Program Administrator*
I. Lilla Connidis	Karen Jackson	Jacques J.M. Shore
Coordinators	*Coordinators*	*Coordinators*
David Laidler	Peter Aucoin	Clare F. Beckton
Donald G. McFetridge	Keith Banting	Ronald C.C. Cuming
Kenneth Norrie*	André Blais	Mark Krasnick
Craig Riddell	Bruce Doern	Andrée Lajoie
John Sargent*	Richard Simeon	A. Wayne MacKay
François Vaillancourt	Denis Stairs	John J. Quinn
John Whalley	Cynthia Williams	
	Gilbert R. Winham	
Research Analysts	*Research Analysts*	*Administrative and Research Assistant*
Caroline Digby	Claude Desranleau	Nicolas Roy
Mireille Ethier	Ian Robinson	
Judith Gold		*Research Analyst*
Douglas S. Green	*Office Administration*	Nola Silzer
Colleen Hamilton	Donna Stebbing	
Roderick Hill		
Joyce Martin		

*Kenneth Norrie and John Sargent co-directed the final phase of Economics Research with David Smith